Posthuman Knowledge

Posthuman Knowledge

Rosi Braidotti

polity

10

Polity Press
65 Bridge Street
Cambridge CB2 1UR, UK

Polity Press
101 Station Landing
Suite 300
Medford, MA 02155, USA

ISBN-13: 978-1-5095-3525-5
ISBN-13: 978-1-5095-3526-2 (pb)

A catalogue record for this book is available from the British Library.

Library of Congress Cataloging-in-Publication Data
Names: Braidotti, Rosi, author.
Title: Posthuman knowledge / Rosi Braidotti.
Description: Medford, MA : Polity, 2019. | Includes bibliographical
    references and index.
Identifiers: LCCN 2018059982 (print) | LCCN 2019014453 (ebook) | ISBN
    9781509535279 (Epub) | ISBN 9781509535255 (hardback) | ISBN
    9781509535262 (pbk.)
Subjects: LCSH: Humanism.
Classification: LCC B821 (ebook) | LCC B821 .B628 2019 (print) | DDC
    144--dc23
LC record available at https://lccn.loc.gov/2018059982

Typeset in 10.5 on 12pt Sabon
by Fakenham Prepress Solutions, Fakenham, Norfolk NR21 8NL
Printed and bound in Great Britain by TJ Books Limited

For further information on Polity, visit our website:
politybooks.com

Contents

Acknowledgements

During the research phase of this book I benefited greatly from the stimulating intellectual environment at the Institute of Advanced Studies at University College London that Tamar Garb and her team set up and where I was Distinguished Visiting Professor in 2017. I am also grateful to Henrietta Moore, Director of the Institute for Global Prosperity at University College London, who invited me as an active Honorary Visiting Professor as of 2017.

I spent two very productive months as a Senior Visiting Fellow at the Internationales Kolleg für Kulturtechnikforschung und Medienphilosophie (IKKM), at the Bauhaus University Weimar in Germany. I am grateful to Lorenz Engell and Bernhard Siegert for their research leadership, and to my research assistant Eduard Kolosoff for his devoted support.

Part of this material was first presented in my Tanner Lectures in Human Values at Yale University in 2017. I want to thank the Tanner Foundation in Utah and the Tanner Lectures Committee at Yale University for their invitation, and especially Yale University President Peter Salovey for his warm and witty welcome. Sincere thanks to Professor Gary Tomlinson and his colleagues and staff at the Whitney Centre for the Humanities for their splendid hospitality. I am grateful to my respondents Joanna Radin and Rüdiger Campe for their insightful contributions during the open discussion, and to many colleagues and students for their formal and informal comments during the sessions. I am also grateful to my friend Moira Fradinger for her moving public introduction.

My sincere thanks to Genevieve Lloyd for her wise and enlightening guidance throughout the drafting process of this book. Thanks also to Matthew Fuller and Keith Ansell-Pearson for their generous insights, theoretical advice and bibliographical details. I am much indebted to Marlise Mensink for her warm friendship. I also wish to thank my personal research assistants Gry Ulstein, Evelien Geerts and Lauren Hoogen Stoevenbeld for their unfailing logistical and organizational assistance. I am indebted to Linda Dement for introducing me to Jessie Boylan's photograph of the 2015 'Ngurini', an immersive installation by the Nuclear Futures Arts Program with the Yalata Aboriginal Community.

Sections of this book were published in my chapter in the volume *Conflicting Humanities*, which I co-edited with Paul Gilroy in 2016, and in the Introduction to *The Posthuman Glossary*, which I co-edited with Maria Hlavajova in 2018. I acknowledge them both warmly here. An earlier draft of the theoretical framework for the PostHumanities was published in *Theory, Culture & Society* in May 2018.

This book would not have been possible without the loyal support of my publisher John Thompson; I truly thank him for his enduring commitment to my posthuman project.

Finally, my eternal gratitude to my life partner Anneke Smelik for her intellectual, emotional and moral support, and because living together is so much fun.

Acknowledgement of the Cover Image

Ngurini, immersive installation by the Nuclear Futures Arts Program with the Yalata Aboriginal Community, 2015. Photo by Jessie Boylan.

Introduction: Posthuman, All-Too-Human

It is not at all uncommon for users of any kind of websites or digital services to be requested to prove their humanity on a daily basis. The prompt usually reads something like: 'Before We Subscribe You, We Need To Confirm You Are A Human'. And it looks like this:

Having to demonstrate one's humanity assumes as the central point of reference the algorithmic culture of computational networks – not the human. This mundane example demonstrates that in contemporary society the human has become a question mark. Who or what counts as human today?

This is not a simple question and it is best answered in the context of our posthuman times. What or who is the human today can only be understood by incorporating the posthuman and non-human dimensions. By posthuman I mean both a historical marker of our condition and a theoretical figuration. The posthuman is not so much a dystopian vision of the future, but a defining trait of our historical context. I have defined the posthuman condition as the convergence of posthumanism on the one hand and post-anthropocentrism on the other, within an economy of advanced capitalism (Braidotti 2013, 2017). The former focuses on the critique of the Humanist ideal of 'Man' as the allegedly universal measure of all things, while the latter criticizes species hierarchy and anthropocentric exceptionalism. Although they overlap and tend to be used interchangeably in general debates, they are rather discrete and separate events, both in the intellectual genealogies and in their social manifestations.

As a theoretical figuration, the posthuman is a navigational tool that enables us to survey the material and the discursive manifestations of the mutations that are engendered by advanced technological developments (am I a robot?), climate change (will I survive?), and capitalism (can I afford this?). The posthuman is a work in progress. It is a working hypothesis about the kind of subjects we are becoming. Who that 'we' is, and how to keep that collectivity open, multiple and non-hierarchical, will be constant concerns in this book.

Though I can barely conceal my fascination for the posthuman, I do inhabit it with critical distance. The posthuman condition implies that 'we' – the human and non-human inhabitants of this particular planet – are currently positioned between the Fourth Industrial Revolution and the Sixth Extinction. Yes, we are in this together: between the algorithmic devil and the acidified deep blue sea. The Fourth Industrial Revolution involves the convergence of advanced technologies, such as robotics, artificial intelligence, nanotechnology, biotechnology and the Internet of Things. This means that digital, physical and biological boundaries get blurred (Schwab 2015). The Sixth Extinction refers to the dying out of species during the present geological era as the result of human activity (Kolbert 2014). More specifically, this conjuncture positions us between two parallel and to a certain extent specular forms of acceleration: the systemic accelerations of advanced capitalism and the great acceleration of climate change. Striking a balance between these conflicting forces, so as to keep the broader picture in mind, is the current posthuman challenge.

At the core of our predicament – but not its sole cause – is the unprecedented degree of technological intervention we have reached, and the intimacy we have developed with technological devices. And yet, the posthuman condition cannot be reduced simply to an acute case of technological mediation. This convergence, with its distinctive combination of speedy transformations and persistent inequalities, is planetary and multi-scalar (Banerji and Paranjape 2016). It affects social and environmental ecologies as well as individual psychic and shared emotional landscapes. It is not a linear event.

My argument is that we need to learn to address these contradictions not only intellectually, but also affectively and to do so in an affirmative manner. This conviction rests on the following ethical rule: it is important to be worthy of our times, the better to act upon them, in both a critical and a creative manner. It follows that we should approach our historical contradictions not as some bothersome burden, but rather as the building blocks of a sustainable present and an affirmative and hopeful future, even if this approach requires some drastic changes to our familiar mind-sets and established values.

To describe the posthuman location as a convergence of several contradictory speeds of transformation does not even begin to approximate the tensions and paradoxes it generates, nor the pain and anxiety it evokes. In such a context, neither universalistic notions of 'Man' nor exceptional claims for 'Anthropos', are sufficient to explain how we are supposed to cope with this challenge. Such outdated positions do not help us understand how knowledge is being produced and distributed in the era of high technological mediation and ecological disaster, also known as the Anthropocene.[1] Humanistic hubris aside, unless one is at ease with multi-dimensional complexity, one cannot feel at home in the twenty-first century.

The posthuman condition may strike the reader as catastrophe-prone at first sight, but in this book, I hope to balance this negative assessment with a more complex and insightful account of the situation. The book highlights the positive potential of the posthuman convergence and offers tools for coping with it affirmatively. Despair is not a project;

affirmation is. This book is about the forms of self-under-standing and new ways of knowing that are emerging from the convergence of posthumanist and post-anthropocentric approaches. While maintaining the analytical and genea-logical distinction between these two components, I argue that their convergence is currently producing a qualitative leap in new directions: posthuman knowledge production. This is not a single development, but a zigzagging set of pathways, which includes a range of posthumanist positions and also a revision of a variety of neo-humanist[2] claims. A full overview of contemporary enquiries about what consti-tutes the basic unit of reference for the human exceeds the scope of this study; I have explored it elsewhere (Braidotti and Hlavajova 2018).

In this book I want to focus on a double target: first to outline the features of emergent posthuman subjects and second to explore the new scholarship they are producing within and across the fields of the (Post) Humanities. I will present cartographies that detect a number of operative principles and discursive meta-patterns and will attempt to provide a critical framework for analysing and assessing them. The underlying conviction of this book is that the posthuman convergence, far from being a crisis – let alone an indicator of extinction – marks a rich and complex historical transition. Full of risks, it also affords huge opportunities for both humans and non-human agents, as well as for the Humanities, to reinvent themselves. Like all transitions, however, it requires some vision and experimental energy as well as considerable doses of endurance.

The aims of this book are the following: to ground the posthuman in real-life conditions; to detect alternative formations of posthuman subjects; to assess the fast-growing volume of posthuman knowledge production; and to inscribe posthuman thinking subjects and their knowledge within an affirmative ethics.

In chapter 1, I will outline the extent of the posthuman convergence in both theoretical and affective terms. Chapter 2 addresses the question of what counts as a posthuman subject and traces emerging patterns of posthuman subjec-tivity. Chapter 3 assesses the advantages of posthumanist knowledge production. Chapter 4 looks at the rise of the

Critical PostHumanities and situates them in the fast-moving landscapes of cognitive capitalism. Chapter 5 analyses established patterns of posthuman thought and discusses concrete practices to evaluate them. Chapter 6 delves deeper into affirmative ethics and what changes of temporal and spatial scale it requires. In a shorter final chapter, I return to the affective mood of the posthuman convergence. The book finishes with the endless potentialities of posthuman resistance and the inexhaustible quality of life itself.

Perhaps here, at the end of the Introduction, I should answer the question whether I'm a robot. No, I'm not, but some of my best friends are! I am posthuman – all-too-human. This means that I am materially embodied and embedded, with the power to affect and be affected, living in fast-changing posthuman times. What all of that entails will be explained in the pages that follow.

Chapter 1
The Posthuman Condition

A Convergence

Discussions about the human, more specifically about what
constitutes the basic unit of reference to define what counts
as human, are by now part of daily conversations, public
discussions and academic debates. Historically, however,
questions such as 'what do you mean by human?', 'are we
human enough?', or 'what is human about the Humanities?'
are *not* what anybody – let alone we, Humanities scholars,
were accustomed to asking. The force of habit led us to talk
about Man, Mankind, or civilization (always assumed to be
Western) as a matter of fact. We were encouraged to teach
Western civilizational values and to endorse human rights,
delegating to anthropologists and biologists the far more
irksome task of debating what the 'human' may actually
mean.

Even philosophy, which is accustomed to question everything, dealt with the question of the human by casting it
within the protocols and methods of disciplinary thinking.
There it conventionally fell into a discursive pattern of
dualistic oppositions that defined the human mostly by
what it is *not*. Thus, with Descartes: *not* an animal, *not*
extended and inert matter, *not* a pre-programmed machine.
These binary oppositions provided definitions by negation,

structured within a humanistic vision of Man as the thinking being *par excellence*. Whereas the oppositional logic is a constant, the actual content of these binary oppositions is historically variable. Thus, as John Mullarkey (2013) wittily observed, the animal provides an index of death for Derrida (2008), an index of life for Deleuze (2003) and an index of de-humanization for Agamben (1998). But the effect of these variations is to reassert the central theme, namely the pivotal function of the human/non-human distinction within European philosophy.

It is important to keep in mind from the start, however, that the binary distinction human/non-human has been foundational for European thought since the Enlightenment and that many cultures on earth do not adopt such a partition (Descola 2009, 2013). This is the strength of the insights and understandings that can be learned from indigenous epistemologies and cosmologies. As Viveiros de Castro eloquently put it, this theoretical operation implements the Great Divide: 'the same gesture of exclusion that made the human species the biological analogue of the anthropological West, confusing all the other species and peoples in a common, privative alterity. Indeed asking what distinguishes us from the others – and it makes little difference who "they" are, since what really matters in that case is only "us" – is already a response' (Viveiros de Castro 2009: 44). He argues that indigenous perspectivism posits a 'multinatural' continuum across all species, all of which partake of a distributed idea of humanity. This means they are considered as being endowed with a soul. This situates the divide human/non-human not between species and organisms, but as a difference operating *within* each of them (Viveiros de Castro 1998, 2009). This conceptual operation assumes a commonly shared human nature that includes the non-humans. To call this approach 'animism' is to miss the point, because Amerindian perspectivism teaches us that 'each kind of being appears to other beings as it appears to itself – as human – even as it already acts by manifesting its distinct and definitive animal, plant, or spirit nature' (Viveiros de Castro 2009: 68). In other words, each entity is differential and relational. Which, incidentally, is also the source of Viveiros de Castro's explicit – albeit critical – alliance with Deleuze. I shall return to this in the next chapter.

For now, the point is that the posthuman condition encourages us to move beyond the Eurocentric humanistic representational habits and the philosophical anthropocentrism they entail. Nowadays we can no longer start uncritically from the centrality of the human – as Man and as Anthropos – to uphold the old dualities. This acknowledgement does not necessarily throw us into the chaos of non-differentiation, nor the spectre of extinction. It rather points in a different direction, towards some other middle ground, another *milieu*, which I will explore in this book.

Theoretical and philosophical critiques of Humanism have been carried out in an outspoken and explicit manner in modern Continental philosophy ever since Nietzsche. More recently critiques of Humanism have been advanced by movements of thought such as post-structuralism (Foucault 1970); vital materialism (Deleuze 1983; Deleuze and Guattari 1987), critical neo-materialism (Dolphijn and van der Tuin 2012), feminist materialism (Alaimo and Hekman 2008; Coole and Frost 2010), and anti-racist and post-colonial movements (Said 2004; Gilroy 2000).

The posthuman, however, is not just a critique of Humanism. It also takes on the even more complex challenge of anthropocentrism. The convergence of these two lines of critique, in what I call the posthuman predicament, is producing a chain of theoretical, social and political effects that is more than the sum of its parts. It makes for a qualitative leap in new conceptual directions: posthuman subjects producing posthuman scholarship. The point about the convergence of posthumanism and post-anthropocentrism needs to be stressed, because in current debates the two are often either hastily assimilated in a sweeping deconstructive merger, or violently re-segregated and pitched against each other. While insisting that the posthuman convergence is decidedly not a statement of inhumane indifference, it is important to emphasize the mutually enriching effect of the intersection between these two lines of enquiry. At the same time, it is crucial to resist all tendencies to reduce posthumanism and post-anthropocentrism to a relation of equivalence, and to stress instead both their singularity and the transformative effects of their convergence. Unless a critique of Humanism is brought to bear on the displacement of anthropocentrism and vice-versa, we run the risk of setting up new hierarchies and new exclusions.

Stressing the convergence factor helps avoid another risk, namely that of pre-empting the effects of the current juncture, by pre-selecting a single direction for the developments of new knowledge and ethical values. What the posthuman convergence points to instead is a multi-directional opening that allows for multiple possibilities and calls for experimental forms of mobilization, discussion and at times even resistance. The keyword of posthuman scholarship is multiplicity. The range of posthuman options is wide and growing, as the chapters in this book will track and trace. Posthuman knowledge will also provide some guidelines for assessing these developments.

Instead of proposing a single counter-paradigm, the point of the posthuman convergence is to issue a critical call: we need to build on the generative potential of already existing critiques of both Humanism and anthropocentrism, in order to deal with the complexity of the present situation. In this book I stress the heterogeneous structure of the posthuman convergence in order to reflect the multi-layered and multi-directional structure of a situation that combines the displacement of anthropocentrism – in response to the challenges of the Anthropocene – with the analysis of the discriminatory aspects of European Humanism. Considering the perpetuation of violent human activity and interaction, I keep the emphasis on justice as social, trans-species and transnational. In earlier work I have called that *zoe*-centred justice (Braidotti 2006). A *zoe*-centred justice has to be backed by relational ethics. These are key elements of the posthuman agenda, because let us not forget that 'we are in this together'.

Critiques of European Humanism pertain to the very tradition of European Humanism, or, as Edward Said (1994) shrewdly pointed out, you can critique Humanism in the name of Humanism. These critiques are as essential to the Western project of modernity as to the modernist project of emancipation. They have historically been voiced by the anthropomorphic others of 'Man' – the sexualized and racialized others claiming social justice and rejecting exclusion, marginalization and symbolic disqualification.

Relinquishing anthropocentrism, however, triggers a different set of actors and a more complex affective reaction. Displacing the centrality of Anthropos within the European world view exposes and explodes a number of boundaries between 'Man' and the environmental or naturalized 'others': animals, insects, plants and the environment. In fact, the planet and the cosmos as a whole become objects of critical enquiry and this change of scale, even just in terms of a nature–culture continuum, may feel unfamiliar and slightly counter-intuitive.

The critique of anthropocentrism that is entailed in posthuman knowledge is highly demanding for scholars in the Humanities because it enacts a double shift. Firstly, it requires an understanding of ourselves as members of a species, and not just of a culture or polity. Secondly, it demands accountability for the disastrous planetary consequences of our species' supremacy and the violent rule of sovereign Anthropos. Most people with an education in the Humanities and the Social Sciences are neither accustomed nor trained to think in terms of species.

In this regard, Freud's insight about evolutionary theory remains sharply relevant. Freud warned us that Darwin inflicted such a deep narcissistic wound upon the Western subject, that it resulted in negative responses to evolutionary theory, such as disavowal. Thus, scholars in the Humanities uphold as a matter of fact, that is to say as a commonsensical given, the classical distinction between *bios* – human – and *zoe* – non-human. *Bios* refers to the life of humans organized in society, while *zoe* refers to life of all living beings. *Bios* is regulated by sovereign powers and rules, whereas *zoe* is unprotected and vulnerable. However, in the context of the posthuman convergence, I maintain that this opposition is too rigid and no longer tenable. In this book I explore the generative potential of *zoe* as a notion that can engender resistance to the violent aspects of the posthuman convergence.

Although one of the undeniable strengths of Humanism is the multiple forms of criticism that it has historically given rise to, even radical critics of Humanism, with their emphasis on diversity and inclusion, do not necessarily or automatically tackle the deeply engrained habits of anthropocentric thinking. Yet, in order to denaturalize economic inequalities and social discrimination, critical cultural and social theory is also called to task as long as it rests methodologically on a social constructivist paradigm that upholds the binary nature–culture distinction. Perhaps unsurprisingly, a post-anthropocentric sensibility has made only a relatively recent appearance in scholarship in the Humanities (Peterson 2013).

In this book I develop a framework for posthuman knowledge by creating a balancing act between post-humanism and post-anthropocentrism. I do so by building on, but also leaving behind, the established controversy between Humanism and anti-Humanism. This controversy preoccupied Continental philosophy in the second half of the twentieth century, in what became known as the postmodern moment, with consequences that were far-reaching, notably for ethical and political thought and practice. We cannot possibly ignore or dismiss this controversy, some aspects of which are returning to haunt the posthuman convergence. Nonetheless, we could gain by moving beyond the polemic – which is what I try to do in this book. The central challenge that the posthuman convergence throws open is how to reposition the human after Humanism and anthropocentrism. No, I'm not a robot, but that begs the question what kind of human I am, or we are becoming, in this posthuman predicament. The primary task of posthuman critical thought is to track and analyse the shifting grounds on which new, diverse and even contradictory understandings of the human are currently being generated, from a variety of sources, cultures and traditions. Addressing this task raises a number of challenges that defy any simplistic or self-evident appeal to a generic and undifferentiated figure of the human, let alone to traditional, Eurocentric humanist values.

To start accounting for the human in posthuman times, I suggest to carefully ground the statement 'we humans'. For 'we' are not one and the same. In my view, the human needs to be assessed as materially embedded and embodied, differential, affective and relational. Let me unpack that sentence. For the subject to be materially embedded means to take distance from abstract universalism. To be embodied and embrained entails decentring transcendental consciousness. To view the subject as differential implies to extract difference from the oppositional or binary logic that reduces difference to being different from, as in being worth less than. Difference is an imminent, positive and dynamic category. The emphasis on affectivity and relationality is an alternative to individualist autonomy.

Rejecting the mental habit of universalism is a way of acknowledging the partial nature of visions of the human that were produced by European culture in its hegemonic, imperial and Enlightenment-driven mode. Suspending belief in a unitary and self-evident category of 'we humans', however, is by no means the premise to relativism. On the contrary, it means adopting an internally differentiated and grounded notion of being human. Recognizing the embodied and embedded, relational and affective positions of humans is a form of situated knowledge that enhances the singular and collective capacity for both ethical accountability and alternative ways of producing knowledge (Braidotti 2018). The posthuman predicament, with its upheavals and challenges, gives the opportunity to activate these alternative views of the subject against the dominant vision. This is what is at stake in the posthuman convergence.

The posthuman doubles up as both an empirical and a figurative dimension. The posthuman is empirically grounded, because it is embedded and embodied, but it is also a figuration (Braidotti 1991), or what Deleuze and Guattari (1994) call a 'conceptual persona'. As such, it is a theoretically-powered cartographic tool that aims at achieving adequate understanding of on-going processes of dealing with the human in our fast-changing times. In this regard, the posthuman enables us to track, across a number of interdisciplinary fields, the emergence of discourses about the posthuman which are generated by the intersecting critiques of Humanism and of anthropocentrism.

The itinerary is as straightforward as it is breath-taking: the notion of human nature is replaced by a 'naturecultures' continuum (Haraway 1997, 2003). The idea of naturecultures brings to an end the categorical distinction between life as *bios*, the prerogative of humans, as distinct from *zoe*, which refers to the life of animals and non-humans, as well as to de-humanized humans (Braidotti 2006, 2018). What comes to the fore instead is new fractures within the human, new human–non-human linkages, new 'zoontologies' (de Fontenay 1998; Gray 2002; Wolfe 2003), as well as complex media-technological interfaces (Bono, Dean and Ziarek 2008). The posthuman predicament is, moreover, framed by the opportunistic commodification of all that lives, which, as I argue below, is the political economy of advanced capitalism.

On the Importance of Being Exhausted

I fully concede at the outset of my book that the posthuman convergence makes for swinging moods, which alternate between excitement and anxiety. Moments or periods of euphoria at the astonishing technological advances that 'we' have accomplished, alternate with moments or periods of anxiety in view of the exceedingly high prize that we – both humans and non-humans – are paying for these transformations. We are caught in contradictory pulls and spins that call for constant negotiations in terms of time, boundaries and degrees of involvement with, and disengagements from, the same technological apparatus that frames our social relations.

Obviously, none of this is happening in a vacuum. If the public debates at the end of the Cold War in the 1990s were dominated by the dubious – and ideologically loaded – claim to the 'end of history', by the 2020s we seem to be heading for a massive outburst of over-fatigue with just about everything else. We may feel exhausted about a range of issues, from democracy to liberal politics, everyday politics, classical emancipation, the knowledge of experts, the nation state, the EU, academic education – and so on. Critical theory reflects this negative trend by indulging in its own kind of self-pitying lament. What happened to push us towards such millenarian feelings of doom? What is this tiredness all about?

The mutations induced by the posthuman convergence are unsettling and often startling. To come back to the example at the beginning of the introduction, it is daily practice for the slightly exhausted citizen-users of the new technologies to be requested to prove their humanity in order to gain access to specialized websites and other digital services. After you have

seen the prompt 'we need to confirm you are a human' and
you have clicked the 'I'm not a robot' box, you will probably
encounter sentences like 'How would you like to pay? By
mobile phone transfer? Paypal? Bitcoin? We don't take
cash ...'. As Matthew Fuller pointed out, the box ticking on
the reCAPTCHA form is only a pretext.[1] What the software
is actually looking for are certain characteristic response
times and movements of the mouse, track pad or touchscreen
that show the action is not being carried out by another piece
of software but a human. It is not unlikely, however, that a
physical robot may mimic such actions or a piece of code
replicate their effect.

In any case, having to demonstrate one's humanity in order
to access goods and services seems to be the imperative of a
'new' economy, centred on the algorithmic culture of computational networks, not good old Man/Homo/Anthropos – the
human. In our information age the boundaries between
anthropomorphic humans and quasi-human technological
substitutes have been radically displaced. Just consider the
extent to which medicine and health care is now performed by
highly sophisticated human–robotics interaction, centralized
data banks and Internet-backed self-medication.

The prospect is as exciting as it is depressing. The
feeling of dispossession is acute, with so much information,
knowledge and thinking power now being produced and
situated outside the traditional container – which used to be
the human mind, embodied in an anthropomorphic frame.
What happens when thinking, reasoning, assessing risks and
opportunities are executed by algorithmically-driven computational networks instead? And when so much of life, living
processes of cell formation and splitting, is operated syntheti-
cally via stem-cell research? Test-tube babies? Artificial meat?
As the AI and robotics industry are cloning the neural and
sensorial system of other species – dogs for scent, dolphins
for sonar, bats for radar, etc. – the human body strikes us as
a rather old-fashioned anthropomorphic engine, not quite
suited to contain the fast-moving intelligence of our technologies. This is not a 'new' problem in itself, but it is gathering
momentum and speed.

Obviously, the image of the neural human container is
inadequate and needs to be updated and replaced by flows

and distributed processes instead. But a switch to fluid process ontologies alone is not enough, as the postmodern era clearly demonstrated. The posthuman conceals deeper conceptual challenges in terms of bridging the mind–body and nature–culture divides. Thus, neither the holistic organicism of early twentieth-century philosophies of Life, often contaminated by European fascism, nor the dismissal of subjectivity altogether, in favour of protocols of in-human reason, is equal to the challenge. What I propose is a shift towards posthuman subject positions so as to be able to affect these transformations and shape them in the direction of ethically affirmative and politically sustainable alternatives.

Indeed, 'we', the human heirs of Western post-modernity, are increasingly burnt out and fatigued, while 'they' – the technological artefacts we have brought into being – are smarter and more alive than ever (Haraway 1985, 1990). Questions about life, live, liveliness, smartness, of being and remaining alive – and possibly growing even smarter – are circulating widely. They constitute the inevitable and painful knots of contradictions, in the multi-layered ecologies that structure the posthuman convergence. Being a posthumanist is a non-nostalgic way of acknowledging the pain of this transition, of extracting knowledge from it, and reworking it affirmatively.

The constant stress generated by this see-saw of expectation and dejection, euphoria and anguish, boom and gloom, however, leaves us, quite simply, exhausted. On a daily, sociological level, this state of exhaustion has been documented through alarming statistics concerning burn-out, depression and anxiety disorders. The figures are especially high among the youth, with suicide rates also rising at a disturbing pace. Feeling emotionally and physically drained, over-worked and unable to cope, are all-too-familiar conditions in our fast-moving, cynically competitive world.

This system is exhausting in that it pursues an internally contradictory aim: on the one hand, it runs on the 'timeless time' (Castells 2010) of a technologically interconnected society where the economy functions 24/7 and capital never stands still. On the other hand, it functions through a public discourse of health, fitness and care of the self and thus requires a conscious and self-regulating, healthy reserve of labour. Not getting enough sleep forms the nucleus of an unresolved tension: to avoid the state of tiredness resulting from the endless pursuit of production, consumption and constant digital connectivity. The negative fall-out of such a state is the emergence of a dysfunctional, under-performing population, untouched by the healing power of restorative sleep – too tired to even sleep properly.

It is no wonder then, as several social commentators have noted (Fuller 2018), that sleep has emerged as a crucial topic in public policy, management and the popular media. On the corporate side, media mogul Arianna Huffington, after selling her majority shares of the world's largest blog, *The Huffington Post*, is devoting her latest venture to the pursuit of wellness, sleep and mindfulness, as keys to enhanced professional performance. The alternative to such an approach is the widespread consumption of prescription drugs to deal both with insomnia and anxiety.

According to recent reports, the sale of anti-anxiety medication is expected to generate revenue of $3.7 billion by 2010 in the US alone, while the UK is at present the second largest market of illegal online sales of the anti-anxiety medication Xanax (Mahdawi 2018). The World Health Organization estimated in 2016 that, without more treatment, 12 billion working days will be lost because of anxiety every year. For De Sutter (2018), the psycho-pharmaceutical sub-plot of capitalism is central to its success: mood enhancement and chemical control are so manifest as to warrant the quip that capitalism and cocaine work in tandem. The state of exhaustion is real, but it is not a single or linear phenomenon.

Complexity is at work here, too. Provocatively perhaps, I would like to pick out some components of the exhausted condition, which transcend the negative and are capable of producing generative states. These aspects have less to do with what the professionals call 'reduced performance' than with a sense of evacuation of selfhood, a low-energy opening out beyond the frame of ego-indexed identity. Such an opening can be quite liberating and afford the possibility of actualizing yet unrealized potentials.

Approaching the state of exhaustion affirmatively, offers some unexpected options. Exhaustion thus defined is not a psychological mood, but rather an intransitive state that is not linked to a specific object, let alone a mental disposition. As such, it is capable of pervading the full spectrum of our social existence. 'We are tired of something', writes Deleuze in his commentary on Beckett, 'but exhausted by nothing' (1995b: 4). Let me dare to suggest that there is a creative potential here, which means that exhaustion is not a pathological state that needs to be cured, as an actual disorder, but a threshold of transformation of forces, that is to say a virtual state of creative becoming. Of course, I do not mean to disregard the pain, but rather encourage us to see the intensity of the discomfort as a motor of change, expressing also the capacity to open up to non/in-human and other-than-human forces. This ability to sense, grasp and work with the virtual is one of the distinct qualities that makes us human in the first place. Which is not to say that we have always been posthuman, but rather that the specific contemporary manifestation of this particular contradiction need not inevitably breed negative reactions. If the human is a vector of transversal becoming, i.e. reaching across categories, then the posthuman convergence can multiply the possibilities and unfold in a number of different directions, depending on our own degree of action and involvement (Braidotti 1991, 2011a). Differential, grounded perspectives are the motor for differential patterns of becoming.

Let me emphasize that the grounded, perspectivist and accountable approach I am developing in this book in response to the negative aspects of the posthuman convergence neither ignores nor disavows the pain and difficulties involved in our current predicament. It offers a different way of processing this profound discomfort: my vital materialist account of posthuman affirmation provides a remedy to the political fractures and the ethical challenges of posthuman times, while avoiding a return to falsely universalist notions of the 'human'. The posthuman convergence is an analytic tool for understanding the grounded, perspectival and accountable nature of the affective, social and epistemic processes we are currently involved in, and the role of non-human agents in co-producing them. It should not be misunderstood as 'inhuman(e)', or unconcerned with the well-being of all. On the contrary, the posthuman is a workable framework to assist in the elaboration of alternative forces and values that can be generated from the burnt-out core of the old schemes and mind-sets.

What has been exhausted in our world is a set of familiar formulae, a compilation of motifs and mental habits 'we' had embroidered around the notion of the human as a concept and a repertoire of representations. Not unlike the characters in a Beckett text, 'we', the posthumans, have run out of possible combinations by which we can pull out our old tricks, one last time. Confronted with a blank existential space, like the silent passages in a radio play, we may remember, but not necessarily miss, the great clamour of Being, the boisterous self-confidence with which the spokesmen of Logos used to bash our ears with grand proclamations and master theories. How all that has changed!

Not only is theory out of fashion (see the next section), but we are not even capable of sharing the same social space anymore, let alone an acoustic one. Nowadays everyone walks around wrapped inside its own acoustic bubble, supported by personalized earphones and Spotified lists. Segregated but conjoined within the same white noise, we have become quantified selves, that is to say both individualized and divided ('dividuals', as Deleuze would say, or 'fitbits', as others would call it). Caught somewhere between stasis and expectation, we could surrender to despair, or take our chances and re-invent ourselves. Exhaustion can become affirmative, if the conditions for regeneration are shared by a sufficient amount of people, of both the human and the non-human kind, who embrace it as an opening out towards new virtual possibilities and not as a fall into the void. In that case we do need a people, a community, and an assemblage: 'we' – this complex multiplicity – cannot survive or act alone.

In this book I propose a creative posthuman approach and explore the case of posthuman knowledge production and the rising field of the PostHumanities to document it. I will argue that the state of exhaustion has already been activated into the generative pre-condition to learn to think differently about ourselves. Such knowledge can help us build a transversal assemblage of human, non-human and inhuman components. Posthuman knowledge is fuelled by transversality and heterogeneity: multiplicity and complexity shall be our guiding principles and sustainability our goal. The way to get started is by composing a 'we' that is grounded, accountable and active. This is the collective praxis of affirmative politics, which can help us out of the alternation of euphoria and despair, giddying elation and toxic negativity. In these posthuman times, amidst technologically mediated social relations, the negative effects of economic globalization and a fast-decaying environment, in response to the paranoid and racist rhetoric of our 'post-truth' political leaders, how can we labour together to construct affirmative ethical and political practices? How can we work towards socially sustainable horizons of hope, through creative resistance? How are scholars in the Humanities currently reconfiguring their fields of knowledge, in response to the posthuman challenges? What tools can we use to resist nihilism, escape consumerist individualism and get immunized against xenophobia? The answer is in the doing, in the praxis of composing 'we, a people', through alliances, transversal connections and in engaging in difficult conversations on what troubles us. In this respect, our posthuman times, with their large inhuman component, are all too human.

Theory Fatigue

Let me expand on one of the features of contemporary exhaustion that lies close to my experience, namely the manifest fatigue with theory and theorists. Although the definition of theory is never clear or consistent in the polemical debates that surround it, it tends to be linked to critical discourses produced by the Humanities and Social Sciences, especially if left-leaning and prone to use polysyllabic words. The 'post-theoretical malaise' (Cohen, Colebrook and Miller 2012) translates easily into anti-intellectualism in society at large and sets a rather sedate mood that is directly linked to our current socio-political context.

This mood is spreading left and right of the political spectrum and can be roughly described as an advanced state of disenchantment with the unfulfilled promises of

Western modernization and more specifically its political utopias and emancipatory drives. After the official end of the Cold War, the political movements of the second half of the twentieth century have been widely discarded as failed historical experiments and their theoretical efforts dismissed accordingly. At first, the 'new' right-wing ideology of free market economy steam-rolled the opposition, in spite of outspoken protest from many sectors of society (Fukuyama 1989). More recently, new sovereign-ism (Benhabib 2009) took over, as authoritarian nationalism started to prevail in Western democracies. Critical theory, a historical bastion of anti-authoritarianism, intrinsically upholds faith in critical reason, as a tool to apprehend and transform reality. Such faith, however, is being questioned today, when the detractors of theoretical thinking often dismiss it as a form of fantasy or narcissistic self-indulgence, attacking its methodology as well as its aims.

On what is left of the political left, the situation is even more complex. There is a sharp inter-generational dimension at work: as if, after the great explosion of theoretical creativity of the post-World War II years, we were lost in a mournful landscape of repetitions without difference. In some ways, it is a sign of progress: what was blasphemy in the 1980s has by now become banality. The work of Foucault and Derrida 'once discursive bomb-throwers and banes of traditionalists, are now standard authorities to be cited in due course' (Williams 2014: 25). But they also function as regular intellectual scapegoats to explain all the evils that have befallen us.[2] These attacks on French theory made in the United States tend to spread to all theory-inclined Humanities, in the context of a swift loss of public support.

Melancholia is the dominant mood. While the centre falters into self-doubt (Latour 2004), a forensic, spectral dimension has seeped into our patterns of thinking. This is boosted, on the right of the political spectrum, by ideas about the historical triumph of capitalism and the inevitability of civilizational crusades that were triggered by 9/11 (Huntington 1996). On the political left, the rejection of theory has resulted in a wave of resentment and negative thought against the previous intellectual generations. In this context of theory fatigue, neo-communist intellectuals

(Badiou and Žižek 2009) have argued for the need to return to concrete political action, even violent antagonism if necessary, rather than indulge in more theoretical speculations. While a few remarkable and coherent scholars did take the jump and entered political life (Douzinas 2017), other left-leaning thinkers were quite content with both professing their impotence and reverting to youthful Leninist convictions, (Badiou 2013), or stating their all-out attraction to strongmen as a remedy against ineffectual and gendered liberalism (Žižek 2016).

Another way of stating the same case is by looking at the rise and fall of the intellectual class as the self-appointed critical force in society. The figure of the intellectual historically pre-dates World War II but it acquires a sharper edge after the violence and horrors of fascism, the holocaust, Hiroshima and Nagasaki, and the Cold War partition of that world (Braidotti 2016a). The philosophical generation of the existentialists, with Sartre and Beauvoir as figure-heads, made responsibility for the state of society and the world the core business of philosophy throughout the post-war period.

Intellectuals became even more active in the aftermath of the global insurrection known as 'May 1968'. The generation of baby-boomers that was to become my postgraduate teachers – notably Foucault and Deleuze – thought very seriously about their social responsibility. They drew a useful distinction between universal, organic and specific functions for the intellectuals (Foucault and Deleuze 1977). These different models were drawn respectively from the Hegelian–Marxist universal tradition, from Antonio Gramsci's organic model and the engaged thinkers of Sartre and Beauvoir's generation, to end with their own 'specific' understanding of the task of intellectuals. Although the distinction between these categories is not fixed but porous and each can unfold separately, or maybe because of this flexibility, their three-fold scheme is still quite useful as an analytical tool. Let us look at it more closely.

The common denominator for both the organic and the specific intellectual is the rejection of universalism and the ethical-political commitment to provide adequate and reasoned cartographies of power. Power is approached in its immanent and situated historical formations, as are the production of knowledge and discourse. For my generation (Braidotti 2014), that position went hand-in-hand with the critique of European Humanism and its vehement and often belligerent universal pretensions, echoing Lyotard's insight into the decline of master narratives (1979). The specific or situated intellectuals' practice rests on the critique of embedded and embodied relations through cartographies of power that also entail the feminist politics of locations and the critique of racism and colonialism. Intellectual practices generated innovative pedagogical methods, aimed at increasing public literacy and democratic criticism (Said 2004). This resulted in the production of a number of inter-disciplinary research areas that called themselves Studies. I shall return to these in chapter 4, as they will prove crucial for the making of the Critical PostHumanities.

The specificity of the critical task of the intellectual was to undergo quite a few mutations in the decades that followed. The very term 'intellectual' was phased out throughout the late 1980s and replaced by a new class of 'content providers', also known as the regime of experts and consultants (Anderson 1997). This downgrading shift coincided with the increased privatization of research following the official end of the Cold War in 1989 and the impact of a new techno-scientific culture based on information technologies and bio-genetics. As Williams put it: 'Theory got rid of the touchy-feely aura of the Humanities, refurbishing them with an aura of techno-expertise' (2014: 43).

The 1990s in philosophy are also known as the period of the 'theory wars', which saw the beginning of the reaction by the political right and its public media (Arthur and Shapiro 1995). They targeted academics who practised critical theory and especially academic thinkers who are close to French post-structuralist philosophy, reaching a strident peak by the turn of the millennium (Lambert 2001). These virulent campaigns against French theory, notably Derrida, which were re-packaged as 'postmodernism' and made synonymous with theory itself, coincided with the slow but systemic rise of the American far right. Trump and his cohort today are an effect of this development, which they bring to new lows of verbal violence and indecency. But anti-intellectualism and contempt for the university are key components of populist movements the world over.

The successive campaigns against theory, which we are experiencing again today, made of violent attacks and demeaning dismissals, coincided with the transformations of the economy. These changes resulted in far-reaching alterations of the institutional structure of the university itself. The establishment of 'research universities' run according to neo-liberal economic rules and struggling to get classified in a world-ranking order, changed the very terms of academic life. It included the creation of social classes within the university staff, of both academic stars and a new academic 'precariat'.[3] In this respect, the discussion about the status of theory in the Humanities and the right-wing backlash against it, overlaps with broader concerns about the position of the university as an institution in posthuman times.

By the end of the 1990s, it was obvious to all that the only 'content provider' that really mattered was the Internet itself, thus tipping the balance against the critical orientation of the Humanities. The former intellectuals were relegated to the market-oriented position of 'ideas brokers' and, in the best-case scenario, 'thought leaders'. By now the mutation of capitalism into a cognitive differential machine was in full swing (Deleuze and Guattari 1977, 1987; Moulier-Boutang 2012), and anti-theory became a dominant reflex in a neo-liberal economic order (Felski 2015). While only a decade ago Peter Galison (2004) could point out the advantages of this change of mood, welcoming the end of grand systems in favour of more 'specific' theory, more recently Jeffrey Williams was justified in lamenting that 'now we are entrepreneurs of the mind and it wears us down' (2014: 166). Academics are exhausted by over-work and constant competitive evaluations (Berg and Seeber 2016).

But the crisis was far from universal. The uneven fortunes of academic publishing seemed to get compensated by the rise of best-selling non-fiction literature by academic celebrities, who were both commercially successful and media-savvy (Thompson 2005; 2010). Their visibility was often manipulated to conceal the impoverished reality of the field (Collini 2012; Williams 2014). Other academic fields simply boomed. For instance, Matthew Fuller argues that contrary to the general trend, the 1990s was a period of theoretical and practical exuberance for media theory, because of the rise of cyber-cultures, and new areas of research after the end of the Cold War. It is significant that a media theorist would propose such a positive assessment of the side-effects of the end of Communism in Europe, and hence sound so optimistic about the general health of the Humanities (Fuller 2008). Media studies, with its focus on the non-anthropocentric, technological apparatus and on objects of enquiry like networks, codes and systems, is one of the many motors and beneficiaries of the posthuman convergence. It may alone account for a great deal of the vitality of the contemporary Humanities.

The trajectory that traces the descending curve of the status and fortunes of the intellectuals is problematic not only in terms of this particular class of practitioners, but also for what it reveals about the institutional settings and the changing social position of the academic Humanities in particular and the university in general. The often acrimonious nature of the debate about the role of critical intellectuals merely highlighted the institutional vulnerability of the Humanities at the time. But this hostility is directly proportional to the extent to which the university itself simultaneously came under fire (Berubé and Nelson 1995). The 'post-theory' mood, in other words, coincides with the end of public financial support for higher education (Williams 2014) and 'a broader scaling down within the Humanities and Social Sciences, of the kind of radicalism that anti-imperial and postcolonial work often enabled' (Nixon 2011: 259). Surveying this situation, Coetzee suggests that the assault on the Humanities, which started in the 1980s, has successfully rid this institution of all academics that were 'diagnosed as leftists or anarchist or anti-rational or anti-civilisational' (2013). So much so that 'to conceive of universities any more as seedbeds of agitation and dissent would be laughable' (Coetzee 2013).

Government support and funding for the academic Humanities have been reduced in institutions across the Western world, despite their attempt at reinventing themselves as 'research' universities (Cole, Barber and Graubard 1993). The 'last professors' who still believed in their critical intellectual mission (Donoghue 2008) and in academic freedom (Menand 1996) denounced 'the university in ruins' (Readings 1996). Many took a stand against the corporate university and increasing tuition fees for students, refusing to be cast as merely managerial figures. Williams argues that in the last forty years, the public university in the United States has been transformed 'from a flagship of the post-war welfare system to a privatized enterprise, oriented toward business and its own self-accumulation' (2014: 6). The neo-liberal re-organization of the institution of the university was implemented through practices like: the academic star system (Shumway 1997), the research audits, the output metrics and the quantification of impact assessment, the privatization of higher education, the emphasis on monetarization of results through systemic grants and fund-raising, etc.

The question of the public value of the Humanities (Small 2013) has come to the fore, as policy-makers apply narrow economic criteria to assess the academic 'market'. The new labour structure within the university – especially in the US – reflects the hierarchical values of neo-liberal economics. A sharp distinction came into being between a small percentage (in the US less than a third, according to Williams) of tenured staff at the top of the scale that labours under increased pressure to generate income through grant submissions. Then there is a large section of an academic 'precariat' at the bottom of the structure: part-time, temporary, untenured and under-paid teaching staff with heavy teaching loads and few research opportunities or career prospects. This mass of non-staff or temporary staff members experience working conditions of duress, stress and systemic exploitation in the UK (Gill 2010), which Marina Warner describes 'like working for a cross between IBM, with vertiginous hierarchies of command, and McDonald's' (2015: 9).

In an incisive study based in Canada, Berg and Seeber (2016) denounce the frantic pace and standardization of contemporary academic life, which are incompatible with the time for deep thought that scholarly research requires. They point out that the stress in academia exceeds that of the general population and the working conditions are unappealing and counter-productive. The neo-liberal governance of universities means that the much-praised flexibility of hours results in academics working all the time; the precarious contracts cause insecurity and stress. The daily life of academics is threatened by expanding class sizes, pervasive technologies and excessive administration. They argue forcefully against the corporatization of the university and the transformation of the global academic market into a branch of research capitalism, which reduces the university to the status of a firm manufacturing knowledge products.

Progressive academics responded to this situation by pleading for a non-profit approach to the Humanities and to higher education, following the classical Liberal Arts model (Nussbaum 2010), while more sceptical voices wondered if there was a future at all for the field (Collini 2012). One of the areas of growth within the Humanities at institutional level today occurs at the intersection between national security matters, issues of surveillance and anti-terrorism. Ever since Lynne Cheney, speaking for the Bush administration in 2001 declared the academics the 'weak link' in the war on terror, much pressure was put on the university to fall in line with official government policy on defence and related matters. The relevance of the Humanities for security studies has been growing ever since (Burgess 2014).

In Continental Europe, the populist right-wing politicians that came to power in the aftermath of 9/11 and the wars that followed it, up till today, are explicitly hostile to the fields of culture and the arts both in society and as an academic curriculum. Art and culture, and the field of the Humanities, for instance, got dismissed as 'left-wing hobbies' by right-wing populist Geert Wilders in the Netherlands and became the target of massive government cutbacks as they are considered worthless investments. This trend continues nowadays in Germany, where the far-right group 'Alternative for Germany' is triggering a 'culture war' against progressive writers, artists and performers.

Literature and the literary critic nowadays are perceived – by management, policy-makers and a large section of the media – as a luxury, not as a necessity, a trend that Marina Warner describes as 'new brutalism in academia' (2014: 42). The pride previous generations could take in the great tradition of literature, music and culture is no longer a point of consensus in a globalized and technologically mediated world. Moreover, a shared sensibility based on the knowledge of the canonical literary texts cannot be assumed or taken for granted, either in the West, or in the rest of the world. Warner's trenchant comment says it all: 'Faith in the value of a humanist education is beginning to look like an antique romance' (2015: 10). This general shift of sensibility is enough to make me almost nostalgic for the days of the modern-postmodern dispute, when Edward Said clashed with Harold Bloom on this very issue and defended an anti-elitist conception of culture, cultural access and production, that favours cultural creativity as a collective activity and a form of democratic participation. Today, the Humanities as a whole no longer occupy a hegemonic position within the hierarchy of knowledge production systems in the contemporary world. Similarly, the critical intellectual, far from representing the idealized self-image of the developed world's subjects, is under severe scrutiny. In this respect, I concur with Redfield who argues that 'theory is a symptom of and a defence against the increasing marginality of literary culture and the bureaucratisation of the professoriat' (2016: 132).

In response to this morose social and academic climate, I first of all acknowledge it and empathize with the struggle to defend the Humanities. At the same time, however, I will adopt an affirmative position, exhaustion notwithstanding. I defend the productivity of the contemporary PostHumanities as pointing to a posthuman future for the field, accounting for the tensions of our times in a manner that is empirically grounded, without being reductive and avoiding negativity. To support my case, I will map out some of the ways in which the PostHumanities are currently being developed in our globally linked and technologically mediated societies. In such a context I intend to keep a strong connection to the critical theory tradition of speaking truth to power and to analyse how authority is formed and operationalized, while helping to ferry it across the posthuman convergence. In spite of its detractors, the work of critique is never done and the critical intellectual is, more than ever, someone who 'represents the powerless, the dispossessed' (Said in Viswanathan 2001: 413). All the more so as many of these, today, are not humans.

The posthuman convergence challenges both the melancholia and the sense of doom that has marked so many recent discussions about the contemporary Humanities. It is vital to note that the quest for an appropriate posthuman image of thought cannot be dissociated from an ethics of inquiry that demands respect for the complexities of the real-life world we are living in. By extension, the development of new scholarly fields and scientific methods in the Humanities, as we shall see in the next chapters, shows that, in spite of alleged exhaustion, the field is highly productive. This creativity reflects the complex and fast-changing position of the university within our technologically mediated, Anthropocene-framed societies. Considering the high productivity rates, I concur with many of my colleagues that the institutional cutbacks on the Humanities have to stop and new investments must be injected. The working conditions in the field also need to be reviewed and improved, because this is not a moment of crisis, but rather of unparalleled growth.

Moreover, the idea of 'crisis' is an inadequate description of the institutional status of the contemporary Humanities, given that this field has historically operated through self-reflection and adaptation to changing circumstances. So much so that the 'crisis' may be taken as the Humanities' *modus operandi*, as Gayatri Spivak (1988) astutely suggested in response to Foucault's analysis of the 'death of Man'. Whether in a strong and self-assertive posture, or as 'weak thought' (Vattimo and Rovatti 2012), the theoretical Humanities are the field that posits itself as a perennially open question, constitutionally Socratic, so to speak. Thus, although it is undeniable that Humanities scholars are investing disproportionate amounts of time defending themselves in the public sphere, there is no reason to despair.

The posthuman convergence evokes a different perception of the scholar and scientist, which is removed from the classical model of the humanistic 'Man of Reason' as the quintessential European citizen (Lloyd 1984). The posthuman challenges us to update this model, by taking in the huge impact of media and technology, moving towards an intensive form of trans-disciplinarity and boundary-crossings among a range of discourses. This movement enacts a transversal embrace of conceptual diversity in scholarship. It favours hybrid mixtures of practical and applied knowledge, and relies on the defamiliarization of our institutionalized habits of thought. Tracking the discursive and material formations of the human within the institutional practice of the Humanities and focusing on the formations of subjectivity remain an integral component of this book project.

Post-Work Fatigue

A sizable portion of the manic-depressive affective economy that we are in is a direct effect of the new economy. Deleuze and Guattari's (1977, 1987) anatomy of advanced capitalism taught us that it functions through deterritorializing flows that destabilize social structures with ruthless self-interested energy. The global economy is all about differential speed of development: it is a spinning machine that perverts global nature as well as global culture and subsumes all living materials – human and non-human – to a logic of commodification and consumption (Franklin, Lury and Stacey 2000). This results in the proliferation of commodified options, constant consumption and quantified selves, and makes for an unsustainable system – a 'future eater' (Flannery 1994) – that erodes its own foundations and sabotages the conditions of possibility for endurance (Patton 2000; Braidotti 2002; Protevi 2009, 2013).

At the same time, as feminist and post-colonial theories (Grewal and Kaplan 1994) pointed out, global consumerism, while promoting an ideology of 'no borders', implements a highly controlled system of hyper-mobility of consumer goods, information bytes, data and capital, whereas people do not circulate nearly as freely. As a result of such speed of differential mobility, a global diaspora (Brah 1996) has replaced the exemplary condition of 'exile' (Said 1994), producing dramatically different nomadic subject positions: migrant workers, refugees, VIP frequent flyers, daily commuters, tourists, pilgrims and others. The violence of capitalist deterritorializations induces the exodus of populations on an unprecedented planetary scale, which includes evictions, homelessness and systemic dispossession (Sassen 2014). Structural injustices, including increasing poverty and indebtedness (Deleuze and Guattari 1977; Lazzarato 2012) condemn large portions of the world population to sub-human life-conditions. This 'necropolitical' governmentality (Mbembe 2003) is at work through technologically mediated wars and counter-terrorism strategies which, together with the rise of xenophobia and illiberal governance, are defining features of the posthuman convergence. The in-human(e) aspects of the posthuman condition is one of the reasons why I want to foreground the question of the subject and subjectivity, so as to work out what the posthuman may mean for our collective resistance and ethical accountability.

The exceptionally high level of technological mediation we are experiencing is inscribed within the profit axiom (Toscano 2005) that is also known as 'cognitive capitalism' (Moulier-Boutang 2012). This system capitalizes on the production of marketable knowledge, notably data about matter, by increasing the speed of technological innovation and supporting the convergence and combination of different branches of technology. Artificial intelligence, neural sciences and robotics, genomics and stem-cell research; nanotechnologies, smart materials and 3-D printing overlap with and reinforce each other. Algorithmic culture at work everywhere in our daily existence has triggered new financial systems with their own crypto-currencies. They also feed a surge of security and privacy concerns, which has led some critics to speak of "surveillance capitalism" (Zuboff, 2019).

What counts as capital today is the informational power of living matter itself, in its immanent capacity to self-organize. This produces a new political economy: 'the politics of Life itself' (Rose 2007), also known as 'Life as surplus' (Cooper 2008), or, quite simply as the post-genomic economy of 'biocapital' (Rajan 2006). The true capital today is the vital, self-organizing power of converging technologies whose vitality seems unsurpassable. Advanced capitalism has accordingly acquired many names; it is also known as 'capitalism as schizophrenia' (Deleuze and Guattari 1987), 'platform capitalism' (Srnicek 2016), 'Psychopharmacopornocapitalism' (Preciado 2013), or 'narco-capitalism' (De Sutter 2018). It is a system where high degrees of technological mediation encounter deep social and economic inequalities, which engender rage and frustration.

Advanced capitalism has proved more flexible, adaptable and insidious than the twentieth-century progressive political movements predicted. Again, the multi-scalar speed of capital is at work here, so that the double-binds and contradictions multiply. This highly mediated system rests on the financialization of the economy, which entails the split between fast-moving finance and static, grounded labour wages. This discrepancy between the financial and the real economies lie at the core of neo-liberal systems. This in turn implies the suspension of job security and the establishment of precarious, zero-hours labour contracts in all sectors, including the academic world. But it also requires digital skills and algorithmic fluency; it rewards the ability to think outside the box, but without rocking the boat. Thus, the advances at the core of the Fourth Industrial Revolution create as many problems as they solve: issues of egalitarian access to these advanced technologies, and the violence of social inequalities, run parallel to the massive job suppressions the new technologies are triggering in the job market. All these in turn take their toll on the on-going depletion of Earth resources. In this respect, there seems to be no end to the 'wrath of capital' (Parr 2013). Workers' solidarity therefore must go hand in hand with issues of environmental justice and fair partici-pation in a techno-democratic system that is both sustained and threatened by the informatics of domination (Haraway 1990). Hyperbolical speed of mobility of capital, information and data co-exists with blocked realities of no growth and no access. Global migration exemplifies the schizoid double-pull of speed and stasis, movement and arrest. As such, it is a systemic component of the global economy.

Contemporary left-wing social thinkers have singled out the flagrant injustices and the polarization of economic resources of this system, struggling to re-adjust the balance. While sharing their goal, I am not always convinced by their analysis of the current economy, partly because most social theory continues to uphold the modernist and constructivist vision of the social space as defined essentially by anthro-pomorphic conflicts and resistance, vigilance and solidarity. These same qualities are transferred to the class of the intel-lectuals and activists who historically embody the struggle to critique the system. These are worthy ideals, which I fully share, but the problem is they do not fully grasp the contradictions of the posthuman convergence.

For instance, in *Platform Capitalism*, Srnicek (2016) analyses it within a conventional Marxist frame of reference, based on a social constructivist method that pitches humans in an antagonistic relationship to their own technologies. This results in a classical socialist proposal for a 'post-work' cybernetic society (Srnicek and Williams 2015), in which humans will be liberated from their dreary tasks through advanced technologies. This analysis, however, fails to address the defining features of the Fourth Industrial Revolution, namely the fact that it rests upon the bio-genetic capitalization of all living systems, and a pervasive use of self-correcting technologies, driven by artificial intelligence. What this 'smart' system of technologically mediated life systems achieves is the suppression of labour itself. It is estimated that by the early 2030s, 30% of jobs in OECD countries could be at risk because of automation. So the burning issue of the systemic divide between the financial and the wage economy remains unchallenged by Srnicek's analysis. It is not work as a whole that will be terminated as much as the economy of salaried human labour (Brown 2016). Adopting an old-fashioned understanding of technology as instrumental, rather than intimately interwoven in the social fabric, results in failing to account for the full extent of technological impact on our daily lives, or our sense of subjectivity and our imaginings.

Taking a different stance, Terranova (2004) stresses the importance of developing a political agenda fit for the contradictions of contemporary networked societies and their 'hypersocial' structures. Bringing the full impact of technological mediation to bear on her analysis of the new economy and the ways in which it both structures and fragments, unifies and divides categories and classes, Terranova proposes to build on the progressive and unprogrammed potential of the on-going transformations. They offer opportunities to refocus the economy in post-capitalist directions, based on enhanced social cooperation, and the sharing of wealth and resources, of the financial, technological, environmental and affective kind. The old dream of socialist cybernetics needs to be replaced, argues Terranova (2018), by a contemporary revision of both labour and social welfare in the form of posthuman 'commonfare' – new digital, ecological and social commons. Moreover, access to 'commonfare' resources and facilities needs to be equally distributed, not only across social classes, but also along the lines of sexualized, racialized and naturalized others.

Another original approach to the analysis of social relation of labour starts from feminist politics of embodiment. Arguing that even the most advanced theories of post-industrial labour do not deal adequately with embodied realities, Cooper and Waldby analyse the embodied labour involved in the new reproductive economy. That includes surrogacy, the sales of body tissues, organs, blood and the participation in clinical trials of what they call the 'biomedical economy' (Cooper and Waldby 2014: 4). This covers the pharmaceutical industry that feeds the new reproductive market and the stem-cell industry that feeds the life sciences sector. Arguing that these forms of labour are unacknowledged and certainly underpaid, they call them 'clinical labour'. They call for critical analyses of this new class phenomenon through feminist and de-colonial frames. In an affirmative twist, however, they see them also as materially embedded contributions to a new economy that overstresses its disembodied and disembedded structure, the better to disavow its debt to the biological resources of contemporary humans, non-human and techno-mediated subjects. The emphasis of this analysis falls on the distinctive character of contemporary labour formations and on their affirmative potential.

Deleuze and Guattari's anatomy of advanced capitalism as schizophrenia (1987) is a relevant and necessary tool to seize the complexity and multi-scalar movements of speed and stasis of capital. But it is not sufficient as a social cartography of contemporary posthuman scholarship. In order to capture the systemic oscillations of cognitive capitalism and its swinging moods, we need to account both for the profoundly logophilic character of this system, the generative powers it mobilizes, and also for its insidious logo-phobic core. Given the over-abundance of data, and research-driven information and knowledge, reactive forces of disciplining and punishment are also at work in the complex, technologically mediated structures of our social system. Usually packaged under the term 'security', these restrictive bio and necro-political tendencies are co-extensive with the vitality of cognitive capitalism. The dividing line between the negative, entropic, self-serving spins of capitalist greed and scientific knowledge at the service of sustainability is provided by a relational ethics of affirmation that I develop in this book.

I submit that we need posthuman theory, less fatigue and more, far more conceptual creativity. It is not by relinquishing the practice of subjectivity altogether that we are likely to even produce an adequate cartography of these shifting conditions, let alone begin to sketch a possible solution for them. On the contrary, we need to re-cast ethical and political subjectivity for posthuman times.

Democracy Fatigue

The social fractures induced by the new economy run deep and cause a radicalization of political and social movements. Populism is rising right and left of the political spectrum, as if democracy no longer succeeded in igniting the popular imagination. Mindful of Husserl's comments about the crisis of European Humanities and Social Sciences in the 1930s, I do wonder about the suicidal tendencies of the democratic system and whether representative democracy is at all immunized against its own reactionary elements (Brown 2015). The sobering awareness that democracy in itself is not enough to save us from its electoral majority is crucial at a historical time when the political momentum seems to be on the side of illiberal movements. We need a stronger ethical stamina to deal with this kind of pressure.

Far too many people today are voting democratically for anti-democratic movements. Contemporary Western politicians – ranging from Donald Trump, the Brexiteers, to the Visegrad group's attraction to Vladimir Putin[4] – have perfected the art of manipulating public resentment and discontent, channelling it towards xenophobia and racism. These exploitative politicians only 'empathize' with the pain and despair of their electorate to the extent that they encourage them to scapegoat their built-up anger onto women, LBGTQ+, migrants, foreigners, asylum-seekers and other figures of despised 'otherness'.

Former liberal thinkers turning arch-conservative, in response to the current US administration's preference for white supremacy, is becoming a salient feature of the contemporary American theory wars (Lilla 2017). The blanket-term 'political correctness' is resurrected and adopted as a term of abuse by both right- and left-wing populist movements, with leftists like Žižek not only supporting President Trump but also blaming the progressive Liberals for the rise of the far-right. This perverse political climate of over-indulgence for illiberal, authoritarian systems and movements also results in the resurgence of the anti-theory tactic that was widely used back in the 1990s. Namely the double charge of cognitive relativism and of anti-scientific methods, against any critical discourses that reflect the experiences and interests of social minorities and those who are excluded from the new economy. These tactics, spearheaded today by gurus of white masculine prowess like the Canadian clinical psychologist Jordan Peterson (2018), are particularly harmful for the Humanities, as they challenge their scientific credibility. In keeping with the bigotry of the times, these neo-conservatives adopt a heavily moralizing language, accusing the critical and theoretical Humanities of nothing less than 'corruption' and betrayal of their allegedly moral mission.

But cultural differences across the Atlantic persist and, in a spectacular reversal of a time-honoured reactionary tradition, right-wing populist movements in the European Union have come out in favour of feminist and gay rights. This is the case notably in France, where the National Front, under the influence of its former deputy leader and gay activist Florian Philippot took a firm stand against the ancestral homophobia of Jean-Marie Le Pen's party. This turnabout happened even earlier in the Netherlands, where Pim Fortuyn first, and later the Freedom Party of Geert Wilders embraced the LBGTQ+ cause. The most recent phenomenon occurred in Germany, where Alice Weidel, an out lesbian, became the leader of the Parliamentary group of the far-right party Alternative for Germany. These hyper-nationalist and racist political organizations make an instrumental use of LBGTQ+ and feminist issues, as an example of alleged Western superiority over Islam. This opportunistic tactic – which is also known under a variety of terms, including 'sexual nationalism', 'homonationalism' and 'queer nationalism' (Puar 2007) – is an attempt to enlist the transformative and radical social project of feminist and LBGTQ+ rights to a xenophobic civilizational campaign against Islam.

The appeal to strong nationalist values and the incitement to xenophobia, promoting detention, expulsion and exclusions, produces what Deleuze and Guattari call *micro-fascism* (1977), both on the left and the right. The manipulations currently practised by populist movements and their reckless leaders aim at spreading hatred, divisiveness and racism. Nationalistic anti-intellectualism is on the rise again, with the Internet facilitating not only instant communication, but also daily outpourings of vitriol. It is both objectionable and exhausting on at least two grounds: in terms of its unabashed stupidity and because it has happened before in European history (I am here borrowing the words of Hannah Arendt, 2006).

In response, in this book I will attempt to re-ignite a democratic imaginary, by emphasizing affirmative political passions and a collective pursuit of freedom. I will start from the acknowledgement of the fractures and disenchantments of our times, but re-work them within an affirmative ethical praxis.

This is not a simple or pain-free process, of course, but anger and opposition alone are not enough: they need to be transformed into the power to act so as to become a constitutive force. The crucial question is: who and how many are 'we'? Resisting the bellicose appeal of *the* people, I argue that politics begins with assembling just *a* people, a community constructed around a shared understanding of their condition. This space of encounter is also where forms of action can be produced, about our shared hopes and aspirations. Critique and creation work hand-in-hand. This productive relational approach is all the more important considering the contradictions of our times. 'We' may well be both excited about our technological advances and injured by the social fractures and injustices of our system. But even before we can agree on what we want to build together as an alternative, we have to confront the question: to what extent can 'we' say that 'we' are in *this* together?

In other words, in order to activate solidarity and resistance, it is better to avoid hasty recompositions of one 'humanity' bonded in fear and vulnerability. I prefer to work affirmatively and defend grounded locations, complexity and a praxis-oriented, differential vision of what binds us together. It is it important, for instance, in the era of the Anthropocene, to see the close links between neo-liberal economic politics and a system of disenfranchisements and exclusion of entire layers of both the human population and the non-human agents of our planet. We need to think through *both* the Fourth Industrial Revolution *and* the Sixth Extinction

Small wonder then that the predominant mood in our social existence is a see-saw of exhaustion and of pervasive anxiety. It is as if our psychic landscape were framed by a manic-depressive emotional economy that leaves us all hanging in there, somewhere. Many people feel on the margins of the much-heralded 'new' economy, and dread its immediate social effects. Geo-politically, all sense of security had already left our lives during the Manhattan project of the 1950s and 1960s, but the contemporary transformation goes further and strikes deeper. After the Cold War, global warming.

And global warnings as well – some of them ecological, others geo-political. Now that the West no longer has just one major Soviet enemy, but only a diffuse target called 'war on terror', we are suffering a series of break-ins of our collective immunity systems, through a mode of governance that works by fear and mistrust. And we are also experiencing a regression of our civic bonds and political ties, a breakdown of the trust that used to unify us. It does not bode well for twenty-first-century democracy (Rorty 1998). Enemies seem to emerge everywhere: home-grown boys turn terrorist against their own societies, neighbours become murderous opponents. There is danger everywhere, and it remains unspecified, so that we live in the expectation of the catastrophe: a virus, of the organic or of the technological kind, or just the next computer crash. The point is that the accident is both imminent and immanent to our lives; it will happen, it is only a question of time (Massumi 1992).

In the same spirit, Jean-Luc Nancy (2015) is rightly worried about the extent to which the interdependence of contemporary systems – ecological, social or technological, but also in terms of warfare and security systems – get translated into joint infrastructures and common use of resources. What really binds these systems is their shared dependence on the connection to capital, defined as the accumulation and exchange of profits. For Nancy this high degree of interdependence on an all-pervading capitalism is the true catastrophe. For him, it is an on-going deployment of planetary risks to which we all are exposed, although he does not question the universality of that 'we'.

While Massumi and Nancy stress the immanence and imminence of the catastrophe, I prefer to draw out different elements of the notion of immanence, for example its virtual capacity to engender resistance. In keeping with my affirmative project for posthuman subjectivity, I advocate a different kind of politics of immanence. Rather than taking flight into some vulnerable pan-humanity, I plead for an immanent – and yet fluid – re-grounding of ourselves in the messy contradictions of the present. My term for this position is: materialist immanence. Moreover, far from marking the rejection, extinction or the impoverishment of the human, the posthuman condition is a way of reconstituting the human.[5] But this regeneration of the human is not unilateral or universal, but rather situated, perspectivist and hence internally fractured and potentially antagonistic. For some it becomes a form of trans-human enhancement, for others a Gaia-oriented down-sizing of human arrogance. For most, it demands some sort of acknowledgement of solidarity with other humans but also an embrace of the non-humans. This range of options indicates that there are many dynamics of redefinition of the human and of posthuman subject formation coming into being in this convergence.

What is at stake in this frenzy of potential redefinitions of the human after Humanism and anthropocentrism, is the issue of how contemporary power is being constituted, how it impacts on what we know and on the ways we may or may not feel that 'we' are in *this* together. We need to start with constructing a plane of encounter for multiple differential positions, which acknowledge their situated and hence partial perspectives. The project rests on the preliminary agreement that we need to re-negotiate – beyond Humanism and anthropocentrism – the terms by which the human is composed, conceptualized and experienced socially in our day and age. We need to negotiate who 'we' are.

The challenge that lies ahead is multiple: posthuman times call for and are sustained by posthuman subjects of knowledge constituted within them across a number of rather exhausting contradictions and paradoxes. And yet, they are producing new social imaginaries and social relations best exemplified by dynamic fields of transdisciplinary posthuman knowledge, which I call the Critical PostHumanities. They give me hope for the future.

Chapter 2
Posthuman Subjects

All differences notwithstanding, most posthumanists would agree that we currently need an enlarged, distributed and transversal concept of what a subject is and of how it deploys its relational capacities. Moving beyond humanist exceptionalism, subjectivity has to include the relational dependence on multiple non-humans and the planetary dimension as a whole. Transversality is the operational concept that helps to conceptualize the subject across multiple axes. Yet, scholars in the posthuman field differ as to how far it can be pushed: trans-sex and transgender are by now well-known categories (Stryker and Whittle 2006; Stryker and Aizura 2013), but trans-species (Tsing 2015), multi-species (Kirksey and Helmreich 2010) and trans-corporeality (Alaimo 2010) may be a step too far for the Humanities. Is subjectivity still an adequate notion in response to the posthuman convergence?

To find some answers, I turn to the empirical evidence provided by the collaborative discursive production of posthuman research and scholarship. Clearly, a new array of distinctly 'smart' objects has entered our existence, as well as the fields of academic research. They emerge from the fast-expanding universe of digital data, that is now coterminous with so many aspects of our daily lives, through 'the Internet of Things',[1] in the fast-devolving world of the Anthropocene.

The themes of current research in the Humanities reflect this conflictual non-human diversity of object of enquiry: today we have animal studies, critical plant studies and eco- and geo-criticism, as well as algorithmic studies, to mention just a few. Humanities scholars nowadays are dealing with objects such as forests, fungi, dust and bio-hydro-solar-techno entities, but also codes, software and digital waste. The wealth of posthuman and neo-materialist scholarship is such as to prevent any synthesis. The best we can do for now (see the next chapter) is to offer a comprehensive cartography of what posthuman knowledge is in the process of producing and becoming (Braidotti and Hlavajova 2018).

For many working in the field, however, the issue of subjectivity sits uncomfortably with the posthuman predic-ament. The scholarship tends to be polarized between on the one hand vehement dismissals of the need for a theory of subjectivity at all, and on the other a tendency to reinscribe subjectivity into the humanistic tradition, albeit it with a few revisions and corrections. I am rather uncomfortable with such a polarization and seek some middle ground. We need a subject position worthy of our times. This means to prioritize issues linked to social justice, ethical accountability, sustain-ability and to trans-species and intergenerational solidarity (Braidotti 2006, 2013). By 'posthumanizing' subjectivity, it can be re-positioned as a dynamic convergence phenomenon across the contradictions of posthumanism and post-anthro-pocentrism. Highlighting the advantages and potentials of this shift of perspective helps develop a suitable ethical framework to do justice to its multi-layered complexity. My affirmative vision of the subject offers a useful platform to construct the kind of transversal non-human alliances required for a posthuman subject.

The posthuman predicament requires even more diversified relational skills. Posthuman subjects are a work-in-progress: they emerge as both a critical and a creative project within the posthuman convergence along posthumanist and post-anthropocentric axes of interrogation. They interrogate the self-representations and conventional understandings of being human, which 'we' have inherited from the past. In doing so, they explore the multi-faceted and differential nature of the collective 'we'.

What constitutes subjectivity is a structural *relational* capacity, coupled with the specific degree of force or power that any one entity is endowed with: their ability to extend towards and in proximity with others. They compose a subjectivity without a centralized subject and 'his' ancestral tree of knowledge. No arborescent subjects, but rhizomic ones (Deleuze and Guattari 1994). Bodies are both embedded and embodied, and have relational and affective powers. As such they are capable of different things and different speeds of becoming. Subjects defined as transversal relational entities do not coincide with a liberal individual, but are rather a 'haecceity' – that is to say a degree of power in the affirmative sense of *potentia*, which means an event of complex singularities or intensities (Deleuze and Guattari 1994). Subjectivity is thus both post-personal and pre-individual, relational and hence in constant negotiation with multiple others and immersed in the conditions that it is trying to understand and modify, if not overturn.

A philosophy of immanence, or of situated perspectives, implies an epistemological obligation to reach adequate understandings of the conditions of one's existence. This entails, in turn, the ethical duty to be worthy of one's own times so as to account for, and interact affirmatively with them, in response to changing circumstances. What this practical philosophy offers is the field of problems and questions themselves, that is to say the cartography of the power relations that are currently re-shaping the formulation of the problem of subjectivity and call for new concepts (Deleuze 2006).

But how does the posthuman impact on the question of subjectivity? Is posthuman subjectivity not a contradiction in terms? Is the human still the necessary point of reference to define the knowing subject and if so, how exactly? What does it mean to be a subject in an era that claims to be simultaneously more-than-human and less-than-human? More than human because of its multi-scalar transformations and technological advances, and less than human in its inhumane economic and social polarizations and irreversible environmental devastation. So the question is: who are 'we'?

In geo-political terms 'we posthuman subjects' are situated across multiple fractures and seemingly irreconcilable power differences. These include different degrees of access to the benefits of technological advances. Global flows of migration and the displacement of populations, growing economic disparities, mass evictions, rising racism and xenophobia, extensive warfare and climate change are the markers of our historicity. In this respect it is more productive to think of ourselves as planetary subjects rather than as global agents (Spivak 1999, 2003). The question therefore is both conceptual and ethical: what kind of subjects are 'we' – the human and inhuman inhabitants of this planet – positioned within a technologically driven 'second life', genetically modified food, robotics, synthetic biology, the acidification of the seas and the desertification of the earth? How can we develop a posthuman theoretical framework that aspires to justice, but is made outside the history of society, encompassing instead what we used to call the natural? (Chakrabarty 2009).

As a feminist, I have always been painfully aware that both the production of scientific knowledge and the institutionalized form of political power defended by liberalism and Marxism foreground a notion and a practice of the subject that is still dominated by Eurocentric humanistic assumptions. As an anti-racist, I acknowledge the important contribution of postcolonial and decolonial theories as well as the alternative, more ancient indigenous traditions of Humanism than the European. They offer a painstaking critical analysis of the extent to which racial assumptions and white supremacy have shaped the philosophical discussions about the human, that Western philosophers have come to take for granted (Whyte 2013; Todd 2016).

The challenge then is how to re-define the subject of knowledge and power without reference to that unitary, humanistic, Eurocentric and masculinist subject. Firmly committed to ontological pacifism, I aspire to a politics that opposes violence, while supporting critical contestations. The state's monopoly over violence, military power and the right to kill – key elements of contemporary necropolitics – need to be counteracted by community-driven mobilizations and activities that empower us to act affirmatively.

These operating principles are also concrete ways to apply my opening assumption, namely that the paradigm shift towards the posthuman is already taking place. The posthuman is not a utopian position to come, nor will it emerge from Silicon Valley, profit-driven futuristic programmes of enhancement that aim at transcending human biology and defying mortality (Kurzweil 2006). The transformation towards the posthuman is neither linear nor one-directional, but is rather a multi-faceted experimentation with what 'we' are capable of becoming. It is undeniable that the combined impact of the Fourth Industrial Revolution and the Sixth Extinction is altering the terms of our embodied existence, as well as our self-understanding, but changes and adjustments on this scale are both gradual and constant. We are not in a position yet to fully grasp the complexity of these internally contradictory phenomena. We need much more research on the material aspects that compose those phenomena, on their assumptions and implications. The material aspects refer to *zoe*, but also to the geological and technological aspects of transformation; I call it the *zoe*/geo/ techno assemblage. This process, with its social-economic effects, emotional and ethical impact, is too often presented in an over-simplified manner. Yet, this process of transformation towards the posthuman should not be taken for granted, like a sort of evolutionary destiny or socially inevitable goal. It is more useful to approach it instead as an experiment and ensure that it becomes the focus of public discussions, collective decision-making processes and joint actions. The on-going social transformations are so intense that they will eventually coalesce into a meta-pattern of new modes of subject formation. This project is still on-going and needs to be assessed critically and collectively. All the more reason to acknowledge that the posthuman convergence is already here, being the prime marker of our historicity.

Multi-Scalar Relationality

'We' are in the process of becoming posthumanist and post-anthropocentric, but not in the way of a Silicon Valley delusion, that this is a homogeneous or linear manner conducive to the composition of a more performative and enhanced pan-humanity. Instead, I emphasize the embodied, embedded and transversal selves that we are, bonded by ontological relationality. Embodied and embedded because we are deeply steeped in the material world. Transversal because we connect but also differ from each other. And yet we are structurally related to one another, to the human and non-human world that we live in. We are after all variations on a common matter. In other words, we differ from each other all the more as we co-define ourselves within the same living matter – environmentally, socially and relationally.

The key term is indeed relationality, operating in an embedded and embodied and grounded, multi-directional and multi-scalar manner. We are relational beings, defined by the capacity to affect and be affected. Posthuman subjectivity starts with the acknowledgement that what defines us as an autonomous capacity is not rationality, nor our cerebral faculty alone, but rather the autonomy of affect as a virtual force that gets actualized through relational bonds (Braidotti 2002; Massumi 2002). A vital neo-materialist philosophy is helpful to sustain this project. The capacity to affect and be affected is not to be confused with individualized emotions, as meaningful expression of psychological states and lived experiences. Affect needs to be de-psychologized, and to be de-linked from individualism in order to match the complexity of our human and non-human relational universe. This relational process supports a thick and dynamic web of interconnections by removing the obstacles of individualism. Life is not exclusively human: it encompasses both *bios* and *zoe* forces, as well as geo- and techno-relations that defy our collective and singular powers of perception and understanding.

Posthuman subjects establish relations on at least three levels: to one's self, to others and to the world. The world can be defined as a complex set of environmental, social and affective ecologies. What does it mean to say that subjects are relational? Firstly, that the agency commonly reserved for subjects is not the exclusive prerogative of *Anthropos*. Secondly, that it is not linked to classical notions of transcendental reason. Thirdly, that it is de-linked from a dialectical view of consciousness based on the opposition of self and others and their struggle for recognition. The knowing subject is not Man, or *Anthropos* alone, but a more complex assemblage that undoes the boundaries between inside and outside the self, by

emphasizing processes and flows. Neither unitary, nor autonomous, subjects are embodied and embedded, relational and
affective collaborative entities, activated by relational ethics.

The posthuman convergence introduces complexity on
multiple other scales, by stressing both the unity of *zoe/*
geo/techno-mediated material relations and their differential structure. Because of this multi-scalar relationality,
the subject of knowledge can by no means be framed exclusively by 'Man' and his sexualized, racialized and naturalized
'others'. Posthuman subjectivity is a transversal alliance that
nowadays involves non-human agents. This means that the
posthuman subject relates at the same time to the Earth –
land, water, plants, animals, bacteria – and to technological
agents – plastic, wires, cells, codes, algorithms. This transversal range reflects and sustains the posthuman convergence,
so that the frame and scope of epistemological and ethical
subjectivity is enlarged along the lines of posthumanist and
post-anthropocentric relations and the multiple perspectives
that inhabit them.

This cross-species transversality is quite liberatory and
therefore I am not prone to any sense of nostalgia for
the humanist 'Man of Reason' (Lloyd 1984) or sovereign
'Anthropos'. Posthuman knowledge production is rich and
creative and we should therefore avoid flat equivalences. It
is crucial to acknowledge the embedded and embodied and
hence accountable cartographies of the posthuman discourses
that are currently produced.

My case is then two-fold: firstly, that the posthuman
convergence is already upon us. Secondly that, far from being
a terminal crisis, it is productive, dynamic and inter-relational.
In my view the posthuman subject is a neo-materialist,
grounded thinker of dynamic and complex social and
discursive processes, but with a keen eye for issues of social
and political justice and a commitment to affirmative ethics.

Immanence and Differential Materialism

Posthuman subject-formation signals a change of speed in the
constitution of transversal subjects that extend beyond the
anthropomorphic humans themselves.

An immanent, posthuman project assumes that all matter or substance is one and immanent to itself. This means that the posthuman subject asserts the material totality of and interconnection with all living things. Moreover, vibrant matter (Bennett 2010) is taken as vital, intelligent and self-organizing. Vital matter is driven by the ontological desire for the expression of its innermost freedom; desire itself is a transversal ontological force that displaces categorical distinctions. This understanding of matter animates the composition of posthuman subjects of knowledge as embedded, embodied and yet flowing in a web of relations with human and non-human others. Posthuman subjectivity is an ensemble composed by *zoe*-logical, geological and technological organisms – it is a *zoe*/geo/techno assemblage.

The implications are both epistemological and ethical. The epistemological error of judgement is a form of misunderstanding that betrays the relational nature of the subject. This means that errors result in decreasing the relational power, positivity and activity of the subject. A misreading of the conditions of our un-freedom reduces our ability to become freer. The ethical implication is that reason is affective, embodied and relational. Understanding the passions is our way of experiencing them and making them work in our favour. The reference here is Spinoza who argues that desires arise from our passions (Spinoza 1996 [1677]). Given that affectivity is the power that activates our body and makes it want to act, a passion can never be excessive, provided we develop adequate understandings of its force. The human being's in-built tendency is towards joy and self-expression, not towards implosion. This fundamental positivity is the key to Deleuze's attachment to Spinoza (1988, 1990).

The posthuman subject is then embodied and embedded, and its relational affectivity produces a shared sense of belonging to, and knowledge of, the common world we are sharing. Relationality extends through the multiple ecologies that constitute us. Such webs of connections and negotiation engender a sense of familiarity with the world and foreground the simple fact that we are eco-sophical entities, that is to say ecologically interlinked through the multiple interconnections we share within the nature–culture continuum. The posthuman subject may be internally fractured, but is also technologically mediated and globally interlinked. Vital materialism stresses the affective intimacy with the world and a sense of engagement in a web of ever-shifting relations and perpetual becoming (Bataille 1988). Intimacy with the world speaks of our ability to re-collect it and re-connect to it and hence of our capacity to find our 'homes' within it (Braidotti 2006). It also activates a deep sense of care and compassion for the damaged state of our planet (Tsing et al. 2017), in the particular conjuncture that I define as the posthuman convergence.

Feminist theory is one of the precursors of posthuman thought, especially the neo-materialist and vitalist tradition that stresses the embodied, embedded and sexed roots of subjectivity and their unexplored resources. It put the emphasis on embodiment and lived experience, as well as underlining the intersectional inclusion of other axes of analysis such as race, age and class. Exploring the sophisticated workings of carnal awareness (Sobchack 2004), and the 'sensible transcendental' structure (Irigaray 1984) of human consciousness, neo-materialist feminist theory (Braidotti 1991) has pioneered an original form of relational embodied empiricism and highlighted its role in producing knowledge. In this respect it anticipates what Deleuze (1984) called the 'empirical transcendental'.

Furthermore, this enlarged sense of carnal empiricism has been implemented through a specific methodology: the politics of locations (Rich 1987). For innovative methods and practices of accountability, we can turn to feminist thought. Especially the materialist tradition of differential feminism that runs through 'standpoint theory' (Harding 1986, 1991), 'situated knowledges' (Haraway 1988) and nomadic subjectivity (Braidotti 1994, 2011a), has helped to develop alternative ways of embedding and embodying accountability. Feminism has replaced discriminatory unitary categories, based on Eurocentric, masculinist, anthropocentric and heteronormative assumptions, with robust alternatives. The embedded and embodied empiricism at work in feminist theory acts as the source of counter-knowledges, methods and values.

Another genealogical methodology comes from race and postcolonial theory, which also rest on situated perspectives, to focus on the effects of 'racialized ontologies' upon the construction of 'human-ness' (Wynter 2015). This methodology is a form of non-Western perspectivism (Viveiros de Castro 1998, 2009), which offers a pluriform variety of definitions of the human in multiple embodied locations and thus intersects with but also challenges the Western tradition. As Viveiros de Castro puts it, with reference to Deleuze: 'whether it be Leibniz's or Nietzsche's, or equally, Tukanoan or Jurunoan, perspectivism is not relativism, that is, the affirmation of the relativity of truth, but relationalism, through which one can affirm that *the truth of the relative is the relation*' (2015: 24, original emphasis).

The Anthropocene adds urgently to the issue: as Clark put it in his work on aboriginal cosmopolitanism (2008), we must be 'wary of the risks of aligning indigeneity with the primordiality of the earth, but are also mindful that integrating social history with geological, climatic or evolutionary history has its own potential to destabilise colonial narratives' (2008: 739). Respectful learning from the oldest guardians of the earth is a good place to start. Building some common meeting ground follows from the relational logic of this approach: 'we' differ, but are in *this* together.

The climate change emergency and the general condition of the Anthropocene expose not only the limitations, but also the responsibilities of European Humanism and its scientific culture. The same violence that brought about the environmental crisis, namely unbridled capitalist greed, imperialism and Eurocentrism, is also the source of the dispossession of Indigenous people and the dispersion of their cultures (Bignall, Hemming and Rigney 2016). It is therefore important to acknowledge, as Whyte recommends, that 'climate injustice, for Indigenous peoples, is less about the spectre of a new future and more like the experience of déjà vu' (Whyte 2016: 88). It is necessary to decolonize the debate about the Sixth Extinction of the Anthropocene from the beginning. This is a crucial element of the politics of locations or of radical immanence, which is the favoured method in this book.

Accounting for one's position in terms of space as well as time grounds the subjects in very concrete but also multilayered locations. This method thus includes taking into account both the geo-political or ecological dimension as well as cultural traditions, historical memory or genealogical dimension of one's subject position. Accountability is both epistemic and ethical. Epistemologically, it is a matter of producing adequate knowledge in and for the world. Ethically, it involves generating affirmative relations (Braidotti 2015). Affirmative ethical forces are capable of increasing our relational capacity (*potentia*), as distinct from the protocols of institutional control (*potestas*). Although the two aspects of power are inextricably linked, it is productive to stress the *potentia*, i.e. relational, part of it.

There is another aspect of feminist thought and Indigenous philosophies that is relevant to the posthuman predicament: the extent to which they reconcile critique with creativity and plead for increased visionary insight. Faith in the creative powers of the imagination is an integral part of feminist embodied perspectival knowledge practices from the very early days (Kelly 1979; Anzaldúa 1987; Rich 1987). Vision has been praised by black theorists (hooks 1981, 1990; West 2018) as the imaginary affective force that drives the innovative core of their transformative epistemologies.

The emphasis on immanence, situated perspectives and creativity does not constitute a form of undifferentiated or 'flat' ontology. On the contrary, this neo-materialist vital philosophy foregrounds the unity of matter, or immanence, as a differential principle. It allows for individuation and diversity, while connecting humans to non-human forces. We all partake of the same matter – the 'chaosmos' (Guattari 1995). This interconnected-ness is not so much chaotic as dynamic and self-organizing. The standard objections to vital matter do not hold: vital materialism is neither a form of determinism, nor a manifestation of pietistic holism and hence of un-differentiation (Hallward 2006). On the contrary, it is a way of empowering the specificity and value of being human at a time when the centrality of 'Man' is being historically displaced. At the same time, it subtracts the anthropomorphic subjects from any claim to exceptionalism.

In this context it is important to remember that this 'Life' that the posthuman subject is immanent to, is no longer '*bios*', but '*zoe*'. Where *bios* is anthropocentric, *zoe* is non-anthropocentric and even non-anthropomorphic.

Moreover, in the posthuman convergence, *zoe* embraces geologically and technologically bound egalitarianism, acknowledging that thinking and the capacity to produce knowledge is not the exclusive prerogative of humans alone, but is distributed across all living matter and throughout self-organizing technological networks.

This is not to advocate an undifferentiated vitalist system that would form flat equivalences across all species, all technologies and all organisms under one common Law. Such a holistic approach was the error of the organicist philosophies of Life developed in the first half of the twentieth century. Some of them fed into the exclusionary and imperialist interpretations of a sexualized and racialized hierarchical natural order of domination, which helped to construct European fascism. The fascist worldview favoured esoteric and often obscurantist organicist theories to the rigour of scientific rationality. Fascist forms of vitalism were both opposed to and seduced by technological mechanicism and the rule of technology.[2] In that respect vitalism was historically associated with the pseudo-spiritualist celebration of a cosmic soul or mystical spirit. This is not the way in which the term vital matter or vitalism has entered the posthumanist debate in the twenty-first century; far from it.

As Foucault (1977) pointed out, Deleuze's neo-materialist philosophy of immanence advances a serious critique of the philosophical roots of European fascism. Deleuze is indeed committed to detoxifying the practice of philosophy from the appeal of methodological nationalism and authoritarianism (Beck 2007). Foucault states that Deleuze achieves the de-Nazification of European philosophy and does so in two significant ways. Firstly, Deleuze criticizes the collective desire for power defined as the naturalization of inequalities through sexualized and racialized hierarchies.[3] Secondly, Deleuze introduces heterogeneity and heterogenesis at the conceptual core of what we used to call nature. It is the case that, in a neo-materialist vital perspective, any specified form of individuated organisms can be seen as bounded, yet fluid. An individuated organism is a reduced actualization of virtual inhuman and non-human flows of becoming. Rather than glorifying or even sacralizing a transcendent notion of 'Life', Deleuze stresses the generative material power of living systems (Ansell Pearson 1997, 1999) and proposes quite radically that there is no Life as one system, just on-going flows and transformations of forces. Life is a complex inter-relation of multiple *zoe*/geo/techno-systems. It is a general ecology of complex relations that is constituted by the circulation of transversal modes of assemblage, in a dynamic exchange that defines reciprocal forms of specification or determination. This relational framework is especially relevant to contemporary posthuman subjects, as it supports the re-composition of the human/non-human nexus by inscribing the technological apparatus as second nature.[4]

'We-Are-(All)-In-This-Together-But-We-Are-Not-One-And-The-Same'

In this book I want to stress the multiple perspectives generated by embodied and embedded middle grounds, keeping at bay a naturalistic or holistic sublime on the one hand, and an equally fallacious flat ontology on the other. The middle ground is composed by heterogeneous multiplicities, both human and non-human.

Posthuman subjectivity does not refer to 'the people' as a unitary category, self-constituted as 'we, the people'. The people are not one, not only in the sense of being a quantitative plurality, as Arendt (1958) recommends, but also on qualitative grounds. A people is rather a heterogeneous multiplicity that cannot coalesce into unity on pre-given grounds, such as the claims to ethnic purity that have become a defining feature of both historical and contemporary authoritarian, nationalist and nativist political regimes. A people is always missing and virtual, in that it needs to be actualized and assembled. It is the result of a praxis, a collective engagement to produce different assemblages. We are not one and the same, but we can interact together.

The aggregating factor in the composition of a missing people is neither the built-in oppositional energy of the dialectical struggle for recognition, nor a shared experience of vulnerability and powerlessness (i.e. oppression by *potestas*). The binding force is not reactive, but active and affirmative-it starts with a shared understanding (cartographies) of the embodied and embedded conditions of oppression and subjection. This is expressed in collective imaginings (figurations) that deploy the shared desire to enact affirmative and empowering (both as *potestas* and as *potentia*) alternatives. This affirmative ethics frames the political subjects as transversal assemblages that are not given, but need to be composed and enacted. This, however, does not make them into mere performative utterances in a linguistic sense. Shared affirmative values and passions rather constitute materialist groundings (i.e. embodied and embedded, relational and affective perspectives) that sustain the collective project of composing just a people.

The neo-Spinozist notion of freedom that underscores this project is slightly different from, but not incompatible with, the classical liberal creed that humans are inherently free and that liberty is the natural condition of Mankind (Skinner 2012). The affirmative drive to compose transversal assemblages assumes that freedom comes down to the shared understanding of the conditions of our bondage, and the collective efforts to act upon them. Conceptually, all living entities are driven by *conatus* – that is to say the ontological freedom to express the degree of power (*potentia*) that any entity has been able to actually embody. The crux of the matter however is to activate the collective desire for affirmative alternatives.

Heterogeneity and complexity allow us to think about the production of multiple actualized life-forms that are irreducibly differentiated. When posthuman subjects become individuated, they will become embodied and embedded in the processes of actualization. Such a process can only occur through networks of natural, social, political and physiological relations. We can therefore speak of forces that are above, below and alongside the subjects, in a constant flow of mutual imbrication. Going 'above' the subject points to the supra-subjective face of institutional and social power. 'Below' the subject operate the sub-subjective and affective factors, including the singular psychic landscapes. And 'alongside' the subjects there are the adjunctive bio-technical assemblages of posthuman relationality (Protevi 2009).

The specificity of humans consists in their anthropomorphic capacities and the degree and quality of the relational abilities they can mobilize. Humans cannot defy gravity as easily as some species of insects do, but they dispose specific neural, cognitive, affective and symbolic functions of their own. Anthropomorphism is both the strength and the weakness of what embodied and embrained humans can do.

Humans are defined by the extent to which they apply these abilities to understand, affect and be affected by the multi-layered and multi-scalar ecologies to which they belong. A transversal practice of subjectivity both frames and empowers the specific abilities that anthropomorphic subjects are capable of actualizing.

Let me sum up the key features of posthuman subjectivity that I have developed in this chapter so far. The first feature is a materialist process ontology based on immanence and becoming, defined as a creative praxis of actualization of the virtual. Secondly, posthuman subjectivity is structured by ontological relationality, which is the power to affect and be affected. Thirdly, it involves a critical detachment from both Humanism and anthropocentrism, which respects the force of non-human elements. Fourthly, transversal subjectivities are composed in the mode of eco-sophical assemblages that include non-human actors. Last but not least, I want to stress the grounded, situated and perspectivist dimension, which is enhanced by the ethical aspiration to compose a missing people, defined as a virtual entity. Ethics starts with the composition of transversal subject assemblages – 'we, posthuman subjects' – that actualize the unrealized or virtual potential of what 'we' are capable of becoming. It is a recipe for collectively managed processes of social transformation, which work through de-acceleration and the common construction of social horizons of hope.

Thus, I come to my first concluding proposition: the proper subject of the posthuman convergence is not 'Man', but a new collective subject, a 'we-are-(all)-in-this-together-but-we-are-not-one-and-the-same' kind of subject. This means that humanity is both a vulnerable and an insurgent category. Posthuman subjectivity can be understood as a process of becoming in its own immanence and not in binary oppositional terms. It is a becoming other-than-the *Homo Universalis* of Humanism or other-than-the *Anthropos* of anthropocentrism. To cope with it we need a subtler and more diversified affective range, which avoids the polarization between the apocalyptic variant of mourning and the euphoric variable of celebration.

Posthumanism Is Not Inhumanism

Before I can delve more deeply into the posthuman vision of subjectivity, I need to address the counter-argument raised by many posthuman theorists against the need for a new vision of subjectivity at all. Many of those who are critical of the need for a vision of the subject seem to be particularly struck by a sort of epistemological exhaustion or resistance. They tend to prefer the notion of the inhuman.

There are at least three different inceptions of the inhuman circulating in contemporary scholarship. The first is the recognition of the importance and sentient capacities of non-human actors and agents. One established anti-epistemological tradition is Actor Network Theory (ANT), which for decades has been stressing the importance of non-human actors in knowledge production systems. Bruno Latour (2005) advanced the notion of such collaborative networks, notably the material technological apparatus of science-making practices. This proved inspirational for the hub of Science and Technology Studies. Latour's main contribution has been to challenge the subject–object distinction and more specifically the association of matter with passivity. This destabilizes social constructivism and introduces a non-reductive form of neo-materialism as a realist perspective on truth (Lillywhite 2017), which also partially acknowledges the relational quality of subject assemblages. However, it stops short of providing a qualitative shift of perspective.

Scholars from Science and Technology Studies generally feel little affinity with the posthuman. Part of the difference is due to disciplinary affiliations, because Technology Studies relies on social science methods and scholars in this field are cautious with philosophically inflated terminology (Rose 2013, 2016). A narrow focus on the sociological analysis of protocols and practices, however, is neither grounded nor precise enough. By disregarding the importance of the embedded, embodied subjects at work in the process of knowledge production, they run the risk of failing to grasp what kind of subjects we are in the process of becoming. In this respect, the contemporary revival of interest in Whitehead's process philosophy is significant, in that it provides a new balance between empirical and speculative approaches, as Stengers has been forcefully arguing (2011).

By reducing the notion of agency to the criticism of the subject–object distinction and replacing subjectivity with the idea of a generalized symmetry of actors and objects, Actor Network Theory ended up throwing the baby out with the bathwater. The political strength of the relational interconnection among different entities in the world is disavowed by the flat ontology espoused by Latour and his object-ontologist champions (Harman 2014). By flattening out different degrees of power as *potentia*, Latour relinquishes the subject function altogether. If there are no subjects, in fact, then there is no need for genders, class, race and age-oriented analyses of power relations. These issues have been dropped from the scientific agenda as being over-politicized. This is the point where I disagree: no amount of claim to the equality between human and non-human actors, which ANT has voiced so explicitly, can compensate for the lack of an epistemology that does justice to the power structures of contemporary subjects. In the absence of an adequate understanding of subjectivity, the very possibility of an ethical and political project that would enable us to come to terms with the paradoxes and challenges of our times, is quite simply undermined.

Latour (1991), with an established record of scepticism about left-leaning politics, critical theory and post-structuralist takes on modernity, has answered this charge by foregrounding the strong methodological basis of ANT. The finite and detailed empirical and anthropological observation of the distinct material practices that compose the chain of events resulting in the production of scientific knowledge is the best scholars can aspire to. He has brought the same incisive empirical focus to bear in his recent work on Gaia (2017), which accomplishes a critical task alongside a more creative one. The critical consists in debunking the mystical holism that surrounds ecological discussions. Latour wants to acknowledge the dynamic and historically contingent nature of Gaia, but to avoid sacralizing it. Stumbling somewhat on his mixed metaphors, he argues 'with "Gaia" you are inside it while hearing the loud crashing of outside/inside boundaries. To be a disinterested outside observer becomes slightly more difficult. We are all embarked in the same boat – but of course it is not a boat!' (Latour 2017: 62). Latour's intervention in the climate change discussion consists in thinking connectivity, while avoiding holism and resisting the subject–object divide. He also develops solidarity for human and non-human actors alike. This meticulous method is juxtaposed to what Latour considers as the methodologically 'fuzzy' discussions about knowledge and power, notably in the work of Foucault and his peers. In this respect, Latour's 'theory fatigue' manifesto of 2004 is as much the reiteration of his anti-speculative beliefs, as a statement of fact: enough big theory, let's stick to facts!

In his insightful analysis, Clarke (2017) argues that Latour's case against holism rests on a caricature of the Gaia hypothesis as theorized by Lovelock (2009) and further developed by molecular biologist Lynn Margulis and Dorion Sagan (1995). The latter stress the symbiotic or auto-poietic nature of this living planet, acknowledging its dynamic force, while resisting sacralizing it. In the light of the subtlety and complexity of Margulis's thought, Latour's case on climate change pursues his life-long concern to reject totalities and reassert networked heterogeneities. His case on secular Gaia strikes me as the French ideology of '*laicité*' (state-enforced secularism) applied to the Anthropocene debate.

The point is that the posthuman predicament blurs the distinction between the analytic and normative dimensions of critical thinking, just as it erases the distance between fact and fiction, especially in relation to technology. Thus, the 'facts' about climate change are hotly debated and passionately disputed, just as the separation between science-fictional visions of virtual futures and our social reality is becoming more difficult to uphold. Besides, in the era of 'post-truth' and 'fake news', a flat appeal to empirical 'facts' simply begs the question and fails to take into account the impact of the broader context within which objectionable phenomena such as 'fake news' are occurring.

These discussions about posthuman subjects, and what they are supposed to know, revive the traditional dividing lines between the methodology and disciplinary conventions of respectively the theoretically-friendly Humanities and the hard-nosed Sciences and Technologies. It is highly significant to note that, in posthuman research, the debates about the 'Two Cultures' (Snow 1998 [1959]) which used to pitch the Humanities against the Natural Sciences, are currently recast into a discussion that rather sees the Humanities and the Social Sciences debate their respective methodological approaches to deal with the spoils of Humanism and anthropocentrism.

The second inception of inhumanism constitutes quite a different variation, pointing towards anthropo-fatigue. This trend takes off from the neo-Spinozist insight on the rationalism of one, intelligent and self-organizing matter and focuses on the fact that such intelligence does not by any means coincide with human rationality (Roden 2014; Wolfendale 2014). This school of rationalist inhumanism operates a sort of extraction: it disconnects the thinking capacity from the anthropological human, assigning it instead to the technological apparatus. Intelligence thus conceived as a computational capacity is disembodied and dis-embedded, becoming functionally autonomous from the Human.

Several different approaches emerge from this fundamental disjunction between the human brain and the computational abilities. The first is a speculative sort of posthumanism that concurs with critical posthuman theory that we cannot quite know what the posthuman may be until we conduct multiple experiments on what we are capable of becoming (Sterling 2012; Roden 2018). Where the two approaches differ, however, is in what exactly we are experimenting with. Speculative posthumanism builds on the premise of rationalist inhumanism to argue that autonomous, rather than anthropologically bound intelligence is what the experiment is all about. This is another way of saying that we do not know what posthuman subjects, or their capacities, might be. All we know is that there will be posthumans, some day.

For speculative posthumanism the focus is exclusively on the inhuman rationality at work in the multiple smart objects currently being designed and re-coded. Speculative posthumanists see the *posthuman* condition as something that may come into being in the future, through human-driven technological processes. But for now, they see current humans as having become depreciated to the status of non-human, as a result of our convulsive technical changes. Whereas the trans-humanists, to whom I shall return below, spin the same insight in the direction of moral philosophy, the speculative posthumanists focus on the specific properties of the technological objects themselves, aiming at developing new forms of agency that would centre on the relation to non-human things. They leave out of their picture subjectivity in its embodied and embedded complexity, as being irrelevant to the job of thinking today.

Speculative posthumanism is close to but also substantially different from trans-humanism. They both share the premise about the autonomy of intelligence, but trans-humanism wants to correct the flaws and limitations of the embodied human brain, by applying the new technologies to a programme of enhancement, called 'super intelligence'. Concretely, it combines brain research with robotics and computational sciences, plus clinical psychology and analytic philosophy, to enhance human neural capacity, so that our brain can function at the same speed as the computational networks we have created. In this approach, the human continues to be defined as a meta-rationalist entity, which will evolve through enhancement to become truthfully posthuman, that is to say super-human.

Gathered around the Oxford Institute for the Future of Humanity, directed by Nick Bostrom, trans-humanism combines a humanistic belief in the perfectibility of Man through scientific rationality, with a programme of human enhancement. It proposes an analytic form of posthumanism that accepts the decentring of both *homo universalis* and *anthropos*, but then combines this insight with normative neo-humanism. This intervention upon the human is presented as in keeping with the classical humanist rationalism of the Enlightenment. It extends the humanistic belief in the perfectibility of Man through scientific rationality, with a concrete and heavily industrial robotics and an artificial-intelligence driven programme of human enhancement. In this framework, the posthuman is defined as a super-human meta-rationalist entity. Bostrom is a champion of the Capitalocene in that he advocates the benefits of capitalism and his approach receives ample economic support from both the scientific community – 'Major Science' – and the corporate world.

Another cluster of thinkers takes the idea of the autonomy of rationalist inhumanism in a different direction, to stress a power of thinking and acting that is independent of the human altogether. Objects, whether the 'hyper-objects' (Morton 2013) of the Anthropocene or the smart Internet-bred objects, have capacities beyond the human and have an ontological status in their own terms. They do acknowledge the materialism of these objects, in terms of the mechanisms of production they issue from, and of their own specific qualities, as well as their interactive ability to connect with each other (Harman 2010, Bryant 2011). But that ability is merely connected to the inhuman rationality that flows through them. Ontological realism means the existence of a world independently of the human capacity to apprehend it.

The object-oriented ontologists, as they call themselves, focus their criticism on 'correlationism', that is to say the epistemological assumption of a direct correspondence between thought and being. They also reject the phenomenological tradition, with its emphasis on intentionality and consciousness. Most importantly in the context of the posthuman project, they specifically snub the political possibilities afforded by alternative productions of subjectivity and desire. However, for my conception of posthuman subjectivity, the ethical and political dimensions are crucial.

What is striking in object-oriented ontology is the opposition to vital materialist theories – such as my own – that acknowledge the implications of the convergence of the Fourth Industrial Revolution and the Sixth Extinction. That is to say, they have no comments on the mixture of panic and elation before the massive technological shifts, occurring with climate change and devastation. By claiming there is no need for a vision of the subject, they ignore and dismiss feminism, post-colonialism, race and ecological thinking. Although computational network is a focal point, they provide no analysis of the collusion between technology and finance, or the pervasive rise of xenophobia in our hyperconnected times. As stubbornly anti-humanists, they prefer to locate rationalism outside the human, the better to develop its rationalist capacities and leave everything else to the social scientists.

A third critique of the posthuman subject concerns the suspicion that this notion results in indifference towards and lack of care for humans. Here I can be clear: it is imperative for academic research not to confuse the posthuman with inhumane behaviour and disposition. Paying due attention to a *zoe*/geo/techno-oriented perspective needs to be combined with grounded analyses of the power relations and the social conditions that shape the manifestations of the posthuman convergence. In attempting to develop new subject assemblages within the political economy of neo-liberal subjectivation (Deleuze 1988, 1995a), we are necessarily confronted by the mechanisms of bio- and necropolitical control of advanced capitalism (Foucault 1995, 2008). The analysis of the technologies of control and domination also demands accountability for modern Western forms of colonial sovereignty and unchecked imperialist might. We must decolonize the Anthropocene.

A major component of the posthuman project is the multiplicity of grounded perspectives, which call for diversity and heterogeneity. These are all the more valuable as they struggle within the contemporary geo-political power relations and the regimes of extermination of species and extinction of multiple life-forms, both human and non-human, which mark our posthuman times. These necropolitical consequences are not evenly distributed across the world or across species. The degrees of exposure to the consequences of the Anthropogenic scenarios vary greatly depending on class, gender, race and geo-political locations. Trans-national environmental justice therefore emerges as one of the crucial knots of the posthuman convergence.

Reaffirming Affirmation

The approaches discussed so far are at times infused by negativity and anthropo-fatigue. Especially the object ontologists tend to nurture a sense of alienation from the species so intense that it becomes saturated with nihilism. They are deprived of a political outlet that is worthy of our times. Nor do they develop a sense of ethics. And when it comes to politics, the best they can come up with is a return to Marxist-Leninism to undo the entropy of capitalism.

I do not deny the importance of alienation nor its generative potential, let alone the affirmative nucleus of nihilism, especially with the insights from Nietzsche. Just like the reality of exhaustion, these negative affects engender the conditions for their own overcoming. They are capable of exposing a potentially intransitive core, which recodes the negative state into a vector of transformation. Acknowledging this kind of analytical function for negativity, however, is also a way of dissolving its ontological force. In a vital, neo-materialist framework the negative is not foundational, but functional to the articulation of a practice of affirmation. In this respect, affirmation is not the disavowal of negativity but rather another way of working it, activating it and extracting knowledge from it.

While feeling deep affinity for my colleagues working in posthuman scholarship, and sharing the sense of exhilaration and anxiety about our science and technology, I want to stress the embodied and embedded, relational and accountable structure of being human. In response to the different brands of inhumanists: I see the brain and our thinking capacity as being embodied and the body as being 'embrained' (Marks 1998). Intelligence is not an autonomous computational capacity and not the same as speed of thought. It is the result of a multitude of social, environmental and psychic factors. Moreover, matter is a self-organizing totality to which we all belong.

There is another and quite radical anti-anthropos position that is more affirmative: the 'a-human', a term coined by MacCormack in 2014. It is an explicit, post-Nietzschean reassertion of the death of Man, spoken from the platform of non-human rights for all organisms. MacCormack presents it as a radical critique of the residual human exceptionalism at work, sometimes even in the most outspoken claims to posthumanism Humanism. To avoid further instrumental manipulations of the human/non-human binary, MacCormack proposes to abolish the category of the human altogether. Inspired by, but also concerned about, the humanistic pitfalls of animal rights, this abolitionist movement embraces radical veganism and campaigns for putting an end to the use of animals for commercial, research and food purposes.

Following Michel Serres, MacCormack pleads for a new natural contract (2014) that would neither torment nor fetishize the non-human others. This Epicurean cosmic legacy also connects across to the vital materialist philosophy of Deleuze and Guattari, notably the idea of eco-sophical unity. This produces a formidable case against the necessity of human-centred systems. MacCormack demands with passionate conviction that we deploy forms of imagination that go beyond species hierarchy and the dialectical habits of thought that have defined our relationship to animals, but also their reversal into spurious forms of animal liberation. Abolishing the category of the human is the answer.

Posthumanism is not an inhumanism, though it resonates with some of the speculative aspects of the project – notably the importance of experimenting with what kind of subjects we are capable of becoming. We are indeed becoming posthuman ethical subjects. We do so by overcoming hierarchical dichotomies and cultivating instead our multiple capacities for relations and modes of communication in a multi-directional manner.

Experimenting with what we are capable of becoming, in material and differentiated locations, is a way of resisting the reactive and panic-stricken composition of Humanities as a white panic or dystopian fear of the posthuman convergence. But experimentation is also a formula for acting, a praxis to lead the new subjects that we are capable of becoming away from the violent aspects of European Humanism, most notably the violence of sexualized, racialized and naturalized exclusions and of colonial domination. It is about redefining the human after Humanism and anthropocentrism, as a *zoe*/geo/techno-mediated being, immanently related to and hence inseparable from the material, terrestrial and planetary locations that we happen to inhabit.

At this particular point in our collective history 'we' simply do not know what our enfleshed selves can actually do. We need to find out by embracing an ethics of community-based experiments, which have to start with the careful composition of the transversal subjects that 'we' are, to ground and operationalize the project. Desire as plenitude – as opposed to desire as lack – provides the ontological relational force that drives the posthuman subject-formation. This means that the ethical imagination is alive and well in posthuman subjects, which stresses an enlarged sense of interconnection between self and others, including the non-human others, by removing the obstacle of self-centred individualism and the barriers of negativity on the other. I want to expand on these relational values across all species through an ethics of affirmation based on species equality.

The Force of the Present

Situating our thinking in the world is a relational and affective practice that provides continuity while upholding deeper temporalities that extend in a multi-scalar and non-linear manner. Let me explore this idea further through the notion that the present is not a static bloc, but a continuous flow, pointing in different directions at once. The force of the present – and the core of its intelligibility – is that it does not coincide completely with the here and now. Such synchronization is never complete, because in a neo-materialist vital system, all human and non-human entities are transversal subjects-in-process, in perpetual motion, immanent to the vitality of self-ordering and relational matter.

There is much to be gained by approaching the posthuman present along the parallel plateaus of the actual and virtual, that is to say of what already is and what might become the case (Deleuze and Guattari 1994). This distinction is pivotal for the development of posthuman knowledge, because by positing a time continuum as a process ontology of becoming, the practice of social and cultural criticism of the current crisis can be supplemented by the more affirmative project of constructing sustainable alternatives. The future is literally right here and now and consequently there is no time to waste.

To be even more explicit: approaching time as a multi-faceted and multi-directional effect enables us to grasp *what we are ceasing to be* and *what we are in the process of becoming*. This double approach helps address the injustices and violence of our times and helps us organize to redress them, while it also nurtures an inspiring perception of the actualization of not-yet accomplished virtual options. These intertwined levels of awareness can occur sequentially or simultaneously, in so far as the past is not a frozen block of half-accomplished deeds, but a heterogeneous mass of future pasts awaiting historical actualization. And likewise, the future is the on-going unfolding of an unrealized virtual past, which 'we' are responsible for actualizing by constructing a subject assemblage – an embodied and embedded 'we' – capable and willing to work on the affirmative aspects of a negative and conflict-ridden present. It follows therefore that the task of creating sustainable futures is a collective affirm-ative praxis, that is to say a gesture of undoing negativity which honours our collective obligations to the generations to come. But it is happening right now.

The implications of a posthuman sense of time are far-reaching. If the present is a complex process, critical thought cannot stop at the critique of the actual – that is to say of what we are and are ceasing to be – but needs to move on to the creative actualization of the virtual – that is to say of what we are in the process of becoming. Critique and creativity work in tandem towards the same goals. Thinking subjects are situated in process within the dizzying interplay of boom and bust, crisis and regeneration, extinction and evolutionary leaps. This means that critical thought needs to adapt to this dynamic in a non-linear mode. Some of our thinking addresses critically the injustices and violence of the times in order to redress them. At other moments thinking about the present confronts but also exceeds the immediate conditions we inhabit and aspires to transform them. The conceptual distinction between the actual and the virtual, that is to say the present as the record of the past and also as the unfolding of the future, renews the powers and the margins of intervention for critical thought and creative practice.

The energy needed to generate new conditions and new theoretical and cultural representations is not going to emerge by dialectical opposition to a present one is not happy with (as suggested by Marxist analysis). It can only be generated by a collective practice that confronts and transfers

these conditions, combines critique with creation in actualizing virtual possibilities for evolution and becoming. The
negative logic of dialectics is of no help in bringing about
intensive, qualitative shifts in what a society or a community
is capable of becoming. By foregrounding affirmative ethics
as a praxis, rather than the logic of negativity, posthuman
knowledge moves further and deeper.

Creativity – or the faculty of the imagination – is the key
concept here, because it is the transversal force by definition.
Within a neo-materialist philosophy of immanence this
means the following. In spatial terms creativity cuts across
and interconnects all living matter, of which each organism
is a single variation. In temporal terms, it is the force that
constantly reconnects to the virtual totality of a block of past
experiences and affects, allowing them to get recomposed
as action in the present, thereby realizing their unfulfilled
potential. This mode of affirmative critique is an exercise in
temporary and contingent synchronization, which sustains in
the present the activity of actualizing the virtual. This virtual
intensity is simultaneously before and after us, both past and
future, in a flow or process of mutation, differentiation or
becoming. That process of becoming is the vital material core
of thought – there is no Greenwich Mean Time in knowledge
production in the posthuman era.

The task of thinking as critical and creative is defined
by the following features: co-existence of the actual and
the virtual; the status quo and the possible alternatives;
what is ending and what is about to come into being. By
extension, the posthuman convergence is marked by the
paradox of simultaneous disappearance and over-exposure,
evanescence and insurgency, of the human. This results in a
paradoxical situation where there is a widespread production
of discourses, knowledge and practices, both in the academy
and in society, about a category – the human – at the very
time when this category has lost all consensus and self-
evidence. The 'human' emerges as an urgent issue just as
it enters a terminal crisis. In fact, it does not even hold as
a category other than as an expression of anxiety about
survival and the concomitant fear of loss of privileges.

The perspective changes when we approach the vertiginous mix of over-exposure and disappearance of the human

within the notion of the time continuum. Firstly, there is no extinction/survival binary, because posthuman thought is not about dialectical oppositions 'either/or', but rather about immanent relations of 'and/and'. Secondly, there is no paradox in the simultaneous over-exposure and non-existence of the 'human', because there is no linear time, but a thousand plateaus of possible becomings, each following its own multidirectional course.

The paradox of evanescence and over-exposure therefore dissipates if we approach the posthuman in a neo-materialist, embedded and embodied perspective, and not as an abstract speculative concern. An immanent philosophical framework that posits matter as one, continually differentiating into specific modulations, produces an inevitable effect of resonance between the emergence of a concept and the conditions that make it thinkable.

Let me unwrap what this means for posthuman subjectivity in the context of the convergence of posthumanism and post-anthropocentrism. In his analysis of the end of European Humanism, Foucault (1970) establishes the analytic conditions for a critique of the human in a post-Enlightenment frame of reference. This is illustrated by the image of humanistic 'Man' as a figure drawn on the sand, being slowly wiped out by the waves of history. The irony of the case is not lost on object ontologist Morton who defines this passage as 'a prescient image of global warming, with its rising sea levels and underwater government meeting' (2016: 13).

The strength of Foucault's case is the effect of resonance it establishes between the crisis of a concept – Man, as the referent for humanity – and the posthuman conditions that make it thinkable in a critical vein. A concept becomes thinkable as it loses consistency and self-evidence, and thus ceases to be a ruling principle. That kind of self-evidence is the result of specific power configurations that attribute to dominant notions a strong sense of entitlement: they are all the more powerful in that they remain implicit. It follows therefore that the task of critical theory is to analyse power relations explicitly and to unveil the mechanisms by which they had gained such self-evidence in the first place. This is what is involved in Foucault's idea of speaking truth to power and discourse.

The apparent tension between the thinkability of a concept and its implosion or disappearance shows also the relational nature of thinking as a relational activity. Thinking functions like a chamber of resonance, a space of vibration, between the multi-layered and multi-directional plateaus of our embodied and embedded positions.

Bringing this insight to bear on the posthuman debate, I would argue that the posthuman convergence is not a crisis of extinction and that it is not necessarily negative. The posthuman convergence is the coming into focus of new conditions for knowledge production and consequently new relational encounters. Thus, Foucault's 'death of Man' is less about extinction than it is about announcing a new phase in advanced capitalism, concurrent with the rise of bio-political management of Life as a non-human force. Similarly, Deleuze's analysis of the political crisis around the events of May 1968 succeeds in foregrounding the structural mutations that capitalism was undergoing towards a post-industrial system.[5] The material and discursive conditions that trigger the emergence of a concept are not dialectical, but in perpetual becoming. New knowledge production happens in a praxis of specification or actualization that is situated in a time continuum, where past and virtual futures intermingle to bring about affirmative forces. Being posthuman subjects means striking a balance in temporal as well as spatial terms, between the 'no longer' and the 'not yet'. This requires finding some synchronicity between complex and multiple foldings and different flows of time sequences. All of this points to the composition of a transversal 'we' on a plane of relational immanence, that is to say to the multiple ways in which humanity is currently being recomposed.

Thinking is not the predication of a transcendental truth, but it is a relational activity. In his discussion of this apparent tension between the thinkability of a concept and its implosion, Benjamin Noys (2010) argues that this tension is constitutive of the immanence of thinking. Being relational, thinking is a way of relating to the world. It functions like a chamber of resonance between 'external' reality and 'internal' perceptions. In thinking there is no antinomy outside–inside, no paradox, but a constant unfolding and enfolding of immanent forces (Deleuze 1993). The resonance between these multiple levels shows conclusively the immanent structure of all living matter.

Being material and relational subjects, the processes of our subjectivation coincide with our historical conditions: 'we' are in *this* world together. We are immanent to it as a force of actualization of multiple ways of becoming. Consequently, we can only perceive and thus become aware of the conditions of our historicity as problems or crises as they erupt and become manifest to our mind's eyes. Within an immanent frame of reference, the articulation of historical conditions (external) and subject formation (internal) is a process of mutual imbrication, of enfoldings and unfoldings of the same, resonating material components. The apparent antinomy of internal and external factors is both false and unhelpful, because what is at work is their mutual interdependence and the multiple folds that connect them transversally (Deleuze 1993).

As far as the posthuman debate is concerned, there are no grounds for plunging into melancholy metaphysical ruminations about the end of the world. We need energizing projects that express generative narratives and do not wallow in the rhetoric of the crisis. Especially when the crisis in question is to a certain extent the lament of white European cultures feeling vulnerable after they have become aware of how anthropogenic global risks are likely to affect them. They need to develop some decolonial perspectives.

Taking instead the affirmative path, posthuman knowledge focuses, through critical and creative cartographies, on the margins of expression of yet unrealized possibilities for overcoming both Humanism and anthropocentrism by concentrating on the issue: who is this 'we' whose humanity is now at stake? Recording both what we are ceasing to be and what we are in the process of becoming, posthuman thinking is ultimately about the creation of new concepts and navigational tools to help us through the complexities of the present, with special focus on the project of actualizing the virtual. The non-linearity of posthuman time echoes the non-unitary, multiple and heterogeneous sense of space. The conceptual part of this proposition concerns the materially embedded and embodied structure of posthuman subjectivity. This has methodological implications for providing adequate and differential accounts (cartographies) of multiple subject

positions that are in the process of becoming. But they are
not becoming the same thing, not in the same place, not at
the same speed.

Because of the great diversity of positions within the
posthuman landscape, differences arise among posthuman
scholars. Those working within inhuman rationalism pursue
the anti-subjectivity line and dismiss the question of the
splintered 'we' accordingly. Cohen, Colebrook and Miller
(2016) argue that there cannot be a posthuman subject –
of knowledge or of anything – because such a subject is
constructed retroactively and in the confrontation with the
anxiety evoked by the climate change crisis. It is a subject
that emerges uniquely at the point of its disappearance.

From this extinction-oriented realization, Colebrook
(2014a) then goes on to argue in a more deconstructive
note that the posthuman predicament spells the thinkability
of the extinction of that very entity – Man/Anthropos –
whose sovereignty has already terminated. Putting Derrida to
affirmative use, they also argue that thinking beyond his own
end is Man's very prerogative, and thus conclude that the
Anthropocene ends up reasserting the inhuman core of the
human subject. The metaphysics of presence/absence remains
definitional of Man as thinking being. Much as I appreciate
the theoretical finesse, the lack of concern for the political
implications of such a dismissal of the generative potential
of the posthuman moment is disappointing to say the least.

Compare, by way of contrast, the formulation of the
same paradox of disappearance and over-exposure in the
terms proposed by Dipesh Chakrabarty (2009). Far from
giving in to white panic and proclamations of uniqueness,
Chakrabarty foregrounds the political riddles generated by
the explosion of a category – the human – that was not held
in global esteem or considered universally intelligible to
begin with. The off-shoots of this paradoxical development,
moreover, are not confined to the master discourses of the
leading disciplines, but affect just as strongly the critical
minority discourses of postcolonial, gender and feminist
theories. We are indeed in this epistemic reshuffle together.
In a neo-materialist, immanent universe, there is no extra-
territoriality. Chakrabarty's approach respects indeed the
situated, hence embedded and embodied, specificities of

different angles of entry into the posthuman predicament. This is a far more productive approach than the speculative emphasis on structural inhumanism. The latter is a way of short-circuiting a transversal politics of the posthuman, a differential bio-politics of subjectivity, and an embedded necropolitical analysis of the costs and damages of our current predicament.

Any awareness of a shared predicament such as the posthuman convergence runs the risk of being reduced, in terms of both intellectual understanding and practical outreach, in over-hasty reformulations of a pan-humanity bonded in fear. Such a gesture wipes complexity out of the picture, namely the awareness of how both the Fourth Industrial Revolution and the Sixth Extinction impact differentially upon different categories, classes and groups of humans and non-humans, depending on their geo-political locations and perspectives. Fear of extinction alone is not credible as a unifying factor, considering the degrees of higher mortality and vulnerability suffered by sexualized, colonized, indigenous and naturalized 'others'. There is a reductive tendency at work that turns the Anthropocene into a white, Eurocentric, male entitlement colonizing the very notions of vulnerability and extinction.

At this juncture I want to reassert my main point about the posthuman as a convergence phenomenon rather than a single new paradigm. This means that it mobilizes the insights, resources and methods of *both* posthumanism (as critique of Eurocentric privilege) *and* post-anthropocentrism (as critique of species privilege). The upholding of a convergence, hence a double move, helps to resist any flat equivalence and enables us to study attentively its multi-sided effects. No discussion of the Anthropocene can afford to ignore patriarchal power relations, colonialism and racism. This multi-directional approach is likely to create tensions and disagreements, but such divergences are productive in themselves. It is important to avoid the outpourings of panic we find in so much and ever so Eurocentric 'Learning to Die in the Anthropocene' kind of scholarship (Scranton 2015). There is quite a proliferation of scholarship about the extinction of life on earth (Lovelock 2009; van Dooren 2014) and of the human (Colebrook 2014a, 2014b), which forecloses any posthuman future (Kroker 2014). This necrophilic obsession with one's own death is conceptually short-sighted as it denies the force of the virtual. Such an apocalyptic scenario is politically counterproductive because it spreads the sense of impotence, while it perpetuates Eurocentric habits of thought. It is ethically unsound because it cultivates a black hole of individual despair instead of labouring towards community. Affirmative ethics is an alternative to this disempowering position.

This is not to deny that humanity as a category is at risk, but to stress that some humans just happen to be more mortal than others. Taking the posthuman convergence seriously, therefore, means accepting the multiplicity of perspectives and locations as embodied and embedded. We need relational and affective accounts of ways of being human. We need specific contextual solutions to global problems (Braidotti and Bignall 2018). The materialist and vitalist approaches remain immanent and non-teleological, which means that the process of becoming posthuman is not to be confused with redemptive narratives of 'born again' pan-Humanities, or eschatological scenarios of collective sacrifice. The task of posthuman thought is to account for the different speeds and patterns of becoming. It begins with the realization that the loss of a familiar notion of the 'human', which coincides with the awareness of the present posthuman conditions, is not the end point, but just one point in the time continuum that sustains the process of becoming posthuman. There are dramatically different locations within this continuum and we need to account for them, depending on our point of entry. It bears repeating: this is not relativism but grounded immanence and politics of locations.

The point of a posthuman position is that it envisages the subject as transversal, trans-individual, trans-species, trans-sexes. In short, it is a subject in movement. This kind of subjectivity obviously includes non-human others, of both the organic and the technological kind. The most important aspect here is to find a balance between the acknowledgement of the damages and the pursuit of an ethics of joyful affirmation. This entails an open eye to the virtual possibilities about what one, or a collective 'we', is capable of becoming. Adding this degree of complexity to the public discussion about the posthuman predicament has the immediate advantage of defusing some of the high emotions that are commonly invested in the posthuman convergence – that alternation of excitement and despair that is ever so exhausting.

A 'crisis' on the scale of the Anthropocene is then both about disappearance and over-exposure, about simultaneous extinction and regeneration. It is primarily an injection of lucidity. We need a dose of sobering wisdom about our real-life conditions that resonates with us – and we with it. 'We' become posthuman in *this* awareness of what no longer is the case. 'We' may indeed have lost a unitary definition of the human sanctioned by tradition and customs. But we do remain human and all-too-human in the simultaneous realization that the loss of humanist unity does not set us on the path to extinction, but is the building block for the next phase of becoming-subjects-together. Mindful of the fact that the statement 'we humans' was never neutral, but in fact indexed on sexualized and racialized hierarchies that controlled access to power, we should not plunge into mourning and melancholia at this loss, but rather focus on the new perspectives it opens up.

Thus, the loss of humanist unity is the starting point for alternative ways of becoming-subjects-together. The realization of our inextricable interconnection with both human and non-human others is the epistemological and ethical bonus we gain from the crisis, or rather the transition brought about by the posthuman convergence. Freedom through the understanding of the conditions of our bondage is the ethical value at work here, as Spinoza teaches us (Lloyd 1994, 1996; Spinoza 1996 [1677]). Speaking truth to power is the method to reach an adequate understanding of these conditions.

The process of becoming begins with the realization of the loss of a familiar notion of the 'human', which coincides with the awareness of the present posthuman conditions, but it moves on transversally towards the quest for alternative ways of becoming. These get actualized through new sets of relations posited across the posthuman time continuum, that is to say the on-going task of constructing what we will have been capable of becoming. But because 'we' are not one and the same, the patterns of becoming will necessarily differ. This means that 'we' may always already have been posthuman, or may yet become it, depending on our embedded perspective or point of entry in this time-frame.

Posthuman subjectivity is a practical project. It is a praxis. What matters is to negotiate collectively about *what* exactly we are in the process of becoming, and how much transformation, pain, dis-identification or enhancement our embodied and embrained selves can take. The posthuman is just the question. The answer is what 'we' are capable of becoming. The particular answer can only be a pragmatic one, bound to time and space. It is the praxis that aims at becoming a multitude of missing people. A multiple 'we' becoming-world-together amidst the painful contradictions of the Anthropocene, when the waves of world history – this time round – may be about to erase from the sandy shores of this planet the face of many other species.

Chapter 3
Posthuman Knowledge Production

Post-Natural Objects of Enquiry

Surveying some of the titles and themes of recent scholarship about the posthuman condition, I am struck by a number of recurring features. Firstly, there is an enormous variety of topics and objects of study about the notion of the human itself: for instance, the non-human (Raffnsoe 2013); the inhuman (Lyotard 1989); the post-anthropocentric as a metamorphic entity (Clarke 2008); the trans-species (Tsing 2015); posthuman personhood (Wennemann 2013); the 'new' human (Rosendahl Thomsen 2013); and posthuman performativity (Barad 2007).

Secondly, a stunning and at times provocative mood features in posthuman scholarship, expressed in daring neologisms and a colourful terminology to designate non-human and non-natural objects of study. This includes specimens of the animal, vegetable and mineral kingdoms, as well as samples from the material infrastructure of algorithmic culture. The degree of terminological liberty taken by scholars in the field may strike one as either quite innovative, or distinctively weird, depending on where you stand on the academic political spectrum. Weirdness is a generative notion, with a rich literary and scientific genealogy. Monstrosity and non-humans as well as de-humanized humans have often been interconnected as figures of devalorized difference (Braidotti 2002). The feminist classic *Frankenstein* is the emblem of this alliance, which is currently being redefined in a set of variations on old and new weirdness (Noys and Murphy 2016). In her analysis of weird literature, Ulstein (2017, 2019), argues that the contemporary weird encapsulates an affective dimension of fear and anxiety about the status of the human, combined with the ethical determination to endure and persist. In an apocalyptic brand of realism, Morton (2013) stresses that today's hyper-objects challenge our capacity to understand and to think the unthinkable, which is the end of the world as we knew it.

Thirdly, posthuman scholarship shows great ease and familiarity with interdisciplinary research methods. There is an evolving relationship between the research cultures of the Humanities and the Life sciences, the Neural sciences, Information technologies, and other fields. Many scholars voice the desire to develop new kinds of interdisciplinary and even post-disciplinary alliances across this broad spectrum, in order to develop a culture of mutual respect that may enable them to address the common challenges they face (Åsberg and Braidotti 2018; Lykke 2018).

The point of convergence among different areas of posthuman knowledge production is the recognition of the role of in/non/posthuman actors and objects of study, which acts against the pull of theory fatigue and endorses the calls for more conceptual creativity. It renews the mission of the conventional Humanities, lifting them out of anthropocentric habits of thought by offering more adequate concepts to deal with the ecological environment, media-nature-culture continuums and non-human others. The posthuman sensibility extends also to keeping high on the agenda the importance of the inhumane aspects of the posthuman predicament and the de-valorized and de-humanized others.

Post-natural objects of study are the new normal, as is the proliferation of projects that address a *zoe*/geo/techno-mediated matter. For example, Gary Genosko (2018), following Guattari, draws a diagram of 'post-natural forces', which analyses the effects of the Anthropocene upon the 'matter' of matter. Thus, the atmospheric element, or air, is transformed into greenhouse gases; the earth becomes minerals and mines, then dust; fire goes to ashes, but also to smoke and gas; and water gets redistributed through different vectors of wetness, with oil as the most precious fluid. Atmosphere, geosphere, biosphere and hydrosphere are all invested by the spinning flows of capital that alter their very structure.

This eco-planetary insight and the relationship to non-human life (*zoe*) are compounded by high technological mediation, digital life being a second nature. Given that there is no 'originary humanicity' (Kirby 2011: 233), but rather 'originary technicity' (MacKenzie 2002), what used to be 'naturecultures' has evolved into 'medianatures' (Parikka 2015a) and 'trans-media' practices (King 2011). A media ecological continuum (Fuller 2005, 2008) can sustain a general ecology (Hörl and Burton 2017; Hörl 2018), foregrounding not just any form of materiality, but rather a geological (Parikka 2015a) and terrestrial kind of materialism (Braidotti 2006; Protevi 2013).

Of course, there is a qualitative difference between accepting the structural interdependence among species and actually treating the non-humans as knowledge collaborators. But the point here is that this is precisely what we need to learn to do, because we live in the age of computational networks and synthetic biology on the one hand and climate change and erosion of liberties on the other. The posthuman subject needs to defamiliarize their mental habits. Thus, granting equal status to natural and post-natural organisms is an explicitly post-anthropocentric move that illustrates the far-reaching implications of thinking in a posthuman frame. In this respect a focus on non-human objects or topics of research is a necessary but not sufficient pre-condition for the production of posthuman knowledge. In order to produce a credible qualitative shift, we need conceptual and methodological transformations.

Contemporary posthuman research in the Humanities has proved equal to the task of dealing with such a qualitative shift of focus, as well as the quantitative growth of new – and sometimes weird – objects of enquiry. Significant advances have been made for instance by literary and cultural Darwinism (Beer 1983; Carroll 2004); eco-feminism and animal studies (Donovan and Adams 1996, 2007;

Midgley 1996); and social and cultural studies of evolutionary theories (Haraway 1990, 2003). The evidence of creative and critical thinking is encouraging (Clarke and Rossini 2016). The proliferation of neologisms is telling. If we now are 'humanimals' or trans-corporeal human-animal compounds, then the Earth, its geological strata and geologic subjects (Yusoff 2015) and its cosmos have become a political arena (Alaimo 2010). Each neologism is a conceptual threshold of its own. Thus, Stacey Alaimo's trans-corporeality is a critique of the abstract and immaterialized subject of the Anthropocene. She argues for a material posthuman agency, linked to 'deviant agents', like animals or fish, but also to the full spectrum of the Anthropocene. This is in tune with a posthuman relational subject acknowledging the transversal micro-political connections while aiming at affirmative ethics.

In her study of digital rubbish, which she presents as a 'natural history' of electronics, Jennifer Gabrys (2011) explores the often abstract notion of information technologies in their physical and mineral formations. This explicitly neo-materialist approach objects to the suggestion that technologies are somehow 'immaterial' by opposing to it a detailed, grounded account of how electronic waste is stored, broken down and dis-assembled. Focusing on the multiple spaces where digital waste is disposed of, from containers to landfills to museums and archives, Gabrys engages with the labour relations involved in electronic waste disposal. Thereby she traces the moves of a racialized, digital proletariat tied to this dangerous and exploitative work.

The same method, which I call 'geological materialism', has been adopted in media studies by Jussi Parikka (2015a), who argues against an immaterial – purely semiotic and representational – approach to media studies. Instead, he chooses to focus on the material realities that make media possible in the first place, notably the Earth's history, geological formations, minerals and energy. Parikka reminds us that, literally, there is more mining going on in the world, than just data mining. There is hence an ethical obligation to engage with the thick materiality of media technologies, their hardware, which takes us into the geophysical resources that went into making them.

The implications for scholarship in the Humanities of such approaches are significant, in that they not only require sizable empirical material, but also different sources, such as the scientific mapping of resources of a broad range of earth minerals. Economics also plays its hand, as the financial interests involved in mining are transnational as well as localized. They include social relations of labour and exploitation, through the different eras of industrial culture up to and including contemporary platform capitalism. By exploring the material framework of media culture, geological materialism crosses a number of disciplinary boundaries and throws an original new light on the idea of media archaeology.

Such examples of new scholarship show that posthuman knowledge is engaged with non-human, *zoe*/geo/techno-centred and post-natural objects, themes and topics. Posthuman scholarship also entails a qualitative shift in methods, collaborative ethics and, I may add, relational openness. As argued in the previous chapters, thinking in posthuman times is about increasing the capacity to take in the intensity of the world and take on its objectionable aspects. Thinking is about increasing our relational capacity, so as to enhance our power (*potentia*) for freedom and resistance. Posthuman thinking is post-identitarian and relational: it turns the self away from a focus on its own identity into a threshold of active becoming.

Last but not least the collaborative aspects of the production of posthuman knowledge are significant. New forms of cooperation are developing between academic researchers, art practitioners and activists (Braidotti and Hlavajova 2018). Artists and curators have licence to skilful critical experimentations. As a consequence, they enjoy a degree of freedom with both form and content that academics can only dream of. For instance, under the heading 'That was then, this is now', the Center for PostNatural History in Pittsburgh has been researching the origins, habitats and evolution of organisms that have been intentionally altered by humans (Pell 2015). Pursuing the mission of studying the complex interplay between culture, nature and biotechnology, this centre aims to acquire, interpret and provide access to a collection of living, preserved and documented organisms of post-natural origin.

The 'post-natural' here is defined as the organisms that have been heritably altered by means including selective breeding or genetic engineering. Displays have included glowing fish with genes from bioluminescent jellyfish and coral, 'Biosteel' goats that grow spider silk proteins in their milk, transgenic fruit flies, and a Silkie chicken, bred through the continuation of a recessive gene for its fluffy, fur-like coat. Star exhibits include 'Atomic Age Rodents' and the 'PostNatural Organisms of the European Union'.

Thinking is a gateway to the openness of *zoe* – the non-human life that does not bear a human name, let alone your own individual name. Thinking is the stuff of the world (Alaimo 2014). And by taking place in the world, it is accountable to multiple constituencies, not only the academic community. All the more so today, when knowledge is being produced across a broad range of social, corporate, activist, artistic and mediated locations, as well as in scientific, technological academic settings. Producing knowledge is just as much the stuff of the world.

The qualitative shift enacted by posthuman knowledge is supported by an affective range of conflicting moods that, in keeping with the overall political economy of the times, oscillates between euphoria and despair. For instance, eco-critics are writing eco-elegiac texts to define our changing relationship to the techno-natural-cultural continuum in which we now live (Huggan and Tiffin 2009). Others speak more bluntly of 'eco-horror' (Rust and Soles 2014). In any case, the response is affective and these powerful affects call out for new languages in the scholarship and general literature on these issues. What do you call that haunting feeling of ecological memories of the landscapes of your youth, now transfigured by violent developments: Eco-nostalgia? Remembrance of trees past? Geo-physical semiotics? Portrait of a young wasteland? Colonial transfigurations? Scar wars?

And how should we describe that sinking feeling at the thought of the unsustainability of our future: Post-anthropocentric nausea? Extinction-attraction Syndrome? Terrestrial delirium? Global obscenities overload? No country for any human?

The affective dimension of a posthuman approach resting on *zoe*/geo/techno perspectives both arises and enlists the resources of the imagination, as well as our cognitive abilities to account for our predicament. A lively literary, cultural and aesthetic movement has developed around the Anthropocene, in literature, cinema, new media and the arts. This is geo-art, or rather a 'geopoetics' that doubles up as a geo-politics in that it responds to the shifting relationship between humans and their planet in terms of both poetical and political experimentation (Last 2017). Taking in the cosmic as well as terrestrial elements of a geo-centred approach requires collective efforts to construct different social imaginaries, a task for which literature and the arts are eminently suited in so far as they focus on the analysis of cultural representations and interpretations of what it means to be human. By highlighting the mechanisms that help develop socially empowering images, the literary Humanities also have the ability to affect the public's response to them. This potential for large impact can also support the social process of change necessary to move towards more sustainable social systems and practices. As you will see in the next chapter, it is no wonder that comparative literature and literary studies constitute one of the main hubs of the PostHumanities.

Epistemic Accelerationism

One aspect of posthuman knowledge production that has clearly emerged as distinctive is the speed and the proliferation of neologisms and counter-concepts about and around the human and the posthuman. I find this exuberant growth quite significant in terms of the contemporary knowledge economy. Unsurprisingly, different kinds of posthumanism have already emerged: theoretical (Badmington 2003); insurgent (Papadopoulos 2010); speculative (Sterling 2012; Roden 2014); cultural (Wolfe 2010; Herbrechter 2013); literary (Nayar 2013); trans-humanist (Bostrom 2014); meta-humanist (Ferrando 2013); and a-humanist (MacCormack 2014). Of course, the list is still growing. There is already a posthuman manifesto out there (Pepperell 2003) and a PostHumanities book series with Minnesota University Press (Wolfe 2010).

Another striking example of a term that is accelerating out of control is 'the Anthropocene'. Even as a relative neologism, the Anthropocene has already become another 'Anthropomeme' (Macfarlane 2016), spawning several alternative terms, such as 'Chthulucene' (Haraway 2016), 'Capitalocene' (Moore 2013), 'Anthropo-scene' (Lorimer 2017), 'Anthrobscene' (Parikka 2015b). And there are yet others: Plastic-ene (New York Times 2014), 'Plantationcene' (Tsing 2015) and 'Mis-anthropocene' (Clover and Spahr 2014). The terminological vitality here reflects the accelerationist discursive economy of our times, and expresses both the excitement and the exasperation involved in accounting for the posthuman predicament within the Anthropocenic frame.

Confronted with such frantic pace, I suggest we hold the frame still in a moment of meditative meta-stability. Please consider the following. The social, environmental and affective contexts within which such speeds and accelerations are taking place are anything but abstract. They rather have to do with a set of highly immanent, grounded conditions that structure the processes of becoming-subject within the new knowledge economy of advanced capitalism.

To return to the notion of the Anthropocene itself, I find it wanting not only in scientific precision, but also in cartographic acumen. What is at stake in discussions of the Anthropocene is rather the issue of how power is constructed and distributed today. Alternatively apocalyptic and redemptive lyrical accounts of the on-going transformations express the difficulties of reaching a balanced account of the posthuman convergence. Unless a more complex critical approach is applied to the analysis, the Anthropocene runs the risk of remaining confined within the parameters of hegemonic whiteness and Eurocentric hubris. It would be inadequate, from the scholarly as well as the ethical point of view, to disconnect the posthuman condition from decolonial, feminist and anti-racist critiques of the limitations of technological developments and Western modernization.

What I find problematic about a great deal of Anthropocene scholarship is its distinct bias towards the anxieties of dominant cultures, ethnic groups and classes. There is a touch of white panic about it (Morton 2013), mingled with masculinist fears and Christian eschatological visions (Latour 2017). These visceral reactions end up appealing to an abstract and reunified notion of the 'human' that disposes of the complications of differential materially embodied and embedded analyses. By denying this kind of complexity, they also fail to acknowledge the differential price that different humans are paying in terms of the environmental, social and economic consequences of the ecological disasters.

This neo-universalized and panic-stricken human, moreover, undergoes another make-over by being over-moralized as an agent of generic responsibility towards all things non-human. Morton is a champion of such senti-mental and apocalyptic gestures that unify humanity in fear and anxiety, while reserving hard-hitting criticism of emancipatory politics – such as feminism, anti-racism and anti-fascism – as relics of antiquated modernist concerns. In his analysis of dark ecology, Morton coins the term 'ecognosis' to define the 'weird' process of knowledge production in the Anthropocene: 'Ecognosis is like a knowing that knows itself. Knowing in a *loop* – a *weird* knowing' (Morton 2016: 5; original emphasis).

Much as I empathize with the weirdness, I am reluctant to reduce the posthuman conjuncture to yet another crisis of whiteness, heteronormativity and masculinity, according to the indexation system of the worst aspects of twentieth-century power structures. Much more is at stake, and the political economy of this transformation is not only multi-scalar and transversal, but also, as we saw above, trans-species (Kirksey and Helmreich 2010) and trans-corporeal (Alaimo 2010). Critical and relational posthuman thought promotes a decentred subjectivity, rejects the residual universalism of a wounded and panic-stricken Eurocentric Anthropocene, and challenges the extent to which it upholds all too familiar power hierarchies.

The Anthropocene moment needs to be supplemented by incisive social-political analyses of the combination of fast technological advances on the one hand and the exacer-bation of economic and social inequalities on the other. This critical approach makes for a multi-faceted and conflict-ridden scholarly and social agenda. Unless we are willing to inscribe social and political concerns at the core of the geo-centred discussions, just referring to the Anthropocene begs the question. New notions and terms are needed to address the urgencies and anxieties of the present (as both actual and virtual) and to map operational cartographies for collective interventions. As I argued in the previous chapter, critical thinkers need conceptual creativity as well as renewed trust in the cognitive and political importance of the imagination as a collectively shared resource.

Let me therefore look more carefully into the schizoid *speed* of the terminological and conceptual accelerations that mark posthuman knowledge. Creating new concepts and coining neologisms is positive as the expression of one's relational capacity to 'take in' the world and to 'take it on'. So far, I have listed the proliferation of posthuman terms, concepts and titles – with an exceptionally high level of inventiveness. But is this creativity the full picture? What are the disadvantages of these spinning accelerations?

I propose to deal with this problem conceptually. This means I enlist again vital neo-materialism, which was useful in the previous chapter to resolve the paradox of simultaneous over-exposure and disappearance of the human. If it is indeed the case that the present is both actual and virtual, it means that it both instantiates but also exceeds the immediate conditions we inhabit. In other words: there is more to what is going on than what meets our posthuman eyes.

This insight helps explore contemporary knowledge production through a posthuman lens focused on what is in the process of becoming. My hypothesis at this point is that the posthuman constitutes a trans disciplinary field of scholarship that is more than the sum of its parts and points to a qualitative leap towards the construction of different subjects and fields of knowledge. I call it the Critical PostHumanities. We are facing the conceptual challenge of having to hold simultaneously in our embedded, embodied and relational minds potentially contradictory ideas like materialism and vitality, growth and extinction, the Fourth Industrial Revolution and the Sixth Extinction.

Two consequences follow immediately, so let us get them out of the way. The first is that the 'human' – which so preoccupies legions of thinkers and policy-makers today – never was a universal or a neutral term to begin with. It is rather a normative category that indexes access to privileges and entitlements. Appeals to the 'human' are always discriminatory: they create structural distinctions and inequalities among different categories of humans, let alone between humans and non-humans (Braidotti 2013, 2016a). As a consequence, it is inappropriate to take the posthuman either as an apocalyptic or as an intrinsically subversive category, narrowing our options down to the binary extinction-versus-liberation (of the human). We need to check both emotional reactions and resist with equal lucidity this double fallacy. It is more adequate to approach the posthuman as an emotionally laden but normatively neutral notion. It is a grounded and perspectival figuration that illuminates the complexity of on-going processes of subject formation. This enables subtler and more complex cartographies of powers and discourses. They start by questioning who 'we' might be. And whose anxiety takes centre-stage in public debates about the convergence of post humanism and post-anthropocentrism.

The second consequence is that we need to resist the scholarship of anxiety that tends to either mourn or celebrate the cause of a new humanity, united in and by the Anthropocene, as both a vulnerable and insurgent category: 'we' are in *this* together! The posthuman turn shows that the consensus about the universal value of Eurocentric assumptions about 'Man' has dissipated, and this figuration of the human is in trouble. 'Man' as the taxonomic type has now become 'Man the brand' (Haraway 1997: 74). This 'anthropological exodus' produces a colossal hybridization of the species (Hardt and Negri 2000: 215).

It is indeed the case that the post-anthropocentric shift of perspective is not met with equal enthusiasm in all academic quarters. Social theory literature about the humanist legacy and the future of the human in our technologically advanced times, is anxiety-ridden (Fukuyama 2002; Habermas 2003; Sloterdijk 2009). Recently, Pope Francis (2015) joined this debate, supplementing Catholic dogma on Natural Law, with Naomi Klein's analysis of the destructive role of capitalism (Klein 2014), in a contemporary variation on the theme of 'apocalyptic monotheism' (Szerszynski 2017: 260). Anxiety is more oblique but equally strong in the progressive left, where the legacy of Socialist Humanism provides the tools to re-work anxiety into political rage. In all cases, we see the emergence of a category – the endangered human – which is at the same time evanescent and insurgent. The evidence provided by posthuman scholarship shows no 'crisis', but a remarkable upsurge of inspiration.

Politically, as I argued above, it is difficult not to read this vulnerable pan-humanity as a knee-jerk reaction by the centre, or the Majority. That centre can be defined as: male, white, heterosexual, owning wives and children, urbanized, able-bodied, speaking a standard language, i.e. 'Man' (Braidotti 1991), or rather by now – 'ex-Man' (Massumi 1998). In so far as the Anthropocentric risks of climate change threaten the entire planet, however, one should avoid any cynicism. Radical epistemologies like feminism and post-colonial theory are just as affected by the demise of Man or Anthropos (Chakrabarty 2009) as the universalist ones. We therefore need to deal with the issue critically, but also affirm-atively. As I argued in the previous chapter, vital materialism puts the posthuman subject on a time continuum in which experiences, thoughts and relations flow in a continuous present. This present never fully coincides with an actualized spatio-temporally saturated 'now', but goes on becoming. The posthuman subject always yearns towards the virtual.

Posthuman theory focusses, through critical and creative cartographies, on the margins of expression of yet unrealized possibilities for overcoming both Humanism and anthro-pocentrism by concentrating on the issue: who is this 'we' whose humanity is now at stake? What 'we' could become as a species and a set of technologically interlinked material cultures? The challenge consists in tracking the multiple, grounded and hence specific and diversified ways in which we are becoming knowing subjects. This approach diverges from the 'otherwise other' of the dialectical oppositions and pejorative differences posited by classical Humanist 'Man' and the supremacist assertions of 'Anthropos'.

In order to answer these questions, I will point out the different lines of connection that compose the ensemble 'we', which I participate in. For the sake of the current discussion, 'we' are situated, feminist-minded, anti-racist, post- and de-colonial thinkers and practitioners, who are trying to come to terms with the challenges of the posthuman convergence, while avoiding a universal posture or undue generalizations. Considering, moreover, the contiguity between posthuman knowledge production and cognitive capitalism, new questions need to be raised and clarified.

It is undeniable that posthuman scholarship is contiguous and resonates with bio-genetic and technologically mediated advanced capitalism. How are we to assess the proliferation of knowledge within this specific landscape? Is the product of posthuman knowledge just the expression of the schizoid speed and accelerations of advanced capitalism? Sarah Nuttall provides a sharp analysis of the impact of capitalist accelerations upon posthuman scholarship, in the context of shifting geo-political relations.[1] Nuttall connects the posthuman convergence to the planetary politics and to the need to redefine a black critical thought for our posthuman times, so as to counteract the rising authoritarianism, the resurgence of white supremacism and a range of inhuman modes of violence across the world and especially in the South. The task is both daunting and urgent.

As Noys puts it, 'our immersion in immanence is required to speed the process to the moment of transcendence as threshold' (2014: 7–8). Accelerationism also calls for an inhuman form of rationalism that privileges the computational abilities of technological apparatus – notably its algorithmic logic – in the hope of turning them to the solution of social and economic issues (I discussed this approach in chapter 2 as a form of speculative neo-rationalism).

The accelerationist stance includes a range of different positions from a barely disguised form of optimism to a more grounded affirmative politics. An example of the latter, Williams and Srnicek (2014: 354) argue: 'an accelerationist politics seeks to preserve the gains of late capitalism, while going further than its value system, governance structures and mass pathologies will allow'. This position, in other words, aims not so much to destroy the platform of neo-liberalism, as to repurpose it towards post-capitalist ends and for the common good. It assumes that the capitalist system holds back progress, as it is not the optimal way to work with the technologies we have at our disposal. A different economic system, more egalitarian and based on sharing resources, would be more apt at ensuring the well-being of the population. At its worst, accelerationism is defeatist and cynical, which is worrying in terms of its ethical and political implications. The fatalism is based on a hasty and rather conservative dismissal of the politics of classical liberalism – which the accelerationists believe to have been assassinated by neo-liberal economics, and by the failure of Socialism in its many twentieth-century variations, including Soviet-style Communism. This results in an insurgent form of nihilism (Land 1992).

Furthermore, accelerationists like Nick Land (1993) push their thinking towards a form of epistemic chaos and anarchist politics, which rejoices in destruction for its own sake. It is one thing to argue that one way to defeat capitalism is by exacerbating and radicalizing its contradictions, in the hope of making it implode. The residual Hegelianism of this position notwithstanding, at least this position expresses some concern for the state of the world. But it is quite another to advocate the pursuit of annihilation as the only strategy, coupled with the enjoyment of violence. This position, which Achille Mbembe (2017b) has labelled 'negative messianism', strikes me as an authoritarian position, which I strongly object to. Moreover, such a stance has nothing in common with Deleuze and Guattari's project of defining a non-fascist ethics, an ethics that critiques power and invites us to cultivate empowerment as the actualization of affirmative passions. Feminism, anti-racism and anti-fascism are among the political movements that have clearly stated their commitment to creating alternatives and combining critique with creativity. The accelerationists do not shine for their knowledge or appreciation of the radical epistemologies of feminism, post-colonialism and indigenous philosophies.

Fortunately, the *Xenofeminism Manifesto* managed to bridge that critical gap (Laboria Cuboniks 2015). The post-accelerationist xenofeminists accomplish, in my terms, a very radical transposition of feminism across the great posthuman divide. They boldly combine an anti-naturalistic stance with techno-materialism and binary gender abolitionism, to articulate 'a radical gender politics fit for an era of globality, complexity and technology' (Hester 2018: 7). Adopting a materialist stance, they focus on mundane technologies such as domestic labour-saving devices, as well as larger infrastructural technological systems, to raise key issues of alienation and reproductive labour. Xenofeminism aims at concrete political interventions upon society, following the slogan 'If nature is unjust, change nature!'. This is a critical, affirmative and upbeat response to the challenges of the posthuman times.

To pursue my brand of affirmative politics: this is neither an endorsement of the shallow optimism of advanced capitalism nor an accelerationist strategy, though it is closer to the latter. It rather focuses on the issue of subjectivity as a differential grounded perspective that must encompass non-human forces and strike its own meta-stable alliances within the flows of de-territorialization of advanced capitalism. Applied to the discussion of the political economy of contemporary knowledge production, this means that the crucial problem is the different speeds of de-/re-territorialization by bio-cognitive capitalism and the toxic saturation of the present it enacts, to the detriment of the actualization of the virtual. The violent erasure, or passive-aggressive blockage, of our collective desire to express and materialize virtual potentials affects both subject formation and knowledge practices in society. They actually exhaust us. Their internally contradictory speeds also impact on the contemporary university, the scientific community and the art world. How to tell the difference between affirmative and instrumental or opportunistic modes of knowledge production is the fundamental question.

As a post-disciplinary, relational field, posthuman knowledge production actualizes multiple possibilities which evade the profit-led accelerations of capital and works within it to go elsewhere. This trend results in the making of the Critical PostHumanities. They function at different speeds, move on different timelines and are fuelled by different ethical affects. They involve social and cultural movements, new kinds of economically productive practices and multiple curiosity-driven knowledge formations that do not always coincide with the surplus-value profit motive. In other words, posthuman knowledge designs a horizon of becoming that the contemporary university and especially the academic Humanities will benefit from.

Because power is a multi-layered and dynamic entity, and because as embedded and embodied, relational and affective subjects, we are immanent to the very conditions we are trying to change, we need to make a careful ethical distinction between different speeds of both knowledge production – with the predictable margins of institutional capitalization – and the construction of alternative knowing subject formations.

Please keep in mind – at this crucial point in the argument – the importance of politics of location or of immanence, and of perspectivism as a multi-layered and multi-directional account of what is already happening. This methodology respects different viewpoints from equally materially embedded and embodied locations that express the degree of power and quality of experience of different subjects. We need to acknowledge the multiple and internally contradictory aspects of our own knowledge practices by adopting a diversified materialist approach, which I propose as the antidote to relativism. The difference is a matter of ethics: becoming as the realization of affirmative, collaborative ethics, as opposed to the axiom of profit and maximization of consumers' quantitative options.

Far from calling for a new pan-human order, a new mode of global governance, this approach foregrounds the self-regulating force of situated knowledge, of multiple heterogeneous assemblages, interconnections that plunge headlong into a post-disciplinary world. Affirmative ethics infuses the understanding of our conditions and thus guides our politics.

The proposed praxis is the formation of posthuman trans-subjectivities to sustain the collective counter-actualization of the virtual. They are trans-individual, trans-cultural, trans-species, trans-sexual, trans-national, and trans-human modes of subjectivity. The barrier against the negative, entropic frenzy of the capitalist axiomatic is provided by the grounded and transformative politics that ensue from the ethic of affirmation. In this regard, a neo-materialist vital position offers a robust rebuttal of the accelerationist and profit-minded knowledge practices of bio-mediated, cognitive capitalism.

Taking 'living matter' as a *zoe*/geo/techno-centred process that interacts in complex ways with the techno-social, psychic and natural environments and resists the over-coding by the capitalist profit principle (and the structural inequalities it entails), we end up on an affirmative plane of composition of transversal subjectivities, through the composition of subject assemblages that actualize the unrealized or virtual potential of 'a missing people'. In the old language: decelerate and contribute to the collective construction of social horizons of hope. Neo-materialist immanence expands this transversal collective ability to produce knowledge otherwise, to other species. Zoe/geo/techno-centred egalitarianism is the core of a posthuman thought that might inspire, work with or subtend informational and scientific practices and resist the full-scale commodification of Life by advanced capitalism (Braidotti 2006).

Let us move this argument a step further now: because posthuman scholarship is contiguous with technologically mediated advanced capitalism, it is not confined to the scientific institutions of higher learning and research, which have historically been the gate-keepers and controllers of scientific excellence. Universities, science academies and specialized institutes are by far not the sole owners of knowledge production capacity today. If capitalism has indeed taken a cognitive turn, then cognitive material is being produced in a myriad of ways and in multiple locations that include the corporate sector, the art world, the military, the activist sector, the blogosphere and the Internet.

Such a vitality in producing information, data and claims to knowledge cannot fail to impact on the role of academic knowledge, especially Humanities scholarship and the function of the university as a whole. The cognitive character of advanced capitalism also provides ammunition for the many political forces that want to dismantle them and replace academic higher education with life-long coaching and other privatized forms of tuition. The same forces would not mind seeing the Humanities reduced to personal hobbies, or a high-class info-tainment for the happy few. My counter-argument throughout this book is that the Humanities today, redefined by the posthuman predicament, are about the creation of new ways of thinking, new concepts and social imaginaries that reflect the complexity of the times and the pursuit of affirmative ethics, as well as criticism. This requires an affirmative, not a defensive or nostalgic approach. The Humanities will prosper to the extent that they are willing to change, to enter into unfamiliar territories and become PostHumanities.

Considering the mutual imbrication of advanced capitalism with posthuman knowledge, however, it is crucial to develop criteria to make distinctions between scientific knowledge in the service of affirmation and sustainability, from profit-oriented and opportunistic knowledge claims. This is by no means a new and original problem, but it does encounter novel applications in the present context, given the velocity and intrusiveness of contemporary technologies. This is why it is important to work out an adequate framework to make qualitative distinctions between the different speeds and accelerations. These distinctions are epistemic, in that they concern different kinds of knowledge claims, but their force is ethical.

Please note that this argument assumes and upholds Nietzsche's distinction between morality as the implementation of rules and protocols of acceptable behaviour and ethics, which is about relations, intensities and forces. Ethics is about power, and power relations are multi-layered and pluri-faceted, both as a restrictive force (*potestas*, or entrapment) and as an affirmative one (*potentia*, or empowerment). In other words, these two modalities of power are not mutually exclusive, but rather co-exist as multiple facets of the same process, namely the process of subject formation.

In this frame of reference, therefore, ethics is a praxis that begins with the production of adequate knowledge in the sense of providing qualitative differentiations between different instances, idea and relations. This approach is modelled on Spinoza's ethics of joy in that it connects adequate understanding to the analysis of our bondage, limitations and flaws, i.e. power. Providing criteria to make such distinctions between negative/entrapping modes of relation and the affirmative/empowering ones amounts to mapping different speeds of re/de-territorialization. It also involves the ethical coding of different forms of knowledge, as well as the petrification or re-territorializations which capture, stratify and capitalize on relations, values and knowledge claims. I shall return to the link between adequate knowledge and affirmation in chapter 5. For now, let me pursue my cartography.

Cognitive Capitalism and the New Knowledge Economy

These paradoxical and internally fractured developments do not take place in a void, but rather within the axiomatic and profit-driven system (Toscano 2005) of advanced, or 'cognitive' capitalism (Moulier-Boutang 2012). Let me expand here on the general outline I provided in the introduction.

Considering not only the high degree of technological mediation, but also the material grounding of its infra-structures and the labour relations it engenders, this system has also been called Network Society (Terranova 2004; Castells 2010; Zylinska 2014). It rests on advanced computational systems, pervasive automation and 'smart' objects and ubiquitous mediation of social relations. But it cannot be reduced to technological mediation alone. The economy of advanced capitalism is split between the financialization of the economy and the de-regulation of labour. What used to be labour, in a society that now claims to be post-work (Srnicek 2016), is simultaneously highly sophisticated, as it requires cultural and algorithmic fluency, and also highly unregulated and hence open to abuses and injustice. It is both human capital and bare life (Agamben 1998).

There is nothing particularly 'advanced' about the ruthless exploitation of labour and natural resources that is enacted by contemporary capitalism. The disparity between the financial and the real economy is flagrant, in a system that capitalizes on credit, twists the workings of state institutions towards endless commercialization of all activities and practices, and ends up producing indebtedness on a global scale (Lazzarato 2012). The discrepancy between the highest earning classes and the bottom of the economic scale is at its worst since the First Industrial Revolution. In 2017 the world's eight richest people had the same wealth as the poorest 50%; in 2018 the richest 1% were on target to own two-thirds of all wealth by 2030 (Savage 2018).

This destructive and divisive political economy feeds a global trend towards illiberal and authoritarian populism that in turn fuels new forms of racism, religious warfare and global apartheid (Hall 1979). In her sharp analysis of neo-liberalism as a regime of governmentality, inspired by Foucault's Lectures at the Collège de France, Wendy Brown (2015) argues a bold case: that the inequalities installed by the neo-liberal imposition of the profit motive as the ethos and the regime of power in contemporary societies undoes both the efficiency and the social credibility of social institutions. The state apparatus as a whole is in the grip of corporate finance and this occupation erodes public support for the very institutions of Western democracy.

Because these regimes of governmentality shape the processes of subject formations, a further side-effect of neo-liberal governance is the hollowing out of the democratic imaginary, breeding that fatigue with democracy I analysed in chapter 1. They constitute indebted and exhausted subjects who are subjected to systemic theft of their powers (*potentia*), to shape life outside the parameters of brutal marketization. The quantified subject thus replaces the classical liberal subject, just as competition replaces exchange, inequality replaces equality and entrepreneurship replaces production (Brown 2015). Neo-liberalism is killing our freedom softly.

These conditions are the same that sustain the posthuman convergence, its intense technological mediation, the environmental devastation, the affective anxieties and psychic exhaustion, as well as the populist anger of our times. Which raises the inevitable question of what conditions and activities could re-ignite a democratic imaginary worthy of our times. How does the posthuman convergence point to new forms of democratic participation by humans as well as non-humans?

A branch of posthuman scholarship, best represented by Cary Wolfe, approaches this problem in a sociological frame, contextualizing the relative marginality of the human species in the current configurations of knowledge and power. Wolfe turns to Niklas Luhmann's system theory to account for technological mediation and argues that modernization itself can be understood as a process of 'functional differentiation' of society into discrete autopoietic/self-organizing social systems. Each of these systems has its own governing codes of knowledge and communication, which is sometimes called 'fragmentation' or 'specialization'. According to Wolfe, this over-specialization of discourses and practices all aim at the same thing: to reduce the increasing complexity of a larger environment that they themselves help to produce, in fact, in deploying their own specialized discourses. The reduction of the public sphere is therefore a systemic and not a political issue.

Much as I share Wolfe's diagnosis about the over-specialization and inner fragmentation of contemporary relations of production including the epistemic ones, I do not share his functionalist approach. In the framework of what I have called the posthuman convergence, the production of knowledge is both an index and an agent of complexity. But this complexity does not pertain exclusively to the social and technological apparatus, nor is it generated by it alone. It rather pertains to the multiple ecologies of becoming subjects, in an embodied and embedded, relational and affective manner. These processes of subjectification result in constructing complex transversal posthuman subjectivities – media-nature-cultural subjects. Focusing exclusively on larger techno-industrial systems falsifies the picture, especially if one leaves out the joint impact of a shift that includes *zoe/ geo/techno* perspectives.

The algorithmic sequences and 'smart' objects that swarm the Internet of Things are 'alive' and it is indeed up to the humans to prove their competence in spite of their non-machinic nature. As a matter of fact, the classical divide between nature and culture, first replaced by a 'natureculture' continuum (Haraway 2003), has now become 'medianature' (Parikka 2015a), resulting in converging 'media nature-culture' environments (Braidotti 2016b). These developments both enhance and displace the centrality of the human subject as the 'homo universalis', the anthropomorphic 'Man' of reason. They also relocate the dialectical opposites and opponents of this dominant and normative vision of the human, which historically have been the sexualized others (women, LBGTQ+); the racialized others (non-Europeans, indigenous); and the naturalized others (animals, plants, the Earth) (Braidotti 2002). Neo-liberal governance indeed plays a central role in exacerbating power differences.

Advanced capitalism is schizoid, as Deleuze and Guattari have argued since the 1970s. It is a differential engine that promotes the quantitative proliferation of multiple options in consumer goods and actively produces deterritorialized differences for the sake of commodification. The saturation of the social space by fast-changing commodities short-circuits the virtual charge of the present, by infecting it with the internally contradictory temporality of commodity fetishism (Massumi 1992). Commodities never fully appease or release, but keep us coming back for more. Addictive and toxic, advanced capitalism is an entropic and self-destructive force that eats up the future and the very sources of its wealth and power, undermining the possibility of its own survival (Holland 2011).

The bio-technological pole of this system is based on the economy of 'Life as surplus' (Cooper 2008), which considers as capital value the informational power of living matter itself, its vital, immanent qualities and self-organizing capacity. The information technology side of the same economy constructs smart virtual systems, mostly applied to data-mining, that is to say the accumulation of what used to be called 'vital statistics'. This is a bio-political practice of gathering crucial information about humans and non-human agents, for the purpose of extensive profiling practices and the risk assessments of vast populations.

As a result, cognitive, advanced capitalism enacts a knowledge economy that profits from the scientific and economic understanding of all that lives. Because life, as it happens, is not the exclusive prerogative of humans, this opportunistic bio-genetic political economy induces, if not the actual erasure, at least the blurring of the distinction between the human and other species, when it comes to profiting from them. Thus, seeds, plants, animals and bacteria fit into this logic of insatiable consumption alongside various specimens of humanity.

In such an economic system, the uniqueness of *Anthropos* is displaced, producing a functional form of post-anthro-pocentrism that spuriously unifies all species under the imperative of the market. This is why the excesses of the Capitalocene threaten the sustainability of our planet as a whole.

The new economy is furthermore based on the storage, capitalization and retrieval of data operated by informatics systems, which goes beyond classical modes of exploitation of living matter. It surpasses, for instance, the practice of 'bio-piracy' (Shiva 1997), or the commercial patenting of living entities. Cognitive capitalism goes further and remakes life as code – bio-genetic (Monsanto) and computational codes (Google). This is a case of 'machinic auto-poiesis', as Felix Guattari called it (2000), building on Maturana and Varela's notion of organic auto-poiesis, to indicate the ability of computational networks to self-organize, just like all living organisms. All species are spuriously unified under the imperative of the market economy.

These breath-taking technological advances are taking place on the brink of an ecological disaster on an unprecedented scale. Any remains of euphoria about the technological mastery of what we used to call nature have been replaced by a pervasive sense of unease about the illness suffered by our environment. The spectre of the Sixth Extinction is upon us. Since the nuclear era, highly militarized applications of our science and technology had turned into sources of permanent anxiety over our present and the sustainability of our future. The current technological revolution not only intensifies these fears, but also spreads them to a new dimension, that is both planetary and very intimate.

This shift occurs within the spinning speeds of advanced capitalism and in the background of the climate change threat. The emergence of the Earth as a dynamic political agent has immediate repercussions for posthuman knowledge. Efforts are on-going to redefine the relationship between the geological and the social – Earth and society. A new political geology is being constructed (Clark and Yusoff 2017) that examines 'geontopower' (Povinelli 2016). The core of a geo-centred knowledge practice within the posthuman convergence touches the traditional distinction between the organic life of animals, plants and the inorganic one of rocks and geological strata. Challenging and displacing that distinction enables subtler analyses of advanced capitalism's profit-making excursions into matter. Working with a Deleuzian perspective and therefore with immanence and vital matter, Protevi (2001) acknowledges that Earth forces have now moved to the core of the social agenda. He calls this shift 'political physis', or a geo-politics of non-deterministic naturalism.

The *zoe*/geo/techno perspectives in many ways are not new, as they refer back to the Continental tradition of vital materialism, also known as Continental naturalism that prospered in Europe, and especially in France, from the eighteenth century. This line runs through to Bergson, Canguilhem, Bachelard and their students Foucault, Serres and Deleuze. The emphasis on life and living systems is a central tool of their epistemological projects, which reflect theoretically upon the complexity of living systems. There is a qualitative distinction between holistic vitalism and the sustained critical attempt at rethinking our multiple, immanent ecologies – social, environmental, mental and affective – in the light of contemporary Life sciences.

The *zoe*/geo/techno dimensions, however distinct, are also part of a more general ecology, which is a multi-layered dynamic system that encompasses environmental, social and psychic elements. Hörl defines it as 'the general ecologization of thinking and theory' in a context where 'power is environmentalized by media technologies that are based on distribution infrastructures and begins to operate ecologically' (2018: 172). Protevi also refers to this complex assemblage in terms of 'geo-hydro-solar-bio-techno-politics' (2018). He also adds that the aim of critical thinking today is to politicize posthumanism and to posthumanize politics (Protevi 2013), while decolonizing both of them by exposing the Eurocentric specificity of their assumptions. A consensus emerges in posthuman research, therefore, that it is a case of socializing the Anthropocene and geologizing the social (Clark and Gunaratnam 2017).

The premises of the posthuman knowledge production emerge as a creative interweaving of *zoe*/geo/techno perspectives. They are deeply rhizomic in structure and movement and tend to sound unexpectedly weird. All of them engage critically with the overcoding flows of advanced capitalism and with the neo-liberal economic exploitation of all living matter. All of them struggle, as well, to keep margins of critical distance from the accelerations of cognitive capital.

So far, the argument in this chapter has been made that the Humanities are prospering to the extent that they are willing to change and enter the unfamiliar territories of posthuman knowledge. But more clarity is needed on how to manage this transition, both in terms of individual practices and institutional settings. How is this change taking place? How is it affecting the content and structure of teaching institutions like the university? The next chapter will address some of these rightful concerns.

Chapter 4
The Critical PostHumanities

Transdisciplinary Exuberance

The Humanities have proved perfectly capable of re-inventing themselves. They are already embracing the multiple opportunities offered by the posthuman convergence, by setting new and distinctive objects of enquiry, free from the traditional or institutional assignment to the human and its humanistic derivatives. The field is richly endowed with the methodological and theoretical resources to set up original and necessary debates with the sciences and technologies and other grand challenges of today, in the posthuman era and after the decline of the primacy of 'Man' and of Anthropos.

Critical PostHumanities are currently emerging as post-disciplinary discursive fronts, not only around the edges of the classical disciplines but also as off-shots of the more marginal, interdisciplinary critical discourses that tend to call themselves Studies. The discursive vitality is telling, as shown by even a cursory glance at the terminological diversification emerging in the field of Critical PostHumanities. Today you will find, both at the level of publications and as institutional realities embedded in courses, curricula and research projects, for instance the Ecological Humanities, the Environmental Humanities, sub-divided into the Blue

Humanities, which study seas and oceans, and the Green Humanities which focus on the Earth. They are also known as the Sustainable Humanities and, in more crass variations, Energy Humanities and Resilient Humanities.

Other successful instances are: the Medical Humanities, also known as the Bio-Humanities; the Neural Humanities; Evolutionary Humanities. The Public Humanities are also quite popular and have spawned into the Civic Humanities; the Community Humanities; the Translational Humanities; the Global Humanities; the Greater Humanities. More neo-liberal variations are the Interactive Humanities and the Entrepreneurial Humanities. The Digital Humanities (Hayles 1999, 2005), which are also called the Computational, Informational and Data Humanities, are possibly the most powerful institutional developments of the last decades.

The fast rate of growth has already prompted several meta-discursive analyses, which in turn resulted in another sequence of neo-logisms. For instance: the PostHumanities (Wolfe 2010); Inhuman Humanities (Grosz 2011); Transformative (Epstein 2012); Emerging; Adjectival (De Graef 2016); and Nomadic Humanities (Stimpson 2016).

The underlying assumptions of the Critical PostHumanities are clear. Firstly, they assume that the knower – the knowing subject – is neither *homo universalis* nor *Anthropos* alone. The knowing subject is no longer a singular entity, but a more complex ensemble: of *zoe*/geo/techno-related factors, which include humans. These knowing subjects are collaboratively linked to a material web of human and non-human agents. The subject of knowledge for the Digital Humanities is AI-mediated; for the Environmental Humanities, it is geo- and hydro-centred.

Secondly, posthuman scholarship rests on a positive relationship to the diversity of *zoe* – non-human life – in a non-hierarchical manner, recognizing the respective degrees of intelligence, ability and creativity of all organisms. *Zoe*- and geo-entities are partners in knowledge production. This implies that thinking and knowing are *not* the prerogative of humans alone, but take place in the world, which is defined by the coexistence of multiple organic species and technological artefacts alongside each other. Organisms and computational networks are eco-sophically connected. Understanding this living continuum signals a becoming-world of knowledge practices.

What is critical and what is posthuman about the PostHumanities is a question of thematic, methodological and conceptual aspects. Thematically, the Critical PostHumanities deal not only with a broader spectrum of human subjects, but also with non-human objects and subjects of study. They also focus on transversal, networked apparatus and big data sets. The Critical PostHumanities position terrestrial, planetary, cosmic concerns as serious agents and co-constructors in processes of collective thinking and knowing. These include the conventional naturalized non-human entities like animals, plants and the technological apparatus. This is a major step forward, but also a challenge for the Humanities that historically have resisted acknowledging the thinking powers of non-anthropomorphic entities.

Methodologically, the defining feature of the PostHumanities is their 'supra-disciplinary' character. This is what makes them critical. The driving force for their knowledge production is not the policing of disciplinary purity, but rather the modes of relation and cross-hybridization these discourses are able and willing to engage in. The PostHumanities prosper to the extent that they show the ability and the willingness to question critically institutional boundaries and move on. Their strength is directly proportional to their relational ability to open up to each other and to the world.

Conceptually, the Critical PostHumanities overcome the vision of a de-naturalized social order somehow disconnected from its environmental and organic foundations. They call for more complex schemes of understanding the multi-layered interdependence between 'naturecultures' today. The zoe/geo/techno mediations that sustain the Critical PostHumanities, do not only take the form of a quantitative proliferation of new fundable fields, which could be perceived negatively as fragmentation, but they also entail qualitative and methodological shifts of perspective.

Politically, the Critical PostHumanities represent both an alternative to the neo-liberal governance of academic knowledge, dominated by quantitative data and control, and a re-negotiation of its terms. An essential component of their success and of their relational power consists in the ability and willingness to participate in corporate culture, in finance and industry. In this respect, the PostHumanities are innovative in both themes and methods and they threaten the centuries-old tradition of academic freedom and independence in equal measure. Given such a proliferation of discourses in academic settings, their intense and hybrid cross-fertilization and the speed with which they are over-coded by and interwoven with financial investments, they can appear suspiciously close to the profit-driven logic of advanced capitalism.

The next step of my argument answers this question: the transversal discourses and practices of the Critical PostHumanities cannot be reduced to the epistemic accel-erationism that fuels cognitive capitalism. As I have been arguing throughout this book, the posthuman convergence is complex and multi-layered and presents both negative and positive aspects. It is generating new power formations and also new ways of resisting them. It produces forms and subjects of knowledge that cannot fully be captured by the schizoid speeds and acceleration of capital. This is the politics of immanence at work, in a manner that deepens Foucault's insight about the multi-layered structure of power, that is as both entrapping (*potestas*) and empowering (*potentia*). However, it is not a question of 'either/or', either complicity with capitalist accelerations or academic autonomy. It is rather a matter of 'and ... and'.

The challenge for critical theory consists in being able to tell the difference between these different speeds and flows of mutation, by practising the cartographic accounts of their different locations. We need to situate the knowledge claims very carefully in terms of the power variables that support them. After all, we are not dealing here with relativism, but with immanent perspectives that honour the materiality of discursive production and the relational structure of subjectivity.

By providing a critical genealogy of their emergence out of the posthuman convergence, within but distinct from neo-liberal economics, I will argue for the Critical PostHumanities as a qualitatively different project from the profit-driven capitalization of advanced knowledge. They can constitute a counter-project, that consists in producing knowledge through collective praxis, in the common world, by the constitution of transversal posthuman subjectivity driven by an ethics of affirmation. The Critical PostHumanities are not only the recoding of academic knowledge by capital, though that aspect – majority-led and well-funded – is undeniable. They are also transversal discursive and institutional structures that take in and on today's world, in a transformative and compassionate manner. This aspect is minorities-driven and not profit-minded. To give an example: when approached from hacking culture and media activism, the Digital Humanities look very different from research done at Google campuses or other corporate quarters. Equally, from the angle of environmental activism and transnational land rights, the Environmental Humanities look quite different from corporate green economics. These are two aspects of the same phenomenon, which have both entered the universities as the new or PostHumanities. My effort in this book is to foreground the *critical* potential of the PostHumanities.

The Critical PostHumanities combine understanding and knowledge with training and pastoral care, thus fulfilling both a critical and a healing function in relation to the negative instances of injustice and dispossession, pain and hurt, exhaustion and anxiety, that mark the posthuman convergence. The Critical PostHumanities are critical and creative in equal parts. They are affirmative while embedded in the conditions of the present (as both actual and virtual), which includes the speedy reterritorializations of knowledge. Contiguity, however, is not the same as complicity and qualitative differences can and must be made. I shall do so by first tracing the genealogy of the Critical PostHumanities and then provide a theoretical framework to assess them.

A Genealogy of the Critical PostHumanities

First-Generation Studies
The first building block of posthuman scholarship is only slightly younger than the Anthropocene itself. Over the last thirty years, the core of theoretical innovation in the Humanities has emerged from a number of often radical

and always interdisciplinary practices that called themselves 'Studies' (Braidotti 2013). Women's, Gay and Lesbian, Gender, Feminist and Queer Studies; Race, Postcolonial and Subaltern Studies, alongside Cultural Studies, Film, Television and Media Studies. Science and Technology Studies is a crucial hub (Stengers 1997), which connects to cultural studies of science (McNeil 2007); health and disability (Shildrick 2009); media (Bryld and Lykke 2000; Smelik and Lykke 2008); topologies of culture, and digital media studies (Lury, Parisi and Terranova 2012; Fuller and Goffey 2013; Parisi 2013). These discourses are the proto-types of the radical epistemologies that – over the last thirty years – have voiced the situated knowledge of the dialectical and structural 'others' of humanistic 'Man of reason'. They activate the insights and knowledge generated by multiple, situated, materially embedded locations and carry them into transdisciplinary knowledge production.

The first generation of critical studies paved the road for posthumanism, in stressing that humanistic 'Man' defined himself as much by what he excluded from as by what he included in his rational self-representation. By organizing differences on a hierarchical scale of decreasing worth, this humanist subject justified violent and belligerent exclusions of the sexualized, racialized and naturalized 'others'. They occupied the slot of devalued difference and were socially marginalized at the best of times and reduced to the sub-human status of disposable bodies in the worst-case scenarios. As a result, that humanist image of 'Man' also implemented social systems built on sexism, homo- and trans-phobia, colonialism and racism that turned cultural specificity into a fake universal and normality into a normative injunction. This image of thought shaped the institutional practice of the Humanities as an exercise of hierarchical exclusion and cultural hegemony.

The criticism of Humanism by the critical 'Studies' at the theoretical level, also resonated with major socio-political changes in the real-life world. The structural 'others' of the modern humanistic subject re-emerge with a vengeance in postmodernity, fuelling great emancipatory movements (Braidotti 2002). The women's rights movement, the anti-racism and decolonization movements, the anti-nuclear and

pro-environment movements are the voices of the structural others of Western modernity. The political movements
carried by these new emerging subjects mark simultaneously
the crisis of the dominant subjects, and for conservatives even
its 'cause', and the expression of positive, pro-active alternatives. In the language of nomadic theory, they express both
the crisis of the majority and the patterns of becoming of
the minorities (Braidotti 2011b). In other words, sexualized,
racialized and naturalized differences, far from being the
categorical boundary-keepers of the subject of Humanism,
have evolved into fully-fledged alternative models of the
human subject, on the ruins of the human as defined by
Eurocentric Humanism.

The first-generation 'Studies' share a number of theoretical
premises. They criticize the idea of the human implicitly
upheld by the academic Humanities. They do so on two
grounds: structural anthropocentrism on the one hand and
in-built Eurocentrism and 'methodological nationalism' (Beck
2007) on the other. Spelling thus the end of the 'monocultures
of the mind' (Shiva 1993), they critically disengage from the
rules, conventions and institutional protocols of the academic
disciplines. This exodus from disciplinary 'homes' shifts the
point of reference away from the authority of the past, and
onto accountability for the real-life condition of the present
(as both actual and virtual). This is what Foucault and
Deleuze called 'the philosophy of the outside': thinking of, in
and for the world. This is a becoming-world of knowledge
production practices.

Institutionally, the first-generation 'Studies' have remained
relatively underfunded in relation to the classical disciplines,
yet have provided a range of new methods and innovative
concepts. Many of these Studies – but by no means all
of them – were activated and propelled by the incisive
philosophical, linguistic, cultural and textual innovations
introduced by the French post-structuralist generation since
the 1970s. As such, they were theory-inflected and influenced
by psychoanalysis, semiotics, Marxism, deconstruction,
feminism and gender theory, race and post-colonial studies.
This multi-faceted critical wave became very influential in
the United States, where it was branded as 'French' theory,
and 'French' feminism. The creative proliferation of 'Studies'

is an institutional phenomenon that took place across North America including Canada, Northern Europe and Australia, but not as much in Catholic Southern Europe. It is not the least of paradoxes that the French post-structuralist theories had little impact on the institutional practice of French society and the academy. In fact, especially throughout the 1980s under the Socialist Mitterrand presidency, a specific French form of Republican universalism was reasserted.

Moreover, it is noteworthy that my beloved anti-humanist French teachers – Foucault as much as Deleuze and Irigaray – were very much philosophers, not particularly interested in, or supportive of, the new interdisciplinary Studies that emerged partly in response to their work. Similarly, Edward Said was not very keen on the field of Postcolonial Studies that nonetheless celebrated him as a foundational figure (Braidotti 2016a). They all preferred a classical humanistic education – the better to critique it, of course.[1] The basic objection was that the change of scale and objects of research introduced by these critical Studies may not be enough to introduce a qualitative shift in terms of concepts and methods. They ran the risk instead of promoting just a quantitative growth of identity-related claims and thus reinforcing discursive powers of inclusion and exclusion. I took their warning to heart and, while disagreeing with such a conservative assessment, devoted a great deal of my work to producing both conceptual and methodological shifts, in women's, feminist and gender studies.

These original institutional and theoretical experiments, which ran throughout the 1990s, brought alternative perspectives and sources of inspiration to the academic world. These developments coincided with a profound transformation of the university structure, but they also became the target of a political backlash. In the United States the backlash happened because of the collusion of critical Studies with the contested French theory and elsewhere because of their radical edge.

It is worth noting that not all the critical Studies oppose Humanism, but also offer alternative visions of the humanist self, the human, knowledge and society. Some of the proposed theoretical notions, such as a female and feminist (Irigaray 1993), queer humanity (Butler 2004), and black humanity (Fanon 1967), are examples of this more inclusive kind of neo-humanism (Braidotti and Gilroy 2016). As a reminder, the posthuman subject that I argue for in this book presents quite a different case: beyond Humanism I envisage a leap forward towards a posthuman ethics of collaborative construction of alternative and post-identitarian ways of 'being-in-this-together'.

A second defining feature of these Studies is the fact that they are firmly grounded in the real-life present world, which means that they emphasize the immanence of lived experience. Being situated in the present and grounded in the world, they express original forms of bodily materialist immanence which generates knowledge through sensible (Irigaray 1993) and transcendental (Deleuze 1994) forms of empiricism. The critical Studies trust real-life events and experiences, even and especially the negative ones: oppression, violence and dispossession.

In this respect, the first generation of critical Studies exposes the compatibility of rationality and violence, of scientific progress on the one hand and practices of structural devastation and exclusion on the other. This is not an anti-science stance, but instead a non-binary, multi-layered way of assessing in parallel ways the workings of science, philosophy and the arts, from the standpoint of the excluded. It is crowded on the margins, so it is a permanent challenge to be loyal to these experiences. By grounding their knowing practices and quest for adequate understanding into lived experience, the Studies discourses also take power relations seriously. This generates a further development: by foregrounding the insights and competences of the excluded and marginalized subjects, the critical Studies end up overcoming their starting premises. They may start from the experiences of women, or LBGT+, or colonialism and racism, and fight for the rights of these categories. But what is at stake is an even bigger issue: it is about renewing the common understanding of what it means to be human, to confront the inhuman and to become posthuman.

I want to insist that these Studies are well placed to develop a posthuman practice of self-renewal in a critical and creative manner, because they have already shown themselves capable of complexity, subtlety and versatility in dealing with the negative aspects of the present, as well as its affirmative potential. They have adapted remarkably well to changes in both popular media cultures and in science and the university structure. They fulfil the cartographic obligation of being both critical of dominant visions of knowing subjects, and creative by actualizing the virtual and unrealized insights and competences of marginalized subjects (Braidotti 2002, 2006).

The case of women's, feminist, queer and gender studies is emblematic of both the critical edge and the creative exuberance of posthuman disengagement from dominant ideas about the knowing subject. Contemporary feminism has predicated a concerted exodus from the regime of Man and Anthropos, defined as a species that monopolizes the right to access the bodies of all living entities. Eco-feminists, in particular, were always geo-centred and post-anthropocentric (d'Eaubonne 1974; Griffin 1978; Merchant 1980; Mies and Shiva 1993). But a profound sense of non-belonging, of being 'outsiders within' (Woolf 1939) infuses feminist literature as a whole. Since the 1970s feminists (Kristeva 1980), this resulted in an imaginary political alliance with the 'techno-teratological' world (Braidotti 2002) of the science fiction horror genre (Barr 1987, 1993; Creed 1993; Haraway 2004 [1992]). This alliance promotes the insurrection of women – as the others of 'Man' – and other 'others', like LBGT+, non-whites (postcolonial, black, Jewish, indigenous and native subjects) and non-humans (animals, insects, plants, trees, viruses, fungi, bacteria and technological automata). These alliances of old and new meanings, practices and subjects can be called distinctly 'weird', as we saw in the previous chapter.

Since then, the empathic bond to non-human, including monstrous and alien others, has become a posthuman feminist topos (Braidotti 2002; Creed 2009). This has resulted in the materialist tradition of differential, embedded and embodied feminism that I have defended (Braidotti 2011). Never quite certain as to the human rights assigned to their sex (MacKinnon 2007), feminists and LBGT+ (Hird and Roberts 2011; Gruen and Weil 2012) have grabbed every opportunity of exiting the binary gender system and taking the leap towards posthuman formations (Halberstam and Livingston 1995; Balsamo 1996; Giffney and Hird 2008; Livingston and Puar 2011; Halberstam 2012; Colebrook 2014b). Trans-species alliances enable experiments with sexual diversity, alternative sexualities and gender systems, modelled on the morphology of non-human species, including insects (Braidotti 1994, 2002; Grosz 1995), fish (Alaimo 2010) and micro-organisms (Parisi 2004). There is a genuine embarrassment of riches in references that of necessity cannot make it to my bibliography, but there is no question that contemporary feminist theory is productively posthuman (for an overview, see Braidotti 2015; Grusin 2017).

Feminist theory is of course not the only genealogical source of inspiration to understand and assess the posthuman turn. It is crucial to recognize that contemporary efforts to transform the human and to describe modes of thought adequate to the complexity of the posthuman convergences we inhabit, sit alongside a far older tradition of Indigenous philosophies (Moreton-Robinson 2003, 2009). These traditions resonate widely in the posthuman era in general and in Anthropocene discourses in particular (Todd 2015; Whyte 2017). The conceptual resonance is high and it engenders points of encounter and intersection. As Simone Bignall argues, the indigenous philosophical tradition is likewise materially embedded and transversal in its understanding of the Earth forces that shape human existence (Bignall, Hemming and Rigney 2016). The common denominator is what Viveiros de Castro calls 'a minimum common *multiple* of difference' (2015: 14), that is to say the multiplicity that is common to humans (*humanitas multiplex*). The acceptance of these multiple, differential and materially embedded perspectives plays a crucial role in the posthuman convergence. It is therefore of the greatest importance to the next stage of my argument.

Second-Generation Studies

What emerged around the turn of the millennium is a second generation of Studies that addressed more directly the issue of anthropocentrism. Genealogically indebted to the first generation in terms of critical aims and political affects and commitment to social justice, they adopt different objects of study. Significant examples are: animal studies; eco-criticism; plant studies; environmental studies; oceans studies; Earth studies; food and diet studies; fashion, success and critical management studies. New media proliferated into sub-sections and meta-fields: Software, Internet, Game, Algorithmic and critical code studies and more. An equally prolific field of research concerns the inhuman(e) aspects of our historical condition: conflict and peace research studies; post-Soviet/communist studies; human rights studies, humanitarian management; migration, mobility, human rights studies; trauma, memory and reconciliation studies; security death, suicide studies; extinction studies. And the lists are still growing.

The proliferation of second-generation Studies accelerated with the posthuman turn, when 'Man' came under further criticism as Anthropos, that is to say as a supremacist species that monopolized the right to access the bodies of all living entities. The anthropocentric core of the Humanities was also challenged by the ubiquity and pervasiveness of technological mediation and new human–non-human linkages of biological 'wetware' and non-biological 'hardware'.

As I argued in the previous chapter, decentring anthropomorphic thinking and anthropocentric patterns of thought has difficult implications for the Humanities in particular. Their structural anthropocentrism means that the Humanities suffer from a lack of adequate concepts to deal with the ecological environment, media-nature-culture continuums, and non-human others. At the same time, it is paradoxical that the Humanities provide most of the terminology, metaphors and representations for posthuman agents and objects. There is a methodological issue at stake here as well, because the dominant model, both for traditional Humanities and most of the critical Studies areas alike, is the social constructivist approach based on a nature–culture divide. This method does not always help to deal with the challenges of our eco-sophical, post-anthropocentric, geo-bound and techno-mediated milieus.

A change of perspective is needed if 'we' – posthuman critical theorists – want to bring all those 'others' into posthuman knowledge production. This means repositioning terrestrial, planetary, cosmic concerns, the naturalized others like animals and plants, and the technological apparatus, as serious agents and co-constructors of transversal thinking and knowing. This achieves a veritable *zoe*/geo/techno-bound perspective indeed. Such new ways of knowledge production may sound counter-intuitive, and of course there is a qualitative difference between accepting the structural interdependence among species and actually treating the non-humans as knowledge collaborators. But my point is that, in the age of computational networks and synthetic biology on the one hand, and climate change and erosion of liberties on the other, this is precisely what we need to learn to do, in addition to all that we know already. We need to embrace the opportunities offered by the new technologies and steer them towards new forms of solidarity and democratic debate and dissent.

What both the first and the second generations of Studies have in common is the commitment to voice the experiences, insights and understandings produced by the excluded and marginalized. They are extracting knowledge from oppression and pain. In so doing they also open up to broader concerns about epistemological and ethical subjectivity and alternative definitions of what counts as the human.

Having come to the end of my genealogical cartography of the Critical PostHumanities, here is my provisional conclusion: these successive generations of Studies areas are both institutionally and theoretically the motor of critique and creativity. I will argue next that they are currently cross-breeding to generate new discursive practices, which I call the Critical PostHumanities. In moving to the next step of the argument, I want to reiterate some qualitative criteria of distinguishing the various kinds of research and inquiry active in posthuman thinking across species and computational networks. The critical Studies are major building blocks for the minoritary aspects of posthuman knowledge, because they are recording both what we are ceasing to be – the actual, or the 'no longer' – and what we are in the process of becoming – the virtual, or the 'not yet'. The knowledge they produce pertains both to the mainstream, approved by the Majority and capable of attracting research funding, and to the non-profit, minorities-driven margins. In Deleuze's language: they constitute both Royal science and nomad science; in this book I stick to Major and minor science. The point is to devise methods and techniques that allow us to tell the difference and to draw the consequences.

From Critical Studies to the PostHumanities

The proliferation of transdisciplinary discourses – as 'Studies' and as the Critical PostHumanities – is such as to warrant serious scholarly credentials. It entails 'Major Science' formations but also multiple assemblages of 'minor science'. This constitutes not just a quantitative growth of areas of study and quantified non-human objects of research, but also a qualitative shift. This shift is best understood within a vital, neo-materialist philosophy of immanence, based on a nature–culture and media–nature–culture continuum, which positions humans as relational components of larger ensembles.

This framework provides theoretical grounding for the emergence of the Critical PostHumanities as a supra-disciplinary, rhizomic field of contemporary knowledge production, which is contiguous with, but not identical to, the epistemic accelerations of cognitive capitalism. It functions at different speeds, moves on different timelines and is fuelled by radically different ethical affects. The novelty of the Critical PostHumanities, their 'newness', if you wish, is also defined by the split temporality of the present as both actual and virtual, by what we are ceasing to be and what we are in the process of becoming. In other words, this degree of complexity means the PostHumanities are not just territorialized by cognitive capitalism, but also design possible horizons of becoming: they constitute an academic 'minor science'. The contemporary universities can benefit from this development. The minority aspect is multi-directional, involving social and cultural movements, new kinds of economically productive practices in a market economy liberated from capitalist axioms, arts and media activism, and multiple curiosity-driven knowledge practices that do not coincide with the profit motive of cognitive capitalism.

Considering the posthuman convergence, there is nothing left for critical thinkers to do than to pursue the production of critical posthuman knowledge. This includes the all-too-human praxis of speaking truth to posthuman power. Because power is multi-layered (*potestas* and *potentia*) and its time sequences multi-dimensional (the present as both actual and virtual), in the midst of the multiple speeds of cognitive capitalism, the task of speaking truth to power involves complexity and multiplicities. To cope with them, 'we' need sharper focus on the complex singularities that constitute our respective locations. The Critical PostHumanities can be the epistemological vehicle for this project, notably for working towards the composition of planes of immanence for the missing peoples, the 'we' who are committed to posthuman resistance.

'We', the dwellers of this planet at this point in time, are interconnected but also internally fractured. Class, race, gender and sexual orientations, age and able-bodiedness continue to function as significant markers in framing and policing access to 'normal' humanity. The Critical PostHumanities provide a diversified array of the changing perceptions and forma-tions of the 'human' in the posthuman era. This field is not aiming at anything like a consensus about a new humanity, but it gives a frame for the actualization of the many missing people, whose 'minor' or nomadic knowledge is the breeding ground for possible futures. The neo-materialist ethics of affirmation that sustain the complex re-composition of minor science in the Critical PostHumanities are giving us a measure of what we are actually in the process of becoming.

A Theoretical Framework for the Critical PostHumanities

Defining Features

Far from being the symptom of crisis and fragmentation, the Critical PostHumanities open up new eco-sophical, posthu-manist and post-anthropocentric dimensions in contemporary knowledge production. In offering *zoe*/geo/techno-mediated perspectives, they strengthen eco-sophical, posthumanist and post-anthropocentric dimensions for the Humanities. What is crucial for the materialist cartographic method is that these developments are empirically verifiable: they are already here.

It would be intellectually lazy to take the on-going prolifer-ation of new discourses as the mere expression of relativism, let alone of the much despised postmodernism. It may be tempting, but equally fallacious, to take the fast growth of the Critical PostHumanities as self-generating. The fact that rhizomic, web-like, knowledge production backed by the

Internet may be going viral does not make it spontaneous. The Critical PostHumanities today are rather the result of the hard work of communities of thinkers, scholars and activists, who reconstitute the missing links in academic knowledge practices. They form alternative collective assemblages. As such it is a collective praxis that composes a new 'we', a missing people.

There are at least two ways to go about assessing the proliferating discourses of the Critical PostHumanities. The first approach takes them as expressing and reacting responsibly to the epistemic acceleration of cognitive capitalism. More specifically, they express the extent to which the contemporary neo-liberal governance of universities is capitalizing on the posthuman convergence. A new discursive energy emanates from the disciplines, propelling them outwards, towards extra-disciplinary encounters with the kind of knowledge currently produced outside the university. This proliferation of knowledge takes place across a broad spectrum of corporate, civic, public, artistic and activist venues. They support an array of research, development and experimentation with new ways of producing knowledge. These developments are therefore in keeping with the mainstream developments of advanced capitalism.

The second approach takes these developments as an expression of minor science and minoritarian assemblages. They are more autonomous, radical and potentially subversive, and develop through an expansion of less official and often non-institutionalized practices and discourses. DeLanda (2016) offers a sharp analysis of the distinction between Majoritarian, Royal and minor or nomad sciences. The former follows an axiomatic model of scientific experimentation that follows universal theorems and set rules, whereas minor science is postulated in the problematic mode and follows closely the dynamic materiality of the phenomena themselves. This qualitative difference in turn affects the position of the scientist: from the passive application of pre-set technical skills of Royal science, to the relational and open approach in the nomadic mode. Royal science concerns itself with what is stable, whereas minor science focuses on flows of becoming. This rhizomic growth works through relational assemblages and generative cross-pollination, which is likely to continue releasing hybrid off-springs and new heterogeneous assemblages (Deleuze and Guattari 1994). This is a post-disciplinary approach, fuelled by the active desire to actualize unprecedented modes of epistemic relations (Lykke 2011). Nomadic subjects produce nomadic Humanities (Stimpson 2016).

Both aspects of the phenomenon need to be taken into account, like two sides of a coin. While I sympathize more with the second approach, it is more productive for a critical discussion not to uphold the distinction between the traditional disciplines and the different generations of 'Studies' listed above. I would rather treat them as a constitutive block, composed by the transformation of the classical disciplines and the growth of the infra-disciplinary 'Studies' alike. The point is that both of them are shifting quantitatively as well as qualitatively under multiple pressures.

If we take the two pillars of the PostHumanities, the Environmental and the Digital Humanities, the question is what meta-patterns of institutional development can we detect in their recent exponential growth? What can make them alternatively profit-driven and Majority-prone, or transversal, critical and minority-inclined?

Let's look at the Environmental Studies first. If we take a first meta-pattern based on Majoritarian formations, identical with and supportive of neo-liberal economics, we will encounter the dominant institutional narrative and practice. For instance, pushed by the advent of the Anthropocene, Comparative Literature generated first Eco-criticism, animal and plant studies, then joined forces with larger assemblages of Social Sciences, Anthropology, Geology and Environmental Sciences, and corporate ideas of sustainability, and finally recoded its field of activity as the Environmental Humanities. The field is quite prolific and it publishes not one but several specialized scholarly journals and functions like an established academic discipline.[2]

At the same time, the minority-driven field is doing very well too; it is so dynamic it seems unstoppable. It has already sub-divided into the 'Green Humanities', focused on the Earth, and the 'Blue Humanities', concentrating on water issues. They are emerging from eco-feminism and other forms of activism, but also from post- and decolonial theories and practices, as we shall see in the next chapter. As such, they are more inclusive and social-minded areas of enquiry.

Even more striking is the case of the Digital Humanities. The dominant or Molar narrative about them is clearly, albeit not exclusively, linked to Media Studies, via the application of computing methods to areas of content in the Humanities. Examples are the production of databases of Biblical and other classical texts, literary texts, the digitization of musical scores, of audio-visual sources, and archival historical material. The point of origin of the Digital Humanities may be heterogeneous, but it is still connected to traditional empirical techniques of scholarly verification of objects and artefacts, through the development of digitized archives, concordances and other such resources.

Then there are the consumer applications, still in the Majoritarian mode because power is productive as well as prohibitive. The contemporary market economy finds ways to capitalize also on the interface with people's intimate lives, recomposing marginal practices and molecular formations into multiple molarities such as the billions of Facebook pages. The field of the Digital Humanities is by now so advanced that it can boast at least six specialized journals, its own advanced companion, and an international network of institutionalized centres (Schreibman, Siemens and Unsworth 2004).[3] Many major research universities in the world today can boast Digital and Environmental Humanities centres or institutes. Such enthusiasm for transdisciplinary practices can hardly be gratuitous, especially within cognitive capitalism.

But this Majoritarian meta-pattern is not all there is. This dominant meta-pattern driven by the speed of reterritorialization of neo-liberal economics, and thus limited by it, is not the full picture. Saturation by capital does not exhaust the potential of the Environmental, the Digital, or of any other PostHumanities. There is another way of approaching the phenomenon, which points to both the methods and the ethical aspirations of the Critical PostHumanities.

Following the analysis of the critical 'Studies' above, I argue that the Critical PostHumanities are a constitutive block of supra-disciplinary discourses that compose a meta-pattern indexed on the becoming-minoritarian of knowing subjects and knowledge practices. They are carried by affirmative ethical forces. On the axis of minority-driven activity, for instance, the Digital Humanities encompass multiple communities of artists, active citizens, activists of all kinds and denominations (including a sizable right-wing political component). The field is fast-moving and also entering the institutional arena. For example, two recent academic publications featured a strong emphasis on feminist and anti-racist praxis, social justice, design programming and hacking (the Routledge and Johns Hopkins University Press Companions to the Digital Humanities; respectively Sayers 2018; and Ryan, Emerson and Robertson 2014).

Two kinds of knowledge economy are thus at work in the posthuman convergence. The first is contiguous with the epistemic accelerationism of advanced capitalism in the service of dominant or 'Major science' (Deleuze and Guattari 1994). The second engages with minorities, involving an affirmative diversity of knowledge traditions or 'minor nomad sciences'. The relationship between these qualitatively distinct practices is neither binary nor dialectical, but is constituted by constant negotiations and contestations. Their dynamic and often antagonistic interaction fuels the immense energy of the fast-growing field of the Critical PostHumanities.

Institutional Answers

The institutionalization of the Critical PostHumanities is well on its way. The Oxford Institute for the trans-humanist 'Future of Humanity', that I already mentioned in chapter 2, is an example of the majoritarian posthumanist position. It embodies the hegemonic model of the posthuman as analytically post-anthropocentric, but normatively neo-humanist. Based on a research platform called 'Superintelligence', transhumanism proposes a programme of human enhancement within an Enlightenment model of universalist rationality. It combines a humanistic belief in the perfectibility of Man through scientific rationality, with a programme of human enhancement. The director Nick Bostrom (2014) pledges allegiance to the European Enlightenment and adopts a moralizing discourse to combine brain research with robotics and computational sciences, plus clinical psychology and analytic philosophy, to define the posthuman as a super-human meta-rationalist entity.

The 'Cambridge Centre for the Study of Existential Risk' (CSER) is both an extension and a response to the Oxford initiative. CSER is dedicated to the 'study and mitigation of risks that could lead to human extinction and civilizational collapse',[4] notably biological, environmental risk, and risks emerging from artificial intelligence and climate change. Directed by Huw Price and Martin Rees, funded by Jaan Tallinn of Skype, it focuses on managerial and moral solutions to contemporary problems.

There are also more mixed institutional responses to the posthuman convergence. For instance, at Aarhus University in Denmark, the 'Human Futures' project foregrounds a Humanities angle with a strong neural and life science participation, thereby constructing transversal connections (Rosendahl Thomsen 2013). More recently, the 'Posthuman Aesthetics' project (Wamberg and Rosendahl Thomsen 2016) engages literary and cultural analysis through posthumanist lenses. Both projects received funding from National Research Council projects.

A more experimental and in some ways more speculative approach has been adopted by the German Federal government in funding two successive programmes to deal with the posthuman convergence.[5] The first was the 'Anthropocene Project' (2013–14), which addressed the momentous shifts in our understanding of nature. Arguing that humanity forms nature, the project explored the opportunities offered by the Anthropocene to enact a paradigm shift and install a new relationship between the Humanities and the natural. The project also studied new models for culture, politics and everyday life, and it established an arts-based Anthropocene Observatory as well as an on-going Anthropocene curriculum. It was followed up by the 'Technosphere' projects, which explore the growing intimacy in the interaction between human and technological infrastructures on a planetary level. The convergence of live media systems with organic life forms creates a new situation, a *zoe*-centred combination of solar, hydro, earth resources and algorithmic systems. The question the project asks is about the limits of human agency in these self-organizing machinic assemblages. Both projects are run by the German National Museum and the Haus der Kulturen der Welt (HKW) in Berlin.

Sweden has pioneered a minority-minded PostHumanities Hub at the University of Linköping, under the direction of Cecilia Åsberg with a strong critical social theory angle (Åsberg and Braidotti 2018). Bringing the knowledge capital of feminist, postcolonial, anti-racist and environmental theories to bear on the posthuman condition, the PostHumanities Hub promotes transdisciplinary alliances and innovative methods.

Strong local initiatives exist at many other universities, including the Posthumanism Research Institute at Brock University in Canada, with a focus on posthuman ontology under the direction of Christine Daigle.[6] New York University has set up a Posthuman Research Group, again with a philosophical and aesthetic angle, directed by Francesca Ferrando.[7] The New School for Social Research, together with the Los Angeles-based Berggruen Institute, runs a programme on 'The Transformations of the Human', directed by Tobias Rees.[8] And the list goes on.

The field can now also boast two cutting-edge journals, both hosted by the Ewha Institute for the Humanities in Seoul, Korea: the *Journal of Posthuman Studies*[9] and the *Journal of Trans-Humanities*,[10] with a focus on studies on the cultural and social trans-boundary phenomena in the Humanities in the twenty-first century. The website *Critical Posthumanism Network* is building a fast-growing genealogy of posthumanism.[11] A final example of the institutionalization of the field is the first PostHumanities book series (Wolfe 2010).

The different speeds and forms of institutionalization of contemporary knowledge practices demonstrate the extent to which the Critical PostHumanities are both caught in and resisting the accelerating spin of neo-liberal logic of capitalizing on knowledge. They are developing faster than the academic institutions can keep up with. They are growing either from the transdisciplinary 'Studies', or in the 'trading zones' between the university, social movements and corporate interests (Galison 1997).

This multi-faceted mode of development is sometimes described as a 'crisis' of the Humanities, but that is neither accurate nor particularly helpful, because the field shows such growth, vitality and new inspiration. This fast growth requires criteria, codes and modes of reterritorialization of these new, transversal fields of knowledge, which is the topic of the next chapter.

In this chapter I have shown that the Critical PostHumanities coexist with and even co-construct the profit-oriented acquisitions of knowledge as capital – both financial and cognitive – that forms the core of advanced capitalism. It is equally true that the Critical PostHumanities also inflect critically and oppositionally the workings of contemporary capitalism. In the emerging meta-patterns of discursive and institutional development that I have sketched in the Environmental Humanities and the Digital Humanities, we can detect on the one hand the profit-driven and Majority-prone practices, and on the other hand transversal, critical and minority-inclined ones. Because these developments are on-going, it is important that PostHumanities scholars get organized in order to influence the processes of knowledge production in the direction of minor science.

The distinction between Major and minor science is ethical, but its effects are political as well as institutional. 'We' – critical posthuman thinkers – are capable of sustaining affirmative assemblages, knowing that their political force lies in actualizing collective imaginings (Gatens and Lloyd 1999). Complexity becomes the operative word in distinguishing between actualized states of 'Major Science' and the virtual becoming of 'minor science'. In chapter 6 I will further expand on the development of the minor sciences in the context of affirmative ethics. But first I will turn in the following chapter to an elucidation of the main tenets of posthuman thinking and provide examples of concrete practices drawn from a variety of fields.

Chapter 5
How To Do Posthuman Thinking

We cannot solve contemporary problems by using the same kind of thinking we used when we created them, as Albert Einstein wisely reminds us.[1] The challenges of our times call for adequate forms of accountability for the great advances as well as resistance to the injustices and perils of the present, by thinking outside the conventional categories of analysis. The issues are urgent and complex: how to understand and account for the convulsive and internally contradictory transformations we are living through, in the language of linearity and objectivity that is the fundamental tool of scholarly enquiry? How can we practise critical thought in an era that has lost faith in critique and even more in theory? How can researchers in the Humanities produce sensible advice, amidst populist disdain for self-professed and certified experts? With so much knowledge generated in society at large, at times even in the most unexpected areas and domains, what does academic research stand for today? In times of war, conflict and social upheavals, what is the suitable way to pursue social justice, critical feminist thought, radical ecologies, anti-racism, equitable sustainability and education for peace? How can new styles of thought be developed, knowing that style in philosophy is not decorative, but is rather a navigational tool that traces the force and movement of concepts? This chapter will explain the theoretical principles and present practices of affirmative posthuman knowledge production. It aims to bridge the epistemology and the ethics of posthuman knowledge.

Posthuman thinking is a relational activity that occurs by composing points of contact with a myriad of elements within the complex multiplicity of each subject and across multiple other subjects situated in the world. Thinking takes the form of cartographic renderings of embedded and embodied relational encounters. These encounters can be with texts, institutions or other concrete social realities, or people. In this book, for instance, it is obvious that I am assembling a great deal of scholarship by others, in order to highlight possible points of dialogue with the project of establishing a critical framework for the posthuman convergence. This method of working draws explicit and acknowledged cross-connections in the hope of being able to constitute planes of encounter and shared work platforms.

This relational activity is not dependent solely upon the super-vising control of a transcendent consciousness that centralizes and ordains the information according to a hierarchy of sensorial and cognitive data. This transcendentalist vision of reason is in fact gathering renewed momentum today, for instance in the work of the trans-humanists I described in the previous chapter. It is also being revived by Enlightenment fundamen-talists like Steve Pinker (2007), who follows evolutionary psychology, cognitive science and Chomsky's linguistics in ascribing innate characteristics to human reason and language. Taking by contrast the pathway of immanence, posthuman thought activates a distributed model of consciousness. This means a web of multi-layered and multi-scalar relations that co-construct states of heightened receptivity and intelligence. Thinking is about acknowledging, capturing and working with extensive and intensive ethical relationality. This book argues that thinking involves the creation of new concepts and adequate figurations to express them.

Major Science and Minor Science

The 'minor' developments I aspire to within the Critical PostHumanities do not prevent the recurrence of patterns of exclusion, as we saw in the last chapter. For example, few or no institutions have made Feminist, Queer, Migrant, Poor, Decolonial, Diasporic, Diseased, Disabled, Humanities official. These discourses remain the crucial pillars of the many critical 'Studies' areas that proliferated, but they are not included in the current reorganization of the PostHumanities. In other words, the theories about these minority discourses do exist, and thrive, but are not officially funded realities. The speed of deterritorialization of these minor subjects of knowledge is therefore of an altogether different order than the majority-driven epistemic acceleration of Majority-funded science. Cognitive capitalism cannot or does not want to over-code these minoritarian subjects to the same extent as it territorializes the more profitable ones. But it does pick 'star specimens' from these minor areas, without granting them organizational charts and institutional funds. This disjunction between dominant and minor can also be a strength in that it decelerates them, thus granting minority subjects the time and political potential of actualizing alternatives. These include alternative modes of becoming subjects, but also different ways of knowing, which design a different meta-pattern, supported by a different 'we', 'the missing peoples'. I will return to them after a brief theoretical clarification of this disjunction between Major science and minor science.

In chapter 3 I argued that thinking is the conceptual counterpart of the ability to enter modes of relation, to affect and be affected. Thinking accordingly sustains qualitative shifts and creative tensions. Escaping the gravitational pull of dominant systems of thought, critical neo-materialist thought pursues the actualization of transversal relations. Posthuman thought is inhabited by a vitalist and materialist multi-directional affectivity that works in terms of transpositions, that is to say generative cross-pollination and hybrid interconnections (Crist 2013; Bastian et al. 2017). Thinking is indeed the stuff of the world (Alaimo 2014).

This stance produces a crucial distinction between quantitative or extensive and qualitative or intensive states (Deleuze 1988). For instance, my cartography of the Critical PostHumanities shows clearly a quantitative proliferation of discourses generated from posthuman locations. As we have seen in the previous chapter, the Critical PostHumanities have produced a series of new objects of study, many of which are not about the human, but rather non-human agents: technological artefacts, animals, things and smart objects. What is happening now is that these objects have been itemized and quantified for the neo-liberal academic market, generating new fields of enquiry. Does that mean that anybody researching objects can claim to be doing the Critical PostHumanities, in a posthumanistic and post-anthropocentric manner? Is such a quantitative proliferation of discourses enough to sustain the claim to a paradigmatic shift? I hardly think so.

A merely quantitative spread without qualitative shifts is an insufficient condition for the production of new concepts and conceptual practices. In order to set up credible and rigorous Critical PostHumanities, we need a qualitative move. The zoe-driven, eco-sophical, geo-centred and techno-mediated ontological basis that sustains posthuman knowledge, supports and even requires qualitative and methodological shifts. In a world haunted by regressions of all kinds, the Critical PostHumanities actualize an immanent politics that offers progressive tool-kits to address the situated and complex singularity of contemporary subjects of knowledge.

The qualitative criteria for evaluation are the following: supra-disciplinarity, non-profit, critical reflexivity, material locations, community-based, transversality and emphasis on generative forces and affirmative ethics. These general principles get operationalized in a series of methodological guidelines ranging from cartographic accuracy, with the corollary of ethical accountability, to the combination of critique and creativity, with a flair for paradoxes and the recognition of the specificity of art practices. Other criteria are: non-linearity, the powers of memory and the imagi-nation, and the strategy of defamiliarization (Braidotti 2013).

As there is no space here to discuss all of these criteria in detail, let me highlight the crucial ones. Non-linearity is in-built into the multi-directional logic of the media–nature–culture continuum. It is therefore necessary to cope with the complexity of contemporary, highly mediated social relations and the fact that the global economy functions in a web-like, scattered and polycentred way. The heteroglossia

of contemporary digital data production and collection intensifies the trend. It defies the logic of the excluded middle
and demands complex topologies of knowledge, for subjects
structured by such high degrees of multi-layered relationality.

Translated into temporal terms, following Deleuze and
Guattari (1994), linearity is the dominant mode of *Chronos*
– the keeper of institutional time and upholder of the
authority of the past, as opposed to *Aion*, the dynamic,
insurgent and more cyclical time of becoming. Applied to
knowledge production practices, *Chronos* supports 'Royal' or
'Major' science: institutionally implemented and well-funded
because it is compatible with the economic imperatives of
advanced capitalism and its 'cognitive excursions into living
matter' (Bonta and Protevi 2004). *Aion*, on the other hand,
produces 'nomad' or 'minor' knowledge: underfunded and
marginalized, but ethically transformative and politically
empowering. While Major science is sedentary and protocol-
bound, minor science is situated, perspectivist and able to
combine critique with the creation of new concepts.

The vital materialist continuum sustains the epistemology of becoming that is the conceptual motor of the
Critical PostHumanities. It can be served by establishing
a new parallelism between philosophy, the sciences and
the arts (Deleuze and Guattari 1994). But it can do much
more: Bonta and Protevi (2004) stress that a materialist
'geo-philosophy' helps to redefine the relationship between
the 'two cultures' of the 'subtle' (Humanities) and 'hard'
(Natural) sciences. The Critical PostHumanities encourages
new creative engagements between them. DeLanda (2002)
praises the intensive mode of Deleuzian science for its anti-
essentialism and points out that 'minor' science also replaces
typological thinking. The virtual and intensive becoming
supplants the ruling principle of resemblance, identity,
analogy and opposition.

Non-linearity also takes the form of breaking up established conventions. The combination of supra-disciplinary
hybridization with the force of the vital *zoe*/geo/techno
framework pushes the task of de-familiarizing our habits
of thought to the edge of a qualitative shift. The postcolonial injunction of 'unlearning our privilege as our loss'
(Spivak 1990: vii) is more relevant than ever in that it can be

expanded to sustain a qualitative assessment of our relational deficits and injuries, notably towards non-human others. The frame of reference becomes the world, in all its open-ended, inter-relational, transnational, multi-sexed, and trans-species flows of becoming. This is a native or vernacular form of cosmopolitanism (Bhabha 1996; Braidotti 2006, 2013).

These are the subjects and leading actors of qualitative shifts and practices towards the Critical PostHumanities, as opposed to the exploitation of quantitative non-human objects of study. The notion of immanence supports a different vision of *zoe*/geo/techno-mediated subjectivity, which requires a different kind of thinking. Understanding such a material and vital continuum entails coming to terms with non-human agents, providing cartographies of their locations and also extracting margins of negotiation for the virtual, within the actual reterritorializations and networked clusters of interest of cognitive capitalism. The crucial idea is that the overflowing codes of capital never fully saturate the processes of becoming, just as the present is not static, but ever open to the virtual. Consequently, the minor discourses always contain margins of disenfranchisement from Major science, because power is not a single entity, but a multi-layered, dynamic and strategic process.

Thus, we could say that the Critical PostHumanities on the plateau of Major science are propelled by powerful financial interests. On the axis of minor science, however, the growth takes the non-profit form of interbreeding and cross-pollinating through multiple missing people and marginal spaces. This does not mean that anything goes, but rather that transversal multi-directionality is the rule for minor sciences and related knowledge production systems. It is important to keep in mind the central tenet of neo-materialist ontology, namely that these plateaus are not dialectically distinct and opposed, but rather contiguous and co-constructed. To be more exact: the nomadic lines of flight of minor sciences cut across, reterritorialize and recompose the dominant knowledge production systems precisely through creating multiple missing links, opening generative cracks, and visiting marginal spaces. If there is only one matter, then there is no uncontaminated, pure 'outside' to its power. 'We' – critical thinkers – perform the stubborn labour of operationalizing critical spaces within, beneath and beyond the present, as the record of both what we are ceasing to be and what we are in the process of becoming. The challenge consists firstly in activating subjects to enter into new affective transversal assemblages, to co-create alternative ethical and political forces. In other words, our challenge is to compose a new 'we', the missing people. A second related challenge is how to express this in a language that remains accessible to most actual people and to represent it in adequate theoretical schemes.

Posthuman Legal Practice
It may be useful to illustrate these more abstract principles with a concrete example from practice. The posthuman convergence has prompted some significant changes and advances in the theory and practice of the Law. In his work on Human Rights, for instance, Patrick Hanafin (2018) argues that a posthuman approach subverts the majoritarian model of human rights, modelled on the vision of the subject as a white neo-liberal male. Such a contestatory move raises issues of law and bio-power, which are best served by a counter-model of transversal subjectivity drawn from Deleuze. Such collective vision implements the creative and collective praxis of jurisprudence, which, contrary to the abstract conceptualizations of legal codes and rules, is work-in-progress. As Deleuze teaches, jurisprudence is an active mode of resisting established protocols and concepts. It is a dynamic element that allows for an immanent conception of rights, open to collective interventions aimed at changing and troubling the law.

Hanafin connects this approach to a micropolitics of becoming that, in the posthuman convergence, addresses basic issues of life and death, ranging from the bio-political management of reproduction, via technological assistance, to necro-political interventions upon ways of dying, including euthanasia and assisted suicide. Posthuman rights embody the claims of transversal assemblages of individuals who do not see a binary cut between thought and action, life and death, environment and humanity, or animality and humanity. This allows us to think of a micropolitics of life as *zoe* (as material embodied singularity) which contests the ordering molar politics of Life as *bios* (understood as transcendental and always already male).

These disruptive elements connect legal matters to society and thus raise political questions of power and entitlement. Hanafin argues that a posthuman approach is of assistance in transforming the canon of liberal rights discourse, by introducing a relational notion of rights, which is not exclusive to anthropomorphic subjects but also includes animals and the environment. The displacement of this fundamental distinction impacts strongly on the Law, which can take distance from the bio-political ordering on individuals and allows them a broader field of intervention beyond individualism, thus enacting an active and contestatory form of citizenship.

On a different note, Ingrid Wuerth (2017) argues that, in a posthuman era, International Law becomes more relevant. This is due to a combination of factors. On the negative side, there is a relative decline of human rights, not so much as a doctrine, but as a practice. This can be demonstrated by the increasing number of authoritarian governments, the decline in international human rights enforcement and multi-lateral treaties, the growing power of China and Russia over the content of international law, and the rise of nationalism and populism across the Western world. On the positive side, the need has emerged not only for more international law, but also for a strengthening of it in a posthuman rights era. The two main content areas of expansion concern peace and security, though this leaves open the question of what power mechanisms could assist in the implementation of new, posthuman rights legal frameworks.

Jannice Käll (2017) focuses on the notion of a Posthuman Data Subject, modelled on the environmental subject, to explore the implications of the posthumanist turn. Starting from the critique of the idea of an inherent difference between persons and things, Käll dismisses human exceptionalism and how it informs human subjectivity as distinct from all others. Arguing that such distinctions across categories of human, and between human and other species, are always an effect of a differential set of powers, Käll proposes to question these boundaries as they are always in flux. This is all too true in relation to digital technology, which, through the Internet of

Things and smart objects have penetrated what used to be the private sphere, producing a whole array of new legal issues. They range from the rights of digitized personhood and personalized data, to online security and privacy questions. Käll argues that all these issues would profit by having anthropocentric and humanist liberal individualism displaced from the centre of the legal scene.

This advance is presented as part of a wider movement in legal theory, which extends the notion of legal subjectivity to non-human agents. The most striking example is the granting of legal personhood to 'nature'. For instance, New Zealand now recognizes a right to personhood for a river, India acknowledges the rights of waterfalls, and Ecuador grants rights to the environment as a whole. Käll focuses especially on the 'Right to Be Forgotten' case, as setting a useful precedent in digital privacy in that it separates data about the body from the actual human bodies. This is an important conceptual move, which rests on the analysis of contemporary advanced technologies as accomplishing the dematerialization of human bodies and the counter-materialization of digital bodies. Understanding that this separation is, in itself, an effect of advanced capitalism, and that corporations like Facebook own and control the data about the dematerialized body, Käll relies on posthuman theory to rethink the human as part of a technologically mediated assemblage, and then devise a legal framework worthy of this complexity. Rights to communication and privacy, in their capacity as fundamental human rights, now must be understood and developed in relation to the digital sphere by upholding the dematerialization of human bodies and the materialization of digital bodies. The control over data as a commodity controlled, to any extent, by market actors, needs to be continuously questioned and ultimately abolished. Critical vigilance is crucial for posthuman resistance.

Desire for Adequate Understanding

The posthuman convergence challenges our powers of thinking on two fundamental levels. The first is the sheer spatial and temporal scale of the issue the posthuman convergence evokes and the paradoxes it engenders. The second is more affective: the posthuman pushes to the furthest edges the thinkability of the extinction of our species. The spectre of a world without 'us' is haunting the human horizon of thought; death is famously the unimaginable event, but even the unimaginable is not what it used to be. As if imagining a world without humans were not within the realm of our collective and individual reason, a melancholy mood surrounds efforts to think what was once unthinkable – our extinction (Ghosh 2016).

Yet, in the tradition of philosophical stoicism, which has greatly influenced the ethical dispositions of Foucault and Deleuze, the contemplation of our own mortality was posited as the key guideline to constructing an ethical life. Living each day as the last one and accounting critically for one's readiness to die form the core of this ethical school. More recently, the ethical formula of postmodern subjects was deep scepticism about the foundational credibility of any category, including that of subjectivity itself and its inhuman component (Lyotard 1989). The ethical formula of post-nuclear subjects – apocalypse from now on – played with the simultaneous evocation and deferral of the extinction of their own and other species (Derrida 2007). As an event with a high statistical possibility of occurrence, extinction ought to be acknowledged, the better to be avoided.

For posthuman subjects, however, the ethical injunction is more complex, because it is interconnected with changing what counts as 'we' – the subjects of thinking and of knowledge. Considering the schizoid double pulls and swinging moods, as well as the scale of issues triggered by the convergence of the Fourth Industrial Revolution and the Sixth Extinction, the epistemological challenges overlap with the need to broaden accountability beyond Man and Anthropos. We have to learn to think differently about what kind of relational subjects 'we' are in the process of becoming, in a multitude of different perspectives. We need to readjust our understanding in order to meet the multiple challenges.

Adequate understanding provides the subjects with an increase in their power to act, which is experienced as joy and the renewed desire to go on knowing more and better.

But, as I argue throughout the book, all knowledge, being embedded, embodied and situated, is inevitably perspectival and hence limited. By extension, knowledge is flawed and contains errors and failures. Humans tend to be transported by passions and prejudices. This means that the quest for adequate understanding is both epistemological and ethical. Epistemologically, understanding requires critical elucidation of one's conditions. Ethically, the posthuman subject needs to stay in tune with one's innermost essence. Combining them expresses the fundamental freedom, which is experienced as a joyful passion. As Deleuze put it: 'ethical joy is the correlate of speculative affirmation' (1988: 27).

Crucial to this project is the distinction between thinking as the epistemic and ethical praxis of forging affirmation and the attachment to transcendental consciousness. For immanent philosophers like myself, transcendental consciousness is an illusion. Deleuze calls is 'a dream with one's eyes open' (1988: 20). At the same time, that consciousness is a normative injunction loaded with discriminatory principles. I want to therefore contrast it with thinking as the critical and creative activity of constituting a transversal subjectivity. This means doing away with transcendental consciousness. Instead, posthuman knowledge brings about a communal and distributed subjectivity, supported by the shared desire for reaching adequate understanding of the conditions that limit our freedom. Thinking is always active: by understanding your life conditions you strive to change them affirmatively.

Posthuman knowledge engages its relational capacity in order to produce adequate understandings of the interconnection with all matter. It does so at a historical time when science and technology have revolutionized knowledge of matter in a multi-scale manner. The pursuit of adequate knowledge needs to stay attuned to and work in tandem with the ethical pursuit of the power to act in transversal alliances with human and non-human actors. Posthuman ethics starts with the pursuit of the unrealized potential of complex assemblages of subjects, within a fast-moving present.

Artistic Practice
The best example of how the resources of the creative imagination come to the rescue of the posthuman knowledge project

can be drawn from literature and art practices. For instance, Lau (2018) argues that posthuman literary criticism marks a fundamental change of paradigm towards transdisciplinary. The reference to neo-materialist vitalism and the emphasis on creativity not only liberates critical thinking across a range of disciplines within the academy, but it also positions literary studies as a crucial field in retraining readers to think outside anthropocentric and humanistic habits. Posthuman literary theory builds on key methodological tools such as defamiliarization, non-linearity, the role of figurations, critique of dogmatic truth. It is displayed in genres such as speculative and science fiction and refers to wide-ranging fields like eco-criticism (Glotfelty and Fromm 1996), transnational justice, racial equality, climate change, and afro-futurism. According to Lau, posthuman criticism has all the makings of a feminist, postcolonial, minor science as an ethically transformative inquiry that exposes the violence of advanced capitalism and its obsession with economic imperatives and discrimination.

The next example comes from art practice. Throughout this book I have pointed to some pertinent examples from posthuman aesthetics (Wamberg 2012) and art theory and practice (Davis and Turpin 2015; Braidotti and Hlavajova 2018). I have also discussed some of them explicitly, as in the case of the post-natural museum (Pell 2015). There is also ample evidence that architecture and design are taking the posthuman turn seriously (Radman and Sohn 2017). For the sake of brevity, let me highlight just one other example, drawn from the field of posthuman art practice, to illustrate its inventiveness and rigour.

Cameron (2018) discusses how the posthuman convergence affects curatorial practice in general, notably by challenging the anthropocentric assumptions of all museological exhibitions and spaces. The space is organized around objects that are displayed for humans to see, enjoy and interpret. The background information provided privileges the social, ideological, historical and cultural constructions of the objects. The only exception is some of the Indigenous collections, as a consequence of Indigenous curatorial agency. A posthuman approach challenges the dominant view of museum practice by critiquing both the Eurocentric humanistic universalism and the implicit anthropocentrism of these practices.

The example Cameron gives is the exhibit of a melted green plastic bucket in Museum Victoria in Melbourne, in the Black Saturday bushfire collection.[2] This item is both framed by, and helps us to contextualize, the survivors' accounts of their ordeal. It is consequently presented in function of the human subjectivities involved, as a static element in a natural disaster in the service of the human. This constitutes for Cameron a double disadvantage: firstly, because it reinstates the binaries between nature and culture, humans and non-humans, and secondly, because it narrows down the scope of the event, denying the other material, discursive, technological, biological and non-human aspects of surviving the bushfires.

If we shift to a posthuman perspective that acknowledges the human world in a continuum with other forces and actors, this kind of museum practice appears not only incongruous, but even deceptive in terms of framing the event it purports to represent. In a *zoe*/geo/techno-oriented framework, in contrast, many other layers of the problem come into focus: material, technical, conceptual, ecological, social and emotional components. These begin with the processes of production of the plastic bucket itself, its geographical location, the industrial genealogy, the weather and climate history.

The human subject is therefore only one of many forces that compose the distributed agency of an event that the museum is trying to account for. These forces cannot be reduced to social conventions of language and representation, but must be approached as components of a relational continuum with natural, terrestrial, climatic and cosmic forces, as well as interspecies connections and intercultural relations. Cameron advocates new exhibition methods and documentation procedures that do justice to these multiple agencies and independences. She suggests that the best way to account for them is through cartographic mappings representative of their performativity as emergent processes.

This point has been forcefully made by the 'Forensic Architecture' programme at Goldsmiths College London, notably by Paulo Tavares, who synthesizes the changing role of artistic practice in the posthuman convergence by looking at 'murky objects'.[3] These are ecological objects and systems that have been transformed into legally relevant evidence in national and transnational discussions about environmental degradation and justice. This transformation of both natural objects (trees, rivers, etc.) and artefacts (fire-melted plastic buckets) into forensic evidence changes their ontological status to that of legal witnesses. It also alters artistic practice accordingly, instituting new protocols of detection, archiving and mobilization of evidence to demonstrate what Tavares calls 'the messy assemblages of scientific practices, NGO advocacy, international law and global geopolitics that gather around nature.' A renewed emphasis on global nature as forensic evidence intersects with artistic and curatorial practice on the one hand, and legal human and non-human rights on the other.

A Different Empiricism

Another theoretical principle of affirmative posthuman knowledge production is how to redefine empiricism within a neo-materialist perspective. The example of a melted green plastic bucket shows the advantages of a philosophy of immanence, with its emphasis on transversal processes and assemblages of human, inhuman, non-human and faster-than-human forces and agents. This allows connecting notions and practices that were often kept apart. The humble example of the melted green plastic bucket includes not only *zoe*/geo/techno components of an ecologized and mediated continuum, but also the terrestrial and cosmic dimensions, i.e. the weather.

This applied neo-materialist perspective is inspired by an updated version of Spinozism.[4] By not privileging one single vantage point, which inevitably coincides with the assumed white male spectator, a more democratic field of vision can open up. This more inclusive approach expresses a kind of ontological pacifism, that is to say, that one cannot blame external circumstances alone, like the bush fire, for one's own misfortune. In fact, trust in our intimacy with and knowledge of the world brings into focus a whole sequence of factors, including our own consumeristic habits. This makes the negative habit of apportioning blame not only ineffectual but also unjust. In other words, apportioning blame, or scapegoating, is wrong double-over: in terms of understanding and in terms of ethics. Within a posthuman framework, the subjects' ethical core should not be defined in terms of intentionality, but as its forces and affects. Ethics is defined as the pursuit of affirmative values and relations, and politics as the pragmatic practice of implementing them. Ethical power can only be understood in terms of *potentia*, the empowerment.

A neo-materialist approach attempts to strike a balance between seemingly conflicting demands: to resist grand theories while staying grounded through embodied and embedded perspectives. At the same time, our methods should resist retreating into narrow and flat empiricism, in the form of sociological reductions or a mere recourse to big data. The favoured approach is an enlarged empiricism that respects the phenomenology of experience, while avoiding exclusive references to identity-indexed claims. Immanence and accountability are key terms here and ethnographic observations a concrete case in point.

Critical and creative cartographies can assist methodologically in bringing forth alternative conceptual personae or figurations of the kind of knowing subjects currently constructed. All figurations are localized, situated, perspectival and hence immanent to specific conditions: they function as material and semiotic signposts for specific geo-political and historical locations. As such, they express grounded complex singularities, not universal claims in a form of transcendental empiricism that broadens the spectrum of what counts as 'evidence-driven' thinking.

The figurations supported by cartographic accounts aim at dealing with the complexity of power relations. They expose the repressive structures of dominant subject formations (*potestas*), but also the affirmative and transformative visions of the subject as both grounded and flowing, or in process (*potentia*). In some ways a figuration is the dramatization of processes of becoming, without referring to one single normative model of subjectivity, let alone a universal one. It allows us to say that 'we' are in *this* together, but we are not One and the same.

With cartographies come also the figurations that sustain them. As I have argued throughout this book, although the posthuman is empirically grounded, because it is embedded and embodied, it functions less as a substantive entity than as a figuration or conceptual persona. It is a theoretically powered cartographic tool that aims at achieving adequate understanding of the present as both actual and virtual. In other words, cartographies are both the record of what we are ceasing to be – anthropocentric, humanistic – and the seed of what we are in the process of becoming – a multiplicity of posthuman subjects.

The posthuman convergence, in other words, enables us to track, across a number of interdisciplinary fields, the emergence of discourses about the non-human, inhuman or trans-human, which are generated by the intersecting critiques of Humanism and of anthropocentrism. It introduces a *zoe*/geo/techno-mediated form of empiricism that enlists the resources of the planet and the cosmos, in keeping with the vital materialism that supports it.

In this respect, empiricism as a specific way of accessing knowledge through observable evidence drawn from the world at large is not dependent upon transcendental consciousness and its idealist models of thought. The empirical field constitutes instead another middle ground, that extrapolates from experience without being bound to it, and recasts objectivity in the mode of situated practices, or politics of locations. This is the model that Deleuze defends as the empirical transcendental field, constituted by and constitutive of transversal connections and arrangements of a heterogeneous nature, that are grounded and multi-layered, but not reductive.

This has major implications for research methods. In her important work on the link between new materialism and new empiricism, Elizabeth St. Pierre (2016) relies precisely on Deleuze's notion of the empirical transcendental to develop a 'post-qualitative' approach to research methodology. Claiming that empiricism and materialism work hand-in-hand, St. Pierre argues that this interconnection calls into question the ontology that sustained the binary divisions between matter and mind in the first place. This means that they challenge also the dominant and dogmatic image of the scholar and scientist as the subject whose thinking powers (as *potentia*) do not require the binary distinctions implemented by institutional structures (*potestas*). Stressing the importance of experimentation, curiosity and affectivity, St. Pierre emphasizes the need to confront the restrictive methods that are commonly labelled under 'empiricism'. She also highlights the need for ethical affirmation to sustain these experiments, because, in so far as they aim at actualizing what might be and is not yet the case, they call upon collaborative and communal resources. Relationality activated by the desire to potentiate alternatives supports the ethical imperative to compose a 'we' – the ensemble that carries out the task.

The relational model of subjectivity concretely means that it is advisable to make alliances in a transdisciplinary and multidirectional manner, both within and without the academic institutions. The dialogues will not always be easy or harmonious, but they are the indispensable means to proceed. This is all the more urgent within the multiple speeds of re- and deterritorialization of advanced capitalism, which threatens the composition of any alternative plane of collaborative and not-for-profit encounters. It is crucial therefore to explore and experiment with a variety of methods to include non-human components into processes of knowledge formation.

By extension, empiricism cannot be reduced to a set of protocols of verification of scientific truths, though that is part of its uses, especially in the era of big data analysis. In the Humanities, moreover, different skills are required – ranging from the acceptance of textual material as empirical evidence, to the importance of hermeneutical methods and critical thought.

Posthuman Disability Studies

In order to bridge the theory of neo-materialism to a concrete practice, I turn to the field of posthuman disability studies. At the core of disability studies is the refusal to represent otherwise constituted bodies as abnormal. This is concomitant with delinking visions of the subject from normative taxonomies that privilege able-bodiedness. An affirmative approach to disability allows for different practices, ranging from alternative modes of advocacy, to ethical and methodological values (Roets and Braidotti 2012). Critical disability studies are perfectly at ease with the posthuman subject, because disability has always contravened the traditional classical humanist conception of what it means to be human. The converse is also true as disability invites a critical analysis of the posthuman, to the extent that disability epitomizes a posthuman enhancement of the self while simultaneously demanding recognition of the self in the humanist register. Disability politics thus works at the edges of posthuman and humanist politics.

Within the posthuman convergence, disability studies has moved into 'DisHuman' Studies (Goodley et al. 2014, 2018). DisHuman Studies simultaneously acknowledges the possibilities offered by disability to trouble, reshape and re-fashion the human, while asserting disabled people's humanity. Resisting the self-aggrandizing narratives about the human sponsored by Eurocentric Humanism, they focus on the neo-liberal and 'ableist' aspects of the ideal image of the citizen as functional productive unit. As we know from feminist and postcolonial studies, this narrow humanist conception of the human has historically excluded many.

Defamiliarization

The production of posthuman knowledge benefits from the methodological practice of defamiliarization, which has been revived by feminist, subaltern and post-colonial theory over the last decades.[5] It functions as a pedagogical tool to encourage the knowing subjects to disengage themselves from the dominant normative vision of the self they had become accustomed to. Defamiliarization is a way of decoding one's implication in power relations, which Gayatri Spivak (1990) calls 'unlearning one's privileges'. Nowadays, these privileges include one's Eurocentric humanist and anthropocentric habits of thought and the forms of representation they sustain, so as to make room for the new.

Dis-identifications from dominant models of subject formation is a way of decolonizing our imaginary through a radical disengagement from the axes and institutions of power in our society. These include the gender system with its binary representations of femininity and masculinity (Braidotti

1991); white privilege and racialized hierarchies, which are critiqued by postcolonial (Gilroy 2000) and race discourses (Hill Collins 1991; Wynter 2015). Dis-identifications in these cases occur along the axes of becoming-woman (sexualization) and becoming-other (racialization), and hence remain within the confines of anthropomorphism. A further shift is needed to develop post-anthropocentric forms of identification, in response to the posthuman convergence.

Defamiliarization with anthropocentrism shifts the relationship to the non-human others and requires dis-identification from century-old habits of anthropocentric thought and humanist arrogance. This is enough to test the ability and willingness of the Humanities to change their own premises. This anthropological exodus is especially difficult, emotionally as well as methodologically, as it can involve a sense of loss and pain. Dis-identification involves the loss of cherished habits of thought and representation, a move which can be exhilarating in its liberatory side-effects but also produce fear, a sense of insecurity and nostalgia.

Dis-identification leads to post-identitarian politics of location. Defamiliarization also entails active processes of becoming that enact in-depth breaks with established patterns of thought and identity formation. It is a fundamentally anti-oedipal methodology that supports productive forms of conceptual disobedience, echoing Gandhi's idea of civil disobedience. Being disloyal to one's civilization is at times the best way to honour it, out of love for its undeveloped potential as well as its actual norms. The transformative aspects of this project require a radical repositioning on the part of the subject, which is neither self-evident, nor free of pain. No process of consciousness-raising ever is painless, though this does not equate it with suffering. It is rather a way to raise the awareness of both the complexities involved and the need for collaborative relations to sustain the project.

Shifting individual and cultural imaginary identifications is not as simple as casting away a used garment. Changes of this qualitative kind happen more easily at the molecular or subjective level and their translation into a public discourse and shared social experiences is a complex and risky affair. This is where the collective ensembles of a 'we' come into action; these are the transversal assemblages aimed at the production of affirmative politics and ethical relations. What is needed is a differential relational ethics of embodied differences that can sustain this challenge, because an undifferentiated grammar of a unitary humanity simply will not do. What needs to be abandoned once and for all is the notion of undifferentiated unity, totality and One-ness. Socially embedded and historically grounded communities are the motor of a collective sense of democracy in a *zoe/geo/techno*-mediated posthuman frame. They act in common to potentiate their shared desire for transformations to be actualized as a collaborative effort.

Posthuman Pedagogy
Posthuman scholarship is making major inroads into the area of pedagogy. It does so from both methodological and conceptual angles and at all educational levels, including primary schools. The two-pronged posthuman approach targets both Humanism and anthropocentrism and sets on the educational agenda the double challenge of dealing with advanced technologies in an ecologically challenged world (Braidotti 2013; Bayley 2018).

The field of new materialism is especially strong in education in general and in feminist educational practices in particular. The growth and high quality of this research field is so intense as to deserve a study if its own.[6] Let me signal a recent thought-provoking collection that brilliantly assesses the current situation (Ringrose, Warfield and Zarabadi 2019). Challenging the methodological habit that assumes Man to be the focal point of all socio-cultural analysis, Cecilia Åsberg (Åsberg, Koobak and Johnson 2010) was among the first to launch the feminist PostHumanities debate as an intersectional, cross-species, materialist critique of the underlying androcentric and anthropocentric lines of science and technologies studies (Åsberg and Braidotti 2018). Feminist Deleuzian methods have also been applied to the study of the cross-disciplinary redefinition of the boundaries between different branches of knowledge (Braidotti 1994; Coleman and Ringrose 2013). These neo-materialist approaches have also been successfully applied to the discussion of qualitative methodology in the Humanities (Mazzei and McCoy 2010).

Strom (2015) explores the qualitative aspects of posthuman education and argues that the innovation of this approach consists thematically of the emphasis on materialist practice and methodologically of the collaborative mode of production and transfer of knowledge. Splitting the binary teacher–student relationship allows the bypassing of individualism and a broader ensemble to emerge in the process of these joint activities. Collaborative and non-hierarchical teaching also makes room for non-human elements, technological, animal or other, to intervene as heterogeneous forces that connect the educational practice to the wider world (Strom et al. 2018). The emphasis on mixity, hybridity and difference makes for a practically oriented and relational style of teaching.

Working in a South African context, Bozalek et al. (2018) stress the methodological as well as political advantages of the posthuman framework. In their work on socially just pedagogies for posthuman times, they outline some basic ground rules. Firstly, that education has to be consistently posthuman, at both the analytic and the normative levels. This raises in turn the need for a posthuman ontology and a new ethics, as evidenced by movements such as feminist neo-materialism and the affective turn.

Secondly, they insist on the need to foreground the social-political aspects of the posthuman predicament, including the specific forms of de-humanization and discrimination, the inhumane and necropolitical aspects that define our era. Most urgent to tackle are the forms of economic polarization and growing inequality that are engendered by neo-liberalism and the way it has impacted upon university education. Large-scale student movements, such as #Rhodesmustfall in South Africa, have expanded this critical stance to the fight against enduring forms of racism, white supremacy and colonialism in the university world. As a global movement, #Metoo has targeted the persistence of sexual violence and harassment also in university life.

Deleuze's concept of nomadic becoming, as the ontological grounding for the posthuman predicament, has proved especially inspirational for posthuman pedagogy and education. Semetsky has set up an empowering framework for nomadic education (Semetsky 2008; Semetsky and Masny

2013). She builds on the idea of subject formation as an event that takes place transversally, inbetween nature/technology, male/female, black/white, local/global, present/past – in assemblages that flow across and displace binary oppositions. This produces an educational theory based on becoming-other, both in relation to involving the non-human elements of education, be it animals, natural entities or technological apparatus.

Another important displacement in posthuman education builds on the parallelism between philosophy, the arts and science, which Deleuze and Guattari see as three equally worthy attempts to come to terms with and provide adequate framing for the intensities of virtual possibilities. This allows for easier interconnections between these domains, which goes well beyond traditional interdisciplinarity. It also shifts the emphasis of training from representational skills to more embodied performative skills, which entails a more affective approach to education. The emphasis on neo-materialism, which provides the ontological grounding for critical posthuman scholarship as a transversal field of knowledge, is also a way to resist the business model of higher education. Posthuman critical thinkers and educators situate themselves in and as part of the world, defending an idea of knowledge production as embedded, embodied, affective and relational.

Lykke (2018) foregrounds postdisciplinarity as a crucial transformative principle for posthuman knowledge and educational practices. Whereas multi- and interdisciplinarity work signifies collaborations within the framework of disciplines which enter into new synergetic relationships with each other, postdisciplinarity refers to more transgressive ways of producing academic knowledge. They destabilize and disrupt the hegemonic power of distinct disciplines and the hierarchies of knowledge that structure the academic divides between the human, social and natural sciences. Lykke adds that postdisciplinarity requires new institutional modes of organizing as well as new curricula and methodological tools. They need to unfold in transversal conversations between different approaches to matters of common concern, defined in non-binary ways. To establish such transversal conversations, the most appropriate method is collaborative, which requires specific spaces where community work can be enacted.

Echoing some of these concerns, Cole works on posthuman transversality with Guattari (Cole and Bradley 2018). Transversality as an organizational principle criticizes the pyramidal academic structure, which implies a hierarchical chain of command at the core of most institutions of higher learning. Cole explores this notion and argues it has the potential to renew educational practices. This entails firstly a critique of the global educational market as a commercial enterprise, which functions by subjecting education to profit-driven motives. Teaching and learning in the context of global capitalism produce profit for some, but for most people the reality is high debt and under-employment. Mindful of what the working conditions in neo-liberal universities have become, Cole argues strongly against the corporatization of the university and the monetarization of knowledge. Guattari's 'transversality' is the antidote, in that it introduces a model of relationality and affect in education, in the sense of non-vertical and non-horizontal planes of encounter.

In keeping with the politics of immanence, the situated perspective of both teachers and students needs to be stressed, but also the need for cartographic and perspectivist accounts of their respective locations. Moreover, if we work towards the ethical aim of an affirmative plane of composition of transversal subjectivities, which can be redefined as expanded selves, or distributed consciousness (i.e. non-Cartesian), it follows that their relational capacity is not confined within the human species, but includes non-anthropomorphic elements. *Zoe*, the non-human, vital force of Life is the transversal entity that allows us to think across previously segregated species, categories and domains. *Zoe*-centred egalitarianism is the core of a posthuman educational practice that might inspire us to resist the trans-species commodification of Life by advanced capitalism. Transversality facilitates the link to animality, on equal, but rhizomic terms that involve territories, geologies, ecologies and technologies of survival. It relocates both students and educators into the very world they are trying to learn about.

Notes Towards a Posthuman University

All these concrete developments indicate the good state of health of applied posthuman knowledge. They also carry significant implications for the posthuman university. The core value is that we need to organize academic communities that reflect and enhance an ethically empowering vision of the posthuman subject of knowledge. Transversal interconnections across the disciplines and society is the way to implement an ethical praxis that aims to cultivate and compose this new collective subject. This subject is an assemblage – 'we' – that is a mix of humans to non-humans, *zoe/*geo/techno-bound computational networks and earthlings, linked in a vital interconnection that is smart and self-organizing, but not chaotic.

Posthuman university structures of knowledge production run against the spirit of contemporary identity-loaded, consumerist capitalism and its commodification of Life itself. They favour instead non-profit experimentations with how many 'we' – collective transversal subjects – can be currently assembled on multiple planetary locations and what 'we' are capable of becoming.

Our historicity is such that, the very factors that structure these subjects are simultaneously booming on and crashing down. What is new is the scale, the speed and the structure of the transformations, that is to say of what is simultaneously ceasing to be and in the process of becoming. Computational networks functioning at posthuman speed have added a new dimension to the idea that thinking is not restricted to our embrained organisms.

On the other hand, wherever you may care to look, there are convulsive and internally contradictory events in the environment, the technology, the accumulation and polarization of wealth, the flows of mobility, and the building of walls and border check-points, the increased interactivity and the growth of xenophobia and racism. Whichever frame of understanding you may attempt to adopt to make sense of these developments, all thinking appears inadequate to the scale of the issues and their schizoid nature. Thinking seems equally insufficient to address the painful, glaring scale of the injustice, the violence, the disrespect and the indignity of how we deal with each other and with the world. This adds urgency to the project of constructing posthuman knowledge in an affirmative manner.

Bringing together the epistemological and the ethical, it means to develop a methodology for academic work that is collaborative but rigorous. I call it the 'sharable workbench', which is not the common methodology in the Humanities to the same extent it is in the Life sciences. Important notions here are non-competitive sharing and collaboration. Research in the Humanities should be structured as the work of fundamental laboratories with collaborative investigation about the key terms and concepts that are at play in shifting towards a PostHumanities perspective. We should work on language and concepts in the same fundamental ways that our colleagues use in the 'hard' sciences. The PostHumanities are equally experimental.

Here are some guidelines to assist the university in making the transition towards productive posthuman perspectives in research and education.

Firstly, in spite of some superficial similarities, the posthuman convergence is not a revival of the postmodern condition, although both movements of thought are the object of vituperative contempt on the part of the opposition. Today more than ever, 'theory' is a term of abuse, always identified with 'high theory', that is to say, abstractions that are unsubstantiated by any verifiable empirical evidence. The proposition is to make some mutual readjustments: some should drop the aggression and learn to see theory as critical cartographies aimed at the creation of new concepts and affirmative values. In return, the conceptual creators need to improve their communication skills and explain their ideas in a language that resonates with the mainstream of humanity as it now exists, as opposed to what it is in the process of becoming.

Secondly, although the figure of the intellectual is by now anachronistic, the tasks and framework of critical thinking need to be redefined, in a move that combines posthumanist criticism with post-anthropocentric creativity and affirms the continuity of all beings within the PostHumanities. This entails a serious discussion of what, of the Humanist past, can and should be salvaged. Of course, the past and its canonical texts should be respected, but they should not be frozen into sacred nationalistic icons. The past of European Humanism is too rich and important to be monumentalized. The past should be brought to bear on the present, transversally and in a broad, planetary perspective. This supposes delinking the classical canon from ethnocentric, patriarchal and exceptionalist premises to form a different cosmological imaginary for them.

Thirdly, considering their role as building blocks of the PostHumanities, it is important to acknowledge and apply the insights, methods, terminologies and ethical aspirations of radical epistemologies that are too often dismissed in academia as 'activist research'. Feminist, gender, queer, LBGTQ+ theories, post- and de-colonial studies, critical race theory, environmental studies and eco-criticism, disability studies, neo-materialism, and Critical Posthumanism are crucial instruments to help steer the contemporary university curricula and research agenda across the pitfalls of the posthuman convergence.

Fourthly, we need to apply transdisciplinary cross-pollination right across the board, forging a new alliance between the Critical PostHumanities and the Life sciences, the neural sciences and the information technologies. We need to set up a new relationship based on mutual respect and a collaborative morality geared to the joint endeavour of meeting the complexities of our posthuman times. The distributed framework of the Critical PostHumanities can provide renewed confidence in their capacity as a resource for policy-making at all levels, starting from the academic and scientific, but pointing beyond.

Fifthly, it is wise to invest in the generative potential of minor or nomadic sciences and their alternative knowledge production systems. The PostHumanities stand to learn from much older and more elaborate indigenous cosmologies and epistemologies, while resisting neo-colonial appropriation. We need to strike generative alliances, starting with the composition of a transversal, material-embedded and differential 'we'.

Sixthly, we need to resist politically cognitive capitalism's appropriation of the vulnerable field of the academic

Humanities, through the reterritorializations induced by the mainstream PostHumanities. This means backing the minor sciences institutionally. It is a way of being worthy of the challenge of constructing a university that is both the record of what we are ceasing to be and the seed of what we are in the process of becoming.

Another form of resisting neo-liberalism's appropriation of the academic Humanities is to cultivate deceleration. Deceleration – slowing down – allows academic communities to subtract themselves from the malignant velocities of advanced capitalism (Noys 2014). In an affirmative note, Berg and Seeber remind us that academics in choosing their branch of work also chose a lifestyle and an ethics: 'We wanted to work in the university because of the joy of intellectual discovery, the beauty of literary texts, and the radical potential of new ideas. These ideals are realizable, even in today's beleaguered institution, although the ever-increasing casualization of labour makes them harder to attain for many of us' (2016: 3). They propose a deceleration of pedagogical and research cultures, through the 'Slow Professors' movement, which advocates 'deliberations over acceleration' (Berg and Seeber 2016: xviii). Calling for more time to think, for both staff and students, as the core mission of academic research, they also propose a more collaborative model of work for the university. Instead of the fierce competition, self-sufficient individualism and accelerating pace, they call for sharing and communal learning. The time for reflection and open-ended enquiry is a core value and not a luxury.

Lastly, the call for timelessness is not just quantitative, in the sense that it means more research time or more sabbaticals, but rather refers to a qualitatively different use of time that is not indexed on short-term and fast productivity. Ultimately, 'slowness is not a question of duration, as of an ability to distinguish and evaluate, with the propensity to cultivate pleasure, knowledge and quality' (Berg and Seeber 2016: 89). A 'slow' approach honours complexity and resonates with a more embodied and embedded vision of intelligence, as a situational and affective quality. Ultimately, the stakes are ethical: the open-ended nature of thinking is connected to an openness to otherness, which also includes non-human agents.

Cognitive capitalism has vested interests in reorganizing the institution of the universities along corporate principles of monetarization and profit. Noam Chomsky (2014) goes so far as to speak of the death of US universities. Given the distributed structure of knowledge production in advanced capitalism, with so much research – in bio-technologies as well as information and digital media – now being co-extensive with corporate interests, the question of what universities are for is more relevant than ever.

My answer is that universities teach critical thought and creative alternatives. At a time of such momentous changes within the posthuman convergence, a university education needs to provide outlets and possibilities to a broad range of citizens. We need life-long education programmes to train the former working class of an economy that no longer exists. But we also need cutting-edge experimental curricula for the digitally related, non-profit minded youth of today. Refugees and asylum-seekers can be enlisted as educational practitioners at all ends of the educational scale, as they are a great cultural and intellectual resource that should be put to better use.

The Humanities deserve better status within the contemporary university. We can look at it pragmatically; even cognitive capitalism is going to need generalists, dreamers, people who can read and interpret the world freely. If the policy-makers could accept that, they would support, not cut back, the Humanities. They should consider them as a double capital: partly because their creativity is generating waves of critical studies discourses, which are currently coalescing in the 'minor science' strand of the Critical PostHumanities. And partly because they possess a unique and irreplaceable capital: what we academics in the different branches of the university are capable of teaching is how to reflect critically upon our own historical achievements and shortcomings. Humbled and instructed by our culture's historical mistakes, as well as its achievements, Humanities education remains a pillar of democracy through civic academic criticism. Ultimately, the mystery question is: how do you do democracy? That's what the world needs to know. The university has worked on this for over a hundred years of democratic criticism, building up another kind of cognitive capital. The Humanities are written into that capital. To throw away this critical capital would be as myopic as it is suicidal. There is only one way to teach democracy, which is to actually enact it in a community of scholars who work together across borders, bonded by love for their subject areas and a sense of civic responsibility. Universities are part of a community, a city, a country; campuses are not bubbles but fully-fledged civic spaces.

Universities need to take the chance of complexity against populist over-simplifications. This entails ways of speaking truth to power that resonate with the contradictions and complexities of the posthuman convergence. Universities need to think with and for the world, as a process of virtual becoming-world, that is to say increasing the ability to contribute to the growth and well-being of a diverse range of human and non-human others.

We need the university as critical training for democratic criticism. I dream of a possible critical and creative assemblage that would consist of: Edward Said meets Microsoft, meets Gloria Anzaldúa, meets Gilles Deleuze, meets Facebook, meets Donna Haraway, meets the Anthropocene, meets Black Lives Matter, meets #Metoo, meets transnational environmental justice, meets the challenge of thinking affirmatively. I would bring ensembles like this back to the core of university training for teaching and research. What we all need to learn, the world over, is how to become a functioning and inclusive democracy. The model of the Critical PostHumanities, with its emphasis on minor science and affirmative ethics, offers a possible way forward.

In the contemporary illiberal world, it is crucial to stick to some basic rules like academic freedom. University-based criticism has historically been a force for democratic societies. This is all the more important because of the growth of xenophobia and proto-fascism in the EU at present. Just as I was finishing this book, the Central European University, the CEU, was 'forced' to relocate from Budapest in Hungary to Vienna in Austria, in order to accept new students in 2019. Even after a prolonged campaign of resistance bolstered by international support, the CEU had to close down in Hungary. The relocation was due to Hungarian government legislation that has been widely criticized for

imposing unattainable requirements on the university, which
is officially registered in the US. The CEU was founded in
1991 by philanthropist George Soros, who provided a sizable
endowment for it. A champion of progressive causes, Soros
has become the target of attacks by populist governments
both in the region and the US. The Canadian CEU President
and Rector Michael Ignatieff stated that this was a 'dark day
for academic freedom' and that it did not bode well for any
university in the world. Sebastian Kurz's populist government
in Austria repeatedly assured that the CEU was unequivocally
welcome to the Austrian capital, as part of their commitment
to academic freedom and research.

Let us defend democracy as the critical edge of a heterogeneous, differential and yet connected citizenry, as a
'missing people' that is internally differentiated, but works
together. This is a 'we' that is materially embedded – just a
people, coalesced around *this* specific project of bringing the
PostHumanities into twenty-first-century democracy.

In this chapter I have explained some theoretical principles
and presented practices of affirmative posthuman knowledge
production as well as guidelines for a PostHumanities
contribution to the university. The mix of principles and
practices hopefully bridges the epistemology and the ethics
of posthuman knowledge. I have provided examples of
selected practices from a wide range of fields to demonstrate
the kind of theoretical and methodological creativity, as
well as the ethical accountability that is being developed on
the debris of anthropocentrism and human exceptionalism.
They offer multiple tips on what it means to think in and
with the world, when that world seems to be falling apart.
Affirmative ethics is what posthuman subjects need in order
to deal with the conflicting demands that will have been
made on them.

Posthuman subjects will have been all-too-human in that
they are facing, right here and now, an inhuman present and
an a-human future. Learning to think differently about what
we do when we think about the humans that we will have
been, enlists the resources of the imagination, of our deepest
aspirations, of vision and trust. These qualities require a
new understanding of the collaborative and interconnected
'we-are-in-this-together' kind of subject. Ultimately, this

leads us to the need for a new ethics, posthumanist and non-anthropocentric, materially grounded, but differential and above all, relational and affirmative. I will discuss this new ethics of affirmation in the next chapter.

Chapter 6
On Affirmative Ethics

The critical mass and originality of the material I presented in chapters 4 and 5 warranted the tentative conclusion that, far from being a crisis, the posthuman convergence is a highly generative moment for the Humanities. It creates new knowledge production and alternative subject formations. I have pointed out two qualitatively different lines of thinking: Major science as contiguous with the profit-driven reterritorializations of capital; and minor science as more heterogeneous, not-for-profit and curiosity-driven.

In dealing with these differential speeds of knowledge production, I have called for a complex and heterogeneous approach that relies on the composition of active transversal assemblages: 'we, posthuman subjects', who are in *this* particular project together, but 'we are not One and the same'. 'We' are positioned in embodied and embedded differential but material locations, which generate different perspectives about knowledge, subjectivity and the posthuman convergence. I also argued that the task of critical thinking is to provide the cartographies and the navigational tools or figurations to understand the differences as well as the common grounds that compose these assemblages. These transversal links encompass human and non-human agents, but they do remain a function of subjectivity: posthumanist, post-anthropocentric, embedded, embodied, relational, affective and ethically accountable.

Situating the knowing subjects as immanent to the very conditions they are trying to understand, change or resist, means that critical thinking is about being able to make a careful ethical distinction between different speeds and territorializations of both knowledge and subject production. This relies upon critical engagement with the present defined as both the actual – the predictable margins of institutional capitalization by Major science – and with the virtual – the construction of alternative formations by minor science. Because both aspects are operational in the spatial-temporal dimension of a continuous present, the specific challenge for critical theory is to map out and operationalize the margins of possible actualization of the virtual. I provided multiple examples of concrete practices that work in this framework, to provide both encouragement and inspiration.

In this and the next chapter I suggest that a critical posthuman perspective offers a way out of the state of exhaustion, anxiety and fear that characterizes the posthuman convergence. It also provides a strong response to the nihilistic and accelerationist tendencies as well as profit-minded knowledge practices of cognitive capitalism. To assert the force of affirmative ethics, however, does not mean to dismiss the reality of conflict and pain. The negative elements have to be taken seriously. A focus on posthuman subjectivity entails also addressing issues of inequality, discrimination and exclusion. In order to complete a framework of defining posthuman knowledge, it is important to stress the inhuman(e) and the dehumanized aspects of this predicament, as well as the perpetuation of structural injustices on dispossessed people and classes.

The contemporary world has a great deal of injustice to account for. Parr (2018) charts the three overlapping axes of contemporary politics as being: economic life, governmentality and militarism. Their combined violence is devastating and calls for global resistance. The brutality of new power relations has established a necropolitical mode of governing, which targets not only the management of the living, but also multiple practices of dying. Consider the generalized material destruction of human bodies, populations and the environment through the industrial warfare led by the fleet of drones and other unmanned vehicles. Think also of the global effects of migration as a result of dispossession, expulsions and terror. The refugee camps and other zones of detention are multiplying, as are militarized humanitarian interventions. Whole sections of humanity are downgraded to the status of extraterritorial, subhumans, like the refugees trying to cross a hostile sea: alien others, not meant to be here to stay.

Taking stock of the necropolitical logic of our times, opposing its violence, and fighting for justice and solidarity are crucial priorities. Yet, I resist the reduction of posthuman subjects to the wounded, vulnerable aspects alone. This picture needs to be broadened. Again, the project is both to do with knowledge and understanding and with ethical values.

Conceptually, subjects cannot be reduced to their vulnerable mortality, on the contrary: they are essentially subjects of desire. Freedom is written into our system as the desire to expand and enhance our existence; this is desire as *potentia*. Thinking beings keep on flowing out of the frames that attempt to capture them. Incidentally, this vital force is precisely what a system like capitalism is interested in, in order to mine it for information and draw profits from it. Hence the constant flows of reterritorialization and capitalization of knowledge.

Ethically, vital neo-materialist subjects are animated by the positivity of an ontological desire that orients them towards the freedom to express all they are capable of becoming. What grounds this ontological aspiration is the fact that virtual possibilities need to be actualized, by a missing 'we', that is to say a transversal subject that will be composed in concrete historical circumstances, in the open structure of time, with the virtual potentials at its core. Heterogeneity, complexity and multiplicities mark this process of becoming, which opens a myriad of possibilities of both resistance and counter-actualization of alternatives. It is this complexity and heterogeneity that constitute posthuman subjectivity, defined as the composition of posthuman subjects who want to know otherwise and produce knowledge differently.

The cartographies of the Critical PostHumanities I have offered in the previous chapters illustrate the force of affirmative ethics. These new fields of knowledge allow for grounded analyses of how discursive power operates today and how it provides new parameters of knowledge, while also perpetuating traditional patterns of exclusion. The posthuman convergence shows a proliferation of knowledges that differ qualitatively from the epistemic accelerations of cognitive capitalism, in that they carry a generative, affirmative dimension that is connected to the potential for minor science. The Critical PostHumanities can be welcomed for their transversal energy and the margins of affirmation they are capable of mobilizing in resisting the opportunistic epistemic speed of advanced capitalism.

Throughout this book I have defended affirmative ethics as a collective practice of constructing social horizons of hope, in response to the flagrant injustices, the perpetuation of old hierarchies and new forms of domination. It is time now to look more carefully at the affirmative margins that are opened by the posthuman convergence, after the decentring of Anthropos in favour of *zoe*/geo/techno relations, and to assess their ability to process pain and construct an ethical subjectivity worthy of our times.

Are 'We' in this Together?

Clearly 'we' are in *this* posthuman convergence together, but this does not necessarily spell out an ontological kind of Humanism that has unified all the humans and thus flattened out the structural differences that separate us. 'We' are in this posthuman predicament together, but 'we are not One', let alone 'The One', the chosen People, because we are positioned in dramatically different power relations. Situated and immanent practices allow for sharper and grounded analyses of these power differences.

Nonetheless, we do remain confronted by a number of painful contradictions that affect us all: for example, climate change is planetary and digital interconnections breed immediate intimacy, but also hatred and paranoia. For its part, economic globalization results in a resurgence of structural inequalities and new monopolies, but it also engenders counter-movements in the form of economic protectionism and xenophobic fears.

In such a conflict-fraught context, appeals to a unitary sense of Humanity are common, for instance in United Nations humanitarianism and in rather self-interested corporate Humanism. But they sound rather hollow when compared to the scale of the devastation induced by the unequal relations of power. Moreover, such a hasty recomposition of an endangered Humanity reinstates anthropocentrism and fails to do justice to the violence humans are visiting upon all other species, the planet included. Furthermore, much Anthropocene scholarship manifests a state of emergency and a sort of 'white' panic about the dire state of the planet and the chances of survival. There is something ironic to say the least in the spectacle of European civilization, that was the cause of so much devastation and multiple extinctions in its colonial occupied territories, becoming so concerned about extinction and the future of the species. While there is no denying the seriousness of the problems engendered by the posthuman convergence, it is equally true that 'for many people in the global South and in extremely poor parts of the global North, these conditions have long been systemic and chronic. Today the global warming and the Capitalocene are distributing the damage in less stratified ways, including across the global North' (Clarke 2018: 15).

It is therefore important to reiterate a number of notions already mentioned in passing in this book, so as to move them to the next stage of the argument. Statements like 'we humans', or even 'we posthumans', need to be grounded carefully on materially embedded differential perspectives, for 'we-are-in-*this*-together-but-we-are-*not*-one-and-the-same'. 'We' are immanent to, which means intrinsically connected to, the very conditions we are *also* critical of. The posthuman convergence is a shared trait of our historical moment, but it is not at all clear whose crisis this actually is. Because we cannot speak of an undifferentiated humanity (or an undifferentiated 'we') that is allegedly sharing in a common condition of both technological mediation and crisis and extinction, extra work is required of critical thinkers. In response I stress the importance of materially embedded differential perspectives, allowing for diversity and heterogeneity of approaches.

Becoming-posthuman is at the heart of a process of redefining one's sense of attachment and connection to a common and shared world, a territorial space: urban, social, psychic, ecological, planetary as it may be. It is a sort of becoming-world. This grounded perspective accounts for multiple ecologies of belonging. At the level of subjectivity, it requires the transformation of one's sensorial and perceptual self-understanding, in order to make room for the collective nature and outward-bound direction of what we still call 'the self'. This 'self' is in fact a moveable assemblage within a common life-space, which the subject never masters but merely inhabits, always within a community, a pack or an assemblage. For posthuman theory, the *zoe*/geo/techno-framed subject is a transversal entity, fully immersed in and immanent to a network of human and non-human relations.

The ethical ideal is to mobilize the active powers of life in the affirmative mode of *potentia*. This actualizes the cognitive, affective and sensorial means to cultivate degrees of empowerment and affirmation of one's interconnections to others in their multiplicity. The selection of the affective forces that propel the process of becoming posthuman is regulated by an ethics of joy and affirmation that functions through the transformation of negative into positive passions. There are no moral injunctions at work, but rather ethical forces that operate like analytic frames for on-going experiments with intensities that need to be enacted collectively. The experiments in the common world, with what kind of subjects we are capable of becoming, can be accounted for by adequate cartographies of how much bodies can take. In earlier work I have called this 'thresholds of sustainability' (Braidotti 2006).

Affirmative ethics is a collective practice that acknowledges the passing and dying of multiple universes, grounded in embedded and embodied materialist practices. This approach will become all the more relevant as my discussion of the Critical PostHumanities veers towards the resonance currently emerging in the scholarship between Major and minor sciences, including knowledge generated by far older Indigenous epistemologies (Nakata 2007).

The Planetary Differential Humanities

The building blocks for the next step of the argument take us back to chapter 4, where I provided the cartography of the Critical PostHumanities. In that chapter I differentiated between Major and minor science production. I argued there that some of the critical subjects of knowledge are missing from the contemporary institutionalization of posthuman knowledge. I now want to turn my attention to the emerging cross-over fields of minor science that combine feminist, anti-racist, post-colonial and anti-fascist perspectives within a posthuman framework.

Let's start from the idea that humanity is not a neutral term but rather one that indexes access to specific powers, values and norms, privileges and entitlements, rights and visibility (Mbembe 2017a). This insight is one of the sources of the critique of humanist universalism, which were raised from the eighteenth century onwards, for instance by Olympe de Gouges (1791) on behalf of women and Toussaint Louverture (2011 [1794]) on behalf of colonized people (Césaire 1981), to name but a few.

No amount of universalism can conceal the fractures, the internal contradictions and external exclusions that have always composed a notion of the human. Fundamental social categories such as class, race, gender and sexual orientation, age and able-bodiedness have functioned as markers of human 'normality'. They still are key factors in framing the notion of and policing access to something we may call 'humanity'. Who qualifies as a human in that view is the kind of being that skilfully combines high Humanist standards of individual physical and mental perfection with collective intellectual and moral values. This is the generic sweep that turned Humanism into a civilizational standard, positioning Europe as the centre of world progress. Incidentally, that is what makes Eurocentrism into a structural and not just a contingent attitude.

In the first chapter I already touched on the issue of philosophical anti-Humanism as a position developed by European philosophers as a critique of their own cultures. I mentioned the extent to which a critique of Humanism is coextensive with Humanism itself (Said 2004) and, more specifically, that the idea of 'crisis' should be taken as the European philosophers' standard *modus operandi* (Spivak 1988). Far from marking a break, it spells the continuity in the rule of the European 'Man of Reason' (Lloyd 1984) and in his ability to reinvent 'him'self through seemingly radical self-reflection and adaptation to changing circumstances. Gilroy argues that Humanism has not yet achieved its promises, but that the advantages of the emancipatory aspects of Humanism should be shared more fully and inclusively by all humans. He then proposes a reparative planetary Black Humanism (Gilroy 2016). In the same mode Sylvia Wynter (2015) develops a philosophical analysis of the mixed legacy of European Humanism, which she calls its Janus-faced paradox. She critiques the racialized ontology of Man in Western philosophy as being non-representative of humanity. Instead, she endorses a revision of Humanism in relation to concepts of Blackness.

These thinkers remain critically within Humanism. They resist the idea of posthuman subjectivity, because they argue that many sectors of the world population have not achieved the human status yet. They fear that the posthuman will short-circuit the process of humanistic emancipation. I fully share this concern (in fact, I have run analogous arguments in relation to the position of women in *Patterns of Dissonance*, 1991). Yet, in the context of the posthuman convergence, it is becoming painfully clear that the dispossessed and oppressed sections of the world population are missing out on the benefits of the Fourth Industrial Revolution, while they are the most severely hit by the climate change and the Sixth Extinction. Because of this double disadvantage it is urgent to establish encounters between posthuman knowledge and black, postcolonial and anti-racist theories, as well as indigenous philosophies.

Examples of bridge-making are ample in scholarship, starting from the towering work of Edouard Glissant (1997), whose take on the poetics of relations is foundational. Deleuzian post-colonial theory and studies is another significant development (Bignall and Patton 2010; Burns and Kaiser 2012). Postcolonial and race theory positions on Humanism have been revised earlier by Ann Stoler's work on gender and race (1995); Robert Young's careful readings of both Foucault and Deleuze (1990, 1995); and by the deconstructive post-colonial work of Homi Bhabha (1994). Finally, there is a new wave of intersectional postcolonial studies (Ponzanesi and Leurs 2014; Wekker 2016) and postcolonial eco-criticism (Huggan and Tiffin 2009).

Let me stress that to place different orders of knowledge and different traditions of subject formation in dialogue with each other does not mean creating false equivalences. It rather aims at amplifying possible resonances between them, for instance, in relation to different ways of understanding the 'missing people'. The empirically missing people are missing because they have been eliminated, disqualified or, in Wynter's terms, 'deselected'. The question is how to bring the capital of critical theory to bear on the Critical PostHumanities, so as to pursue the argument that I started in chapter 4 on minor science and the construction of a missing people.

We can construct a missing people by three steps. Firstly, by agreeing on a cartography of the condition that we are in, and which I have termed the posthuman convergence. Secondly, by developing adequate schemes of knowledge about these conditions, most notably about the power relations these involve. Thirdly, by defining a platform of action on multiple scales in the real world. This is my model of affirmative ethics. Such a praxis can compose a new community, as a virtual entity. The missing people form a 'we-are-in-this-together-but-we-are-not-one-and-the-same' kind of people. The formula 'we-are-in-this-together-but-we-are-not-one-and-the-same' is what I mean by transversal subjectivity.

When we bring to bear the missing people upon the Critical PostHumanities, we accomplish two things. First, we are re-segregating the critical discourses that at the moment are not in dialogue, notably the posthuman platform in its array of techno-studies and multiple forms of posthumanism, and postcolonial, anti-racist and indigenous theories. Second, we are reactivating the disjunction between Major and minor knowledge that I discussed in the previous chapter, so as to counteract the perpetuation of patterns of discrimination against the feminist, queer, migrant, poor, decolonial, diasporic, otherwise-abled Humanities and diseased Humanities, to mention just a few. Incidentally, also missing from the field are non-nationally indexed Humanities and, as Rorty critically noted (1998), poor people, or trailer park Humanities. This shows the disparity in the speed and intensity of the de- and re-territorializations of these missing people.

What does it mean to be 'missing' to begin with? Whether we look at indigenous knowledge systems, at feminists, queers, otherwise enabled, non-humans or technologically mediated existences, these are real-life subjects whose knowledge never made it into any of the official cartographies or genealogies. The struggle for their visibility and emergence drives the radical politics of immanence, aimed at actualizing minority-driven knowledges through transversal alliances. The people who were empirically missing – even from minor science – get constituted as political subjects of knowledge through such alliances.

Stressing the convergence aspect of the posthuman juncture is helpful, precisely because the effects of resonance may result in the composition of sharable discursive spaces, where the critique of Eurocentric imperialism and colonial violence can be written into the new scripts emerging from the posthuman convergence. Convergence does not equate to colonial appropriation or deletion of all situated differences. In the framework of affirmative ethics, the challenge consists in opening up alternative ways of thinking about what kind of humans we are in the process of becoming: 'we' who are not One and the same, but are nonetheless in *this* posthuman convergence together.

The Critical PostHumanities are in constant process, interbreeding through multiple alliances, topics and missing links. This does not mean that anything goes, but rather that rhizomic multi-directionality is the rule. The rhizomic energy of the field is already providing answers: the strength of minoritarian subjects consists in their capacity to carry out alternative modes of becoming and transversal relations that break up segregational patterns. New border crossings are being set up with the aim of actualizing the virtual knowledge and visions of these missing peoples.

Since Rob Nixon's seminal work on slow violence (2011), the missing links between postcolonial theories, the Environmental Humanities and indigenous episte-mologies have been exposed and analysed, resulting in growing convergence between them. Arguing that the status of environmental activism among the poor in the global South has shifted towards the transnational environmental justice movement and the assessment of damage caused by warfare, Nixon proposes to develop new cross-over dialogues between these movements and the – by now already 'classical' – Environmental Humanities. At the level of the political economy of the PostHumanities, this results in the production of new areas of studies that cross over the complex post-anthropocentric axes of enquiry. Postcolonial Environmental Humanities come to the fore; Transnational Environmental literature also emerges as a cross-over between Native American Studies and other Indigenous studies areas.

Similar developments are on the way to fill in missing links in the Digital Humanities. For instance, relying on the work of pioneers like Lisa Nakamura (2002), Ponzanesi and Leurs (2014) claim that Postcolonial Digital Humanities is now a fully constituted field, digital media providing the most comprehensive platform to re-think transnational spaces and contexts.[1] These new assemblages pursue the aims of 'classical' postcolonial studies, across the reterritorialized Digital Humanities platform, into the complexity of minor science. The project of decolonizing new media is timely, considering that the field is coextensive with corporate and institutional interests that make it indispensable for economic growth and the war on terror.

The idea that the adoption of digital technologies can exacerbate the devastation of indigenous ways of knowing is also central to Mignolo's decolonial movement. It results in a call for 'de-linking' digital media from the disastrous legacy of European colonialism and Western modernity (Mignolo 2011: 122–3). This results in new alliances between Environmentalists and Legal specialists, Indigenous and non-Western epistemologies, First Nation peoples, new media activists, IT engineers and anti-globalization forces, which constitute a significant example of new political assemblages.[2] They have produced the Decolonial Digital Humanities, for example the Hastac Scholars Forum, explicitly inspired by Mignolo's work.[3]

Being part of a social minority is no guarantee that one becomes an agent of social transformation. However, it is a better place to start from than any of the centres that compose the grid of power. The examples that were given above illustrate the transversal alliances of heterogeneous elements, because they are not the same culture, the same organism, or even the same species. In this respect, the assemblage is a virtuality that needs to be brought into being.

These assemblages combine sophisticated theories with attention to the earth. They also express enduring care for the people who live closest to the earth – indigenous populations – thus raising the ethical and political stakes. The critique of Western imperialism and racism provides an added critical distance – an extra layer of dis-identification – that positions these posthuman critical thinkers closer to the dispossessed and the disempowered, adding that many of those are neither human nor necessarily anthropomorphic.

In my view, relational ethics stresses the compassionate but also the more political aspect of subjectivity. As Cornell West put it recently (2018):

> Race matters in the 21st century are part of a moral and spiritual war over resources, power, souls and sensibilities. There can be no analysis of race matters without earth matters, class matters, gender matters and sexuality matters and, especially, empire matters. We must have solidarity on all these fronts.

Within a neo-materialist frame, the political – that is to say the communal process of composing transversal subjects committed to the actualization of the virtual – is driven by the ethics of affirmation. This entails the overthrowing of negativity through the recasting of the oppositional, resisting self ('I would prefer not to') into a collective assemblage ('we'). This transversal alliance today involves non-human agents, technologically mediated elements, Earth-others (land, waters, plants, animals) and non-human inorganic agents (plastic buckets, wires, software, algorithms, etc.). A posthuman ethical praxis involves the formation of a new alliance, a new people.

If the present is the record of what we are ceasing to be, we now witness the decline of 'Man/Anthropos' and his Humanities. At the same time, the present is also the seed for what we are in the process of becoming-subject. Consequently, the 'missing people' is also an emerging or virtual category. This emergence phenomenon refers to the collective effort to bring into action a complex singularity, a new 'we' that expresses the embedded, embodied, relational and affective forces. This praxis generates patterns of becoming, of minor science, of intensive shifts. The activating factor in the politics of immanence is a plane of transposition of forces in both spatial and temporal terms: from past to future and from the virtual to the actual. It is the actualization of a virtuality, travelling at different speed from capitalist acceleration. We saw in chapter 5 that even international law has to come to terms with it; all the more the rest of us.

The point of this actualization is to provide an adequate expression of what embodied and embrained bodies can do and think and enact. Adequate to what? Adequate to what the missing peoples can do. This comes down to an evaluation of forces, that is to say to what bodies can do in terms of sustaining intensity, processing negativity and producing affirmation. The task of producing adequate understandings and expressions of alternative knowledge is also connected to the ethical task of turning the painful experience of inexistence into generative relational encounters and knowledge production. This is liberation through the understanding of our bondage. It is a way of extracting knowledge and activism from pain, via the transformation of the negative. The process of collectively constructing affirmative ethics involves the composition of planes of becoming for a missing people. Some of these missing peoples were never fully part of the 'Human', understood as the 'Man of Reason', whose crisis so preoccupies the Humanities today. Others are run-away groups that no longer identify with dominant subject formations and Majority-led knowledge. These complex posthuman ensembles that constitute subjectivity are negotiable: the 'human' is just a vector of becoming. 'We' need to compose a new people and a new earth.

The politics of radical immanence – to actualize the emergence of a missing people – exposes the weakness of the reactive recomposition of pan-humanity as a threatened category, the vulnerable cosmopolitanism I criticized in earlier chapters. Instead of taking a flight into an abstract idea of a 'new' pan-humanity, bonded in negative passions like fear of extinction, in a world risk society (Beck 1999), I make a plea for materialist affirmative ethics, grounded in immanent interconnections and generative differences. This is a transversal composition of multiple assemblages of active minoritarian subjects: many 'people' who are no longer missing.

Zoe-Driven Ethics of Affirmation

At this point the insight about the non-linearity of time is important, notably the multi-layered structure of the present as both the record of what we are ceasing to be and the seeds of what we are in the process of becoming. At the ethical level this means that the conditions for political and ethical agency are not dependent on the current state of the terrain: they are not oppositional and thus not tied to the present by negation. Instead, they are projected across time as affirmative praxis, geared to creating empowering relations aimed at possible futures. Saying 'no' to the unacceptable aspects of present conditions cuts both ways: it means both 'I do not want this' and 'I desire otherwise'. Ethical relations create possible worlds by mobilizing resources that have been left untapped in the present, including our desires and imagination. They activate the virtual in a web or rhizome of interconnection with others. We have to learn to think differently about ourselves. This is highly relevant for the posthuman subject, which cannot afford to restrict the ethical instance within the limits of human otherness, but has to open it up to inter-relations with non-human, post human and in-human forces.

Affirmative ethics builds on radical relationality, aiming at empowerment. This means increasing one's ability to relate to multiple others, in a productive and mutually enforcing manner, and creating a community that actualizes this ethical propensity. Within the framework of affirmative ethics, the notion of evil, that is, ethical evil, is equated with negative affects. What is negative about them is neither a psychological mood nor a normative value judgement. In order to understand this crucial point, we need to de-psychologize this discussion about negativity and affirmation and approach it instead in more conceptual, but also more pragmatic terms. The normative distinction between good and evil is replaced with that between affirmation and negation, or positive and negative affects.

Negativity rather has to do with the effects of arrest and blockage that ensue as a result of a blow, a shock, an act of violence, betrayal, a trauma, or just intense boredom. It is the rigidity of catatonia. Affirmative ethics consists not in denying negativity, but in reworking it outside the dialectical oppositions. That is necessary because negative passions diminish our relational competence and deny our vital interdependence on others. They negate the positive power (*potentia*) of our relational ethical essence, of Life as the desire to endure, to continue, by becoming other-than-itself. The black hole of narcissism and paranoia, the despotic glee in humiliating others, the gloom of hatred – all this negativity hurts the victims, but also harms the perpetuators' capacity to pursue the ethical opening outwards.

Fundamentally, negative passions harm the self's capacity to relate to others, both human and non-human others, and thus to grow in and through others. Negative affects diminish our capacity to express the high levels of interdependence, the vital reliance on others that is the key to both a non-unitary vision of the subject and to affirmative ethics. This refers back to the post-identitarian moment of neo-materialist posthuman thought: we need to avoid indexing the process on an individualist notion of the subject, while keeping the complexity in mind.

What is positive in the ethics of affirmation is the belief that negative affects can be transformed. This implies a dynamic view of all affects, including the painful ones. Every present event contains within it the potential for being overcome and overtaken; its negative charge *can* be transposed. The moment of the actualization of its virtual potential is also the moment of the neutralization of the poisonous effects of the pain. The ethical subject is the one with the ability to grasp the freedom to de-personalize the event and transform its negative charge. Affirmative ethics is a clinical practice about detoxing from the poison of un-freedom, servitude and betrayal of our inner nature as dynamic entities of desire. The ethical good is accordingly equated with radical relationality aiming at affirmative empowerment. The ethical ideal is to increase one's ability to enter into modes of relation with multiple others and to create a community that actualizes this ethical propensity.

At the risk of repeating: affirmative ethics consists not in denying negativity, but in reworking it outside the dialectical oppositions. Consequently, affirmative ethics is not about the avoidance of pain, but rather a different way of reworking it. It is about transcending the resignation and passivity that ensue from being hurt, lost and dispossessed, activating it beyond the dialectics of recognition and the politics of resentment. The positivity here is not supposed to indicate a facile optimism, or a careless dismissal of human suffering. The emphasis on the pursuit and actualization of positive relations and the ethical value attributed to affirmation do not imply any avoidance or disavowal of conflict.

Rather than a lack of compassion, it is instead an over-supply of it! Affirmative ethics aspires to an adequate understanding of the conditions of our relational dependency on the negative. Critical thought feeds on negativity, as Nietzsche sharply observed. The ethical relation, however, consists in the active transformation of the negative into something else. Ethics is not just the application of moral protocols, norms and values, but rather the force that contributes to conditions of affirmative becoming.

First one disengages the process of subject formation from negativity and then attaches it to affirmative otherness. This means that reciprocity is redefined outside the dialectics of recognition as mutual specification. This differential modulation occurs within a common matter and in a shared praxis, as the co-construction and also the counter-construction of affirmative values and relations. 'We-are-in-*this*-together' is the ethical formula par excellence and all the more so in a posthuman vital political economy of over-exposure and evanescence, exuberance and extinction.

Affirmation and Vulnerability

We have seen so far that affirmative ethics emerges from engaging with and processing pain and vulnerability and working with other transversal subject-entities to transform them. Joyful or affirmative relations are achieved through the praxis of reaching adequate understanding of our conditions by reworking together the negative experiences and affects that enclose us. Affirmative ethics implies a commitment to duration, both in the temporal sense of continuity and the spatial one of endurance. It implies conversely a rejection of self-destruction. An ethically empowering mode of relation increases one's *potentia* and creates one's ability to take in and on the world, which is the common nature, or rather the common ground, for all living entities.

Affirmative ethics and the positivity of desire neither deny nor cancel pain, violence and suffering, but rather propose another way of dealing with them. In terms of affirmative ethics, negativity – the harm that you do to others – is immediately reflected in the harm you do to yourself. This results, for example, in terms of loss of relational power, self-awareness and inner freedom. In this regard, pain and vulnerability in fact express the deeply affective and relational nature of all living entities. This vital bond is also the core of their generative powers. Affirmative ethics is the motor of that regeneration. It is not propelled by any categorical moral imperative under the aegis of a transcendental consciousness, but is rather co-produced in the acknowledgement of the immanent interconnection of the multiple ecologies that constitute all living systems.

What emerges from this approach is a different practice of ethical care and containment of the other, based on the constitutive affective ability of all entities to affect and be affected, to interrelate with human and non-human others. Alaimo (2016) defines this as a form of exposure, but also of openness and hence availability. In other words, it is the expression of the intensity of our *potentia* or embodied and embedded vital common nature. These form mutually inter-dependent transversal connections within a common flow of *zoe*/geo/techno relations. Vulnerability as the power of exposure is defined as an ethical and political means to come to terms with – rather than disavow – the untenable, painful and unacceptable aspects and disasters of posthuman times. Working within a feminist neo-materialist frame of analysis, Alaimo (2016) stresses the distinctive pleasures, as well as the challenges of trans-corporeal entanglements.

The emphasis falls not so much on vulnerability as a foundational condition, as on the embodied and embedded subjects' capacity to turn it into a generative force. This is achieved through the ability and the commitment to co-produce conditions and practices that transform the negative instance, including hurt and pain. As we have seen above, this requires the constitution of missing people through collective assemblages.

Given that posthuman subjects are defined as radically immanent, embedded and embodied assemblages of forces or flows, intensities and relations, and considering that they involve a range of human and non-human entities, the immediate aim is some form of meta-stability, perhaps in the form of deceleration from the manic speeds of cognitive capitalism. Joyful or affirmative relations, reached through the praxis of reworking together the reactive and negative experiences and affects, are the desirable ethical mode.

Posthuman subjectivity is transversal and active, but it does acknowledge the importance of limits as thresholds of encounters with others, to ensure productive relations and prevent nihilistic self-destruction. To be limitless is the kind of delirious megalomania that is endorsed today by the Silicon Valley gurus of trans-humanism, who pursue the fantasy of unloading an entity they call 'the mind' into computers and computational systems. They strike me as the heirs to the dualistic neo-Cartesian master narratives of cyber-culture, ever so willing to reduce intelligence to a disembodied computational capacity and to 'dissolve the bodily self into the matrix' (Braidotti 2002). If we follow closely a vital neo-materialist scheme on this point, on the other hand, a materially embedded vision of the subject necessarily entails the limitations imposed by its sheer material nature, in so far as being embodied implies a singular spatial-temporal frame: one life, in its radical immanence.

The subject lies at the intersections with external, relational forces; to constitute affirmative assemblages requires the sensibility to and availability for changes or transformation which are directly proportional to the subject's ability to sustain them without cracking. The sense of limit, in the sense of framing a threshold of sustainability, is crucial to the operation of becoming in the sense of actualizing joyful or affirmative forces, or an affirmative ethics. Negotiations have to occur as stepping stones to sustainable flows of becoming.

The bodily self's interaction with his or her environment can either increase or decrease that body's *potentia*. Thinking is a sort of relational sensor that prompts understanding and helps to discern the forces that increase its power of acting and its activity, in parallel physical and mental terms. A higher form of self-knowledge by reaching adequate understanding of the nature of one's affectivity is the key to an affirmative ethics of empowerment. It includes a more adequate understanding of the interconnections between the self and a multitude of other forces. This requires labour so as to increase relational powers and to deal with complexity without being over-burdened. Thus, only a quest for increasing degrees of relational powers can guarantee the freedom of the mind in the awareness of its true, affective and dynamic nature.

Thinking the unity of body and mind, affirmative ethics stresses the power (*potentia*) of affects (*affectus*), which is 'a dynamic articulation' and not merely passive reflection (Lloyd 1996: 31). Affecting and being affected refer to 'the increase or decrease in its powers of acting' (Lloyd 1996: 72). This 'power of acting' – which is in fact a flow of transpositions – is expressed in terms of achieving freedom through an adequate understanding of our passions and consequently of our bondage. Coming into possession of freedom requires the understanding of affects or passions by a mind that is always already embodied.

An ethics that is constructed as the praxis of overturning negativity aims at achieving freedom through the understanding of the conditions that make us un-free, that is to say through the awareness of our limits, of our oppression. Ethics means faithfulness to this *potentia*, one's essence as joy, or the desire to become. The posthuman subject needs to work towards affirmation through the notion of 'endurance', which is the transformative version of the more corporate idea of resilience. As Walker and Cooper argue (2018), resilience theory has ceased to operate as critique and has evolved into a full mainstream methodology of management of the posthuman convergence. Aiming to integrate society, the economy and the biosphere in a new phase of posthuman capitalism called 'panarchy', which aims at continuous adaptive cycles of growth, restructuring and capital accumulation. By contrast, endurance strikes a more critical non-profit note about alternative subject formation processes. It entails temporal duration, thus proposing the notion of the subject as an entity that survives and lasts. It also refers to spatial elements, the ability to withstand and sustain changes and transformation and to enact them affirmatively in environmental, social and affective terms. Endurance involves affectivity and joy, but it also means putting up with hardship and physical pain.

The affirmative and material turn I defend here, far from implying a disavowal of negativity and of the importance of the imaginary and of representations in language and literature, takes them to task for the construction of posthuman critical theory. My affirmative ethics takes equal distance from authoritarian universal moralism as from the *laissez-faire* ideology of neo-liberal politics, with its emphasis on the production of quantified selves and its 'cultural obsession with health and with clean, functional bodies'.[4]

This is why the question of subjectivity is so important and why I do not approve of hasty dismissals of this crucial political factor. Recasting subjectivity in the affirmative mode of a praxis that activates the capacity of transversal subjects to detach themselves from the historically sedimented determinations of power, aims at releasing transversal lines of resistance and not integral lines of power.

Whereas Marxism would argue for ideological rupture, Deleuze and Guattari emphasize that, to actualize this rupture requires subjects who actively desire otherwise and thus break with the *doxa*, the regime of common-sense, in a radical gesture of defamiliarization. The function of the virtual is to actualize the real issues, which means precisely the effort to interrupt the acquiescent application of established norms and values, to deterritorialize them by introducing alternative ethical flows. The virtual is the laboratory of the new. To accomplish this ethics, we need to assemble and enact together a qualitative leap, by understanding how it engenders the conditions of our bondage. Such a leap engages with, but also breaks productively with the present. The virtual or affirmative force is thus also the motor of political change. Being worthy of what happens to us – *amor fati* – is not fatalism, but pragmatic engagement with the present (as both actual and virtual), in order to collectively construct conditions that transform and empower our capacity to act ethically and produce social horizons of hope, or sustainable futures.

Chapter 7
The Inexhaustible

The underlying current of this book has been affective. Throughout I have addressed the complex and internally contradictory alternation of emotions that marks the posthuman convergence. Excitement and exhilaration in view of the Fourth Industrial Age, flip into anxiety and fear at the thought of the huge costs and damages inflicted by a Sixth Extinction, on both human and non-human inhabitants of this planet. The spread and recurrence of the negative pole of this manic-depressive affective economy is quite concerning. Exhaustion and fatigue have become prominent features of the contemporary psychic landscapes. Exhaustion is witness to the daily and nightly struggles that mark our interaction with the complexities of the present.

It is not easy to address these issues. Words, in so many ways, falter and fail. One can only talk about exhaustion in a language reduced to its ossified minimal components, a language that has reached the edge of what it can express, approximating silence, but not falling into it just yet. Exhaustion almost longs for a neutralized style that has perfected ways of de-linking from grand statements of meaningful action. Exhaustion requires a language that is through with power as *potestas*. Such a language is not weak, so much as disconnected from the sovereign power of the master signifier who means what it says and says what it means. Exhaustion is meaning-free and antithetical to judgements and authoritarian injunctions.

In the first chapter I mentioned that exhaustion is its own, intransitive state: one is tired of something, but exhausted by nothing and everything. Being tired leaves open the possibility of rest and recovery, whereas exhaustion just is what it is. In this final chapter I will activate the affirmative ethics and argue that exhaustion is not only negative. Like all affective states, including for instance vulnerability, exhaustion essentially expresses our capacity to affect and be affected by others. As such, it affirms our relational openness to the world and therefore can be very productive.

Accepting one's vulnerability as the starting point for a process of transforming it collectively and socially, expresses a sort of epistemological humility that reiterates the never-ending nature of the processes of becoming. It defends community-based experiments to transform the negative conditions and states into affirmative alternatives. It is a praxis that promotes action and knowledge out of negativity and pain. This pro-active activism manifests the living beings' shared ability to actualize and potentiate different possibilities. This transformative energy is the core of affirmative ethics.

What is inexhaustible is the potential that all living organisms share for multiple actualizations of yet unexplored interconnections, across and with humans and non-humans. This is the immanence of a life that can only be co-constructed and jointly articulated in a common world. What is inexhaustible is not some transcendental and abstract notion of Life with capital letters, but rather the more patient task of co-constructing one's life, alongside so many others. Just one life, following the formula of the ancient Stoics, can only be predicated in a constant, friendly companionship with pain and suffering. This in turn means that ethics is the practice of extracting knowledge and wisdom from the reworking of pain. Pushed to the extreme, it brings us face to face with mortality, the extreme manifestation of vulnerability. Death is the painful event par excellence, but it is also the event that marks our inscription into the time of our life. As such, at the level of awareness, it is the event that has already happened, because to be born means to become mortal. As such, it is a strangely impersonal event. Death marks the outer boundary of the limited time we have at our disposal. Being aware of this limit can be an energizing thought, not a catastrophe.

The co-construction of affirmative ethics actualizes virtual possibilities in the present. It marks a qualitative transformation of our shared sense of becoming in time, by opening into the non-place where the 'no longer' and the 'not yet' reverse into each other, unfolding out and enfolding in their respective 'outsides'. In this continuous flow, the present becomes both a memory and a promise. Actualizing the virtual is a praxis, not a miracle. It is an act that cannot be understood apart from the transformations and the connections it produces. 'Becoming' is a way of configuring this leap itself. It refers to the actual transmutation of values that will propel us out of the void of critical negativity, into the generative encounters with others that also gravitate towards positivity, or affirmation. It is an affirmation of the generative powers of life that involves friendship with impersonal death.

Stoicism is highly relevant for the posthuman convergence, because it teaches us how to work through painful experiences, notably the sense of loss, dispossession and fear for the future. Moreover, stoicism is relational and interactive. Composing just a life and gearing it to affirmation by reworking pain as an ethical praxis does not assume a sovereign individual subject, but rather foregrounds the transversal structure of subjectivity. It lays down the rules for the collective self-styling of alternative subject positions, beyond individualism, Eurocentric Humanism and anthropocentrism. Affirmative ethics encourages us to train for making the most of one's powers and capabilities, so as to become the most affirmative possible version of what one could be, through the pain and the acknowledgement of mortality.

Sceptics will see this as being concomitant with neo-liberal self-management techniques, whereas it is intended to be exactly the contrary. It is a way of decelerating and escaping the multiple speeds of reterritorialization by capital, by focusing on alternative values. What matters most is to intervene upon these speeds and accelerations of advanced capitalism, disrupting their ruthless expansion by introducing different forces. The actualization of the virtual is a concrete political praxis, progressive and liberating when implemented collectively. Escaping velocity by a process of self-exhaustion is a way of turning down one's organized identity and sense of self, the better to resist the lure of acceleration by the spinning machine of capital.

The source of the resistance is the resilience of *zoe*. The point of affirmative ethics is that *zoe* cannot be reduced to devalued and dehumanized life (as Agamben claims), but needs to be opened up to encompass the varieties of non-human lives. In the vital neo-materialist framework, *zoe* is posited as the 'power of life' as *potentia*.

Posthuman resistance must mobilize for the compositions and collective construction of alternative subject formations and forms of life that are not wholly exhausted by the negative force of power. Politics requires not just resistance, but the effort to activate the generative force of virtual possibilities. Indeed, *zoe* as bare life is devalued life, assigned the status of disposable scapegoat. Many lives today are the object of biopower's thanato-politics, doomed to ethnic cleansing or slaughter, to being killed without their killer being held accountable. Many of these lives are not human. My point, however, is that *zoe* exceeds these negative conditions, because *zoe* exists outside and anterior to sovereign power and hence resists subjugation. This is the greatness of affirmative thought as a secular, materialist philosophy of becoming. It is an inexhaustible generative force that potentially can transmute lives into sites of resistance – all lives, also the non-human.

Life as endless immanent power of becoming is inexhaustible, even though specific bound forms of it are not. *Zoe*, as a force exceeding anthropocentric perspectives and humanistic expectations, offers resources to resist the reterritorializations of advanced capitalism. These resources do much more than provide resistance: they are the seeds of alternative forms of empowerment. This is about becoming otherwise other. Life is a generative force beneath, below and beyond what we humans have made of it. *Zoe*/geo/techno perspectives at the core of this heterogeneous definition of life are sites of resistance. They provide multiple alternatives to the devastations of necropolitics and the entrapment of bio-political management of Life as capital.

The desire to persevere in the affirmative project of constructing and empowering just *a* life is thus a praxis of in-depth resistance to macropolitical structures and hierarchical relations of power. It acts as a force of creative replenishment for thought and action. This is the force of virtuality. It opens up a desire that is not predicated on the negative principles of Lack and Law, but on relational affirmation and plenitude. Desire is always social. It follows then that desire also plays a role in the production of political passions, that is to say in the affects that structure our social imaginary and our political aspirations. I have argued in the first chapter that the people living in Continental Europe right now are suffering from theory fatigue, post-work fatigue and democracy fatigue. Neither the European project nor democracy as an unfinished project excites the collective imagination any longer. If anything, illiberalism has acquired a cool status. Kick-starting some positive reconfigurations of becoming-Europeans in the post-nationalistic and minor sense of the term is a way of rekindling the collective desire for democracy.

Collective imaginings and shared desire also play a major role in the social construction of negative political passions. In the context of contemporary Europe, and with its legacy of the disasters of the twentieth century, it is important to name and resist new forms of micro-fascism that are emerging. Microfascism brings about the paradox of a desire that desires its own repression and its un-freedom. This is unfortunately the recipe of contemporary illiberal and populist movements. Defined as the love for a strongman, fascism promises to solve all your problems: to make the trains run on time, to restore the British Empire, to solve the world's problems by tweeting abuse at imagined enemies late at night, and – inevitably – to chase away all foreigners, all transgressive others, all non-aligned subjects.

Contemplating the state of the present, one is struck by the delusional, infantile, but also homicidal quality of a desire that desires its own extinction and marries into the cult of destruction. This is a systemic blockage of the affirmative force of desire. It produces an endless implosion of what could have been a mode of becoming. This is precisely the kind of negativity that anti-fascist subjects need to be on guard against. Importantly, the fascist has to be traced not only in the 'other', but also within yourself. 'The fascist inside you' is this totalitarian entity that dispels relational connections and instils suspicion and hatred. It leads to scapegoating instead of pursuing adequate understandings of our conditions. One can undo the fascist inside by acknowledging one's attachment to dominant identity formations and power structures. This acknowledgement is the precondition for the practical task of changing the negative habit into affirmative relations. This praxis requires opening up to others and co-constructing alternative social structures and alternative desires that sustain the task of transforming the negative. Returning desire to its affirmative structure is a way of learning to live the non-fascist life, that is to say a life guided by the ethics of relational affirmation as outlined throughout this book.

But what a huge task that is! Fatigue, fear and boredom overlap and accumulate to produce a feeling of utter impotence. This closing down of the horizon of possible actions is the symptom of the negativity of our times. Negativity expresses itself in a social and psychological dimming of a sense of possibility, which triggers a systemic fragmentation and a shattering of our relational capacity. This weakening of the desire to act often feeds an appeal to external powers to take over the task of organizing how to live our lives. This negativity ultimately brings about a shrinking of our ability to take *in* and *on* the world that we are in, simply because it hurts too much to take it in and on. We have to dose how much of it we can take, until it gets too much. Too-much-ness is one of the sources of exhaustion, which marks so much of our current predicament.

What is inexhaustible, however, is our desire to persevere in living, against all odds. This is the innermost essence, or *potentia* of all living entities: the life in me that does not answer to my name. This vital sense of life is not to be taken for granted, or be sacralized in religious terms. It remains materialist and secular. 'Just a life' expresses a deep sense of belonging to a common world, the one word we have in common. The desire to get on with it is the fragile yet irrepressible bond that interconnects all living entities. This produces a roar of energy that is mostly unperceived and imperceptible, yet indispensable.

The inexhaustible is linked to the virtual, whose ontological orientation is towards becoming actualized. The virtual fuels the ontological force of affirmation. In this dynamic, vital and material worldview, the process of actualization does not exhaust all possible combinations any one entity is capable of becoming. There is a conceptual explanation for this, though the essence of the matter is ethical. Conceptually, the source of this inexhaustible desire to persevere derives from the fact that the actualizations of untapped alternatives and virtual possibilities can never be exhaustive and all-encompassing. Because affirmation is a praxis that affects and transforms the negative conditions, and because of the infinite range of virtual actualizations, it is logically and materially impossible to exhaust all possibilities.

To push this even further, as stated on several occasions in this book, the process of actualization is not reducible to a dialectical overturning of power relations. That would merely consume one pole of the opposition by activating the other. In a neo-materialist perspective, it is rather the case that the counter-actualization of the virtual potentiates some of what is possible and leaves alone or does not activate other options. It all comes down to what bodies can do, in the sense of both *potestas* and *potentia*. What is left out of their ability to become otherwise does not reverse dialectically into the negative, either as a form of dead matter or non-life or as a latent reservoir of future revolutionary or anarchical energy. It is simply left alone and is taken out of the current equation, the equation being the praxis of composing a people that aims at actualizing affirmative alternatives.

In a vital neo-materialist perspective, these counter-actualizations entail framing possible modes of becoming, which by no means exhaust the sum total of virtuality. The virtual is infinite because life is. The virtual only matters as far as it is actualized, which does not depend on wilful individualism but on community action. This ontological force of affirmation is instantiated as a collective praxis of alternative subject formations. In this respect, it is neither active nor passive, but located in some other middle ground. It is a sort of becoming-imperceptible of the subject.

The ethical implication is to get going. Affirmative ethics puts the motion back into e-motion and the active back into activism. Because of the abundance of yet unfulfilled possibilities, much remains to be done. That may sound insufficient at a time of such deep transformations and never-ending accelerations, coupled with the swinging moods they bring on, the despair and disenchantment alternating with excitement and hope. But acknowledging that the virtual is inexhaustible is a source of inspiration that can be turned into a vector of active becoming. Yes, there is so much to do, and it is exhausting just to think of it. But we need to start somewhere, however humbly.

We saw in the previous chapters that reaching an adequate understanding of the mostly negative conditions of our locations enlists the parallel resources of an embodied brain and an embrained body to the task of increasing our power to act. That is to say, to relate more and better to the world. Ontological desire is activated by the evacuation of the self and the exhaustion of wilful activity. Exhaustion thus marks the demise of the sovereign subject position; it is a practice that aims at deactivating the despotic attachment to power, which marks the dominant model of ethical and political subjectivity in Western culture.

Exhaustion, however, is not a pathology that needs to be cured, let alone sedated by the ever-watchful psycho-pharmaceutical industry. Exhaustion is an intransitive state that allows multiple opportunities to stay afloat in a state of latency, always *in potentia*. What sustains the flow of even such low levels of intensity is the desire to become otherwise and the desire for other ways of living and dying.

Acknowledging this force is the starting point for the more practical task of doing something about it. The virtual needs to be actualized. And to actualize it we need each other. So, let us settle in the immanence of just a life, which will have been ours, on this damaged planet, in the company of many, and not all of them human. What is inexhaustible is our capacity, our power even, to differ within ourselves, as well as between us. We can extract ourselves from this sad state of affairs, work through the multiple layers of our exhaustion, and co-construct different platforms of becoming. This trans-formative praxis can only be enacted collectively, together, as transversal subjects of posthuman times. Shared exhaustion actually unfolds upon a deeper wisdom about what it is exactly that one knows, when one is facing momentous changes in unfamiliar territories. One knows that Life lives on regardless of human pretensions and expectations. 'We' can only intervene in *this* as transversal ensembles, acting collectively: 'We'-who-are-not-one-and-the-same-but-are-in-this-convergence-together.

Notes

Introduction: Posthuman, All-too-Human

1 The term 'Anthropocene', coined in 2002 by Nobel Prize winner Paul Crutzen, describes the current geological era as dominated by measurable negative human impact on the Earth, through technological interventions and consumerism (Crutzen and Stoermer 2000). It was discussed at the International Geological Congress in August 2016, but was rejected in July 2018 by the International Commission on Stratigraphy, in favour of the 'Meghalayan' era.
2 These range from the classical humanism of Martha Nussbaum (1999) to post-colonial (Gilroy 2016); queer (Butler 2004) and critical humanism (Critchley 2014), to name just a few.

Chapter 1: The Posthuman Condition

1 Private communication with the author.
2 The most recent manifestation of this trend is the politically right-wing debate on the alleged responsibilities of postmodernism in the making of contemporary post-truth claims by populist politicians. Many of the tactics of bullying, naming and shaming, displayed by these campaigns, are borrowed from Conservative US think-thanks like the Heritage and other foundations.

3 A portmanteau term obtained by merging precarious with proletariat. It designates the bottom social class in advanced capitalism with low levels of economic, cultural and social capital (*Wikipedia*, consulted 15 June 2018).

4 The Visegrad countries are: Czech Republic, Hungary, Poland and Slovakia. Their alliance, allegedly aiming at enhancing cultural and economic ties in the region, has forged a neo-nationalist and authoritarian group with strong ties to Russia. They are opposed to EU refugees and asylum regulations.

5 The literature of extinction is also proliferating. See, for instance, works on: ceasing to be human (Bruns 2010); extinction of life on earth (Lovelock 2009) and extinction of the human *tout court* (Colebroook 2014a, 2014b).

Chapter 2: Posthuman Subjects

1 This term refers to the network of physical devices, vehicles, home appliances and other items embedded with electronic network connectivity, which enables these objects to connect and exchange data within the existing Internet infrastructure. Experts estimate that the Internet of Things will consist of about 30 billion objects by 2020 and its global market value is estimated to reach $7.1 trillion by 2020 (*Wikipedia*, consulted 23 January 2018).

2 The Futurist movement is emblematic of this double pull.

3 In this respect, Deleuze's analysis is compatible with Erich Fromm's definition of fascism (2001 [1941]) as the abdication of personal responsibility and Wilhelm Reich's (1970) idea of a popular, eroticized desire for a strongman to relieve us from the freedom to make our own choices.

4 Spinoza himself made no distinction between created, born and manufactured objects, given that what matters is their 'power', the forces they affect and are affected by. With thanks to Genevieve Lloyd.

5 In *Anti-Oedipus*, published in 1972, Deleuze and Guattari go so far as to foresee even the financialization of the economy and the emergence of a system based on debt.

Chapter 3: Posthuman Knowledge Production

1 Sarah Nuttall, 'Coeval Time: The Shock of the New Old', unpublished paper delivered at 'The Critical Tasks of the

University' conference, University of Bologna, the Academy of Global Humanities and Critical Theory, 23 June 2017.

Chapter 4: The Critical PostHumanities

1 It should be noted that the French philosophers had strong ideas about the university as an institution and wrote significant platforms for new teaching and research structures: Deleuze for Vincennes Paris VIII and Derrida for the Collège International de Philosophie. See also the work of CERFI (Centre d'études, de recherches et de formation institutionnelles), started by Guattari in 1967 with the aim to develop collective interdisciplinary research in the Humanities and Social Sciences, which published the journal *Recherches*.
2 See the two major ones: http://environmentalHumanities.org/; http://www.resiliencejournal.org/
3 This is the CenterNet Network that publishes the *Digital Humanities Commons*: http://www.dhcenternet.org/
4 https://www.cser.ac.uk/
5 https://www.hkw.de/en/programm/themen/das_anthropozaen_am_hkw/das_anthropozaen_am_hkw_start.php
6 https://brocku.ca/pri/
7 http://www.theposthuman.org/ny-posthuman-research-group.htm
8 https://www.berggruen.org/work/the-transformations-of-the-human/
9 Editors Stefan Lorenz Sorgner and Sangkyu Shin: http://www.psupress.org/Journals/jnls_JPHS.html
10 Editor Ki-Jeong Song: http://www.trans-Humanities.org/
11 http://criticalposthumanism.net/

Chapter 5: How To Do Posthuman Thinking

1 Albert Einstein quote: http://www.brainyquote.com/quotes/quotes/a/alberteins385842.html (accessed 1 September 2018).
2 The Black Saturday bushfires in Victoria on 7 February 2009 was Australia's worst natural disaster (to date).
3 https://www.forensic-architecture.org/lexicon/murky-evidence/
4 Innovative critical perspectives have been offered by the contemporary monistic philosophies of Deleuze (1988, 1990), Guattari (1995, 2000), Serres (2008) and other neo-Spinozist thinkers (Matheron 1969; Deleuze and Guattari 1987, 1994; Wilson

1990; Negri 1991; Balibar 1994; Macherey 2011), and more specifically of their implications for scientific understandings of both materialism and scientific realism (DeLanda 2002) and their implications for the Humanities (Citton and Lordon 2008).

5 Defamiliarization – in German *Verfremdung* – was originally proposed as an aesthetic approach by artists and writers in the twentieth century, notably Bertold Brecht, but also the Surrealists. This critical genealogy exercises a strong subterranean influence, especially in Foucault.

6 See Braidotti, *Posthuman Feminism*, forthcoming with Polity Press.

Chapter 6: On Affirmative Ethics

1 See also the Postcolonial Digital Humanities blog and website at http://dhpoco.org/.

2 See, for instance, the land/media/indigenous project based in British Columbia: Bleck, Dodds and Williams (2013).

3 Coordinated by Micha Cardenas, Noha F. Beydoun and Alainya Kavaloski. See the website: http://www.hastac.org/forums/colonial-legacies-postcolonial-realities-and-decolonial-futures-digital-media. With thanks to Matthew Fuller.

4 With thanks to Christoph F.E. Holzhey, in a seminar delivered at IKKM, Weimar, January 2018.

References

Agamben, Giorgio. 1998. *Homo Sacer: Sovereign Power and Bare Life*. Stanford, CA: Stanford University Press.

Alaimo, Stacy. 2010. *Bodily Natures: Science, Environment, and the Material Self*. Bloomington, IN: Indiana University Press.

Alaimo, Stacy. 2014. Thinking as the stuff of the world. *O-Zone: A Journal of Object-Oriented Studies*, 1.

Alaimo, Stacy. 2016. *Exposed: Environmental Politics and Pleasures in Posthuman Times*. Minneapolis, MN: University of Minnesota Press.

Alaimo, Stacy and Susan Hekman (eds). 2008. *Material Feminisms*. Bloomington, IN: Indiana University Press.

Anderson, Laurie. 1997. Control rooms and other stories: Confession of a content provider. *Parkett*, 49, 126–45.

Ansell Pearson, Keith. 1997. *Viroid Life: Perspectives on Nietzsche and the Transhuman Condition*. London and New York: Routledge.

Ansell Pearson, Keith. 1999. *Germinal Life: The Difference and Repetition of Deleuze*. London and New York: Routledge.

Anzaldúa, Gloria. 1987. *Borderlands/La Frontera: The New Mestiza*. San Francisco, CA: Aunt Lute Books.

Arendt, Hannah. 1958. *The Human Condition*. Chicago: Chicago University Press.

Arendt, Hannah. 2006. *Eichmann in Jerusalem. A Report on the Banality of Evil*. London: Penguin Classics.

Arthur, John and Amy Shapiro. 1995. *Campus Wars: Multiculturalism and the Politics of Difference*. Boulder, CO: Westview Press.

Åsberg, Cecilia and Rosi Braidotti (eds.). 2018. *A Feminist Companion to the Posthumanities*. New York: Springer.

Åsberg, Cecilia, Redi Koobak and Ericka Johnson (eds.). 2010. Post-humanities is a feminist issue. *Nora*, 19(4), 213–16.

Badiou, Alain. 2013. Our contemporary impotence. *Radical Philosophy*, 181, pp. 40–3.

Badiou, Alain and Slavoj Žižek. 2009. *Philosophy in the Present*. Cambridge: Polity.

Badmington, Neil. 2003. Theorizing posthumanism. *Cultural Critique*, 53(1), 10–27.

Balibar, Etienne. 1994. *Spinoza and Politics*. London: Verso Books.

Balsamo, Anne M. 1996. *Technologies of the Gendered Body: Reading Cyborg Women*. Durham, NC: Duke University Press.

Banerji, Debashish and Makarand R. Paranjape (eds.). 2016. *Critical Posthumanism and Planetary Futures*. New Delhi: Springer India.

Barad, Karen. 2007. *Meeting the Universe Halfway: Quantum Physics and the Entanglement of Matter and Meaning*. Durham, NC: Duke University Press.

Barr, Marleen S. 1987. *Alien to Femininity: Speculative Fiction and Feminist Theory*. Westport, CT: Greenwood Press.

Barr, Marleen S. 1993. *Lost in Space: Probing Feminist Science Fiction and Beyond*. Chapel Hill, NC: The University of North Carolina Press.

Bastian, Michelle, Owain Jones, Niamh Moore and Emma Roe. 2017. *Participatory Research in More-than-Human Worlds*. New York: Routledge.

Bataille, Georges. 1988. *The Accursed Share: An Essay on General Economy*. New York: Zone Books.

Bayley, Annouchka. 2018. *Posthuman Pedagogies in Practice: Arts Based Approaches for Developing Participatory Futures*. London: Palgrave Macmillan.

Beck, Ulrich. 1999. *World Risk Society*. Cambridge: Polity.

Beck, Ulrich. 2007. The Cosmopolitan condition: Why methodological nationalism fails. *Theory, Culture & Society*, 24(7/8), 286–90.

Beer, Gillian. 1983. *Darwin's Plots: Evolutionary Narrative in Darwin, George Eliot, and Nineteenth-Century Fiction*. London: Routledge & Kegan Paul.

Benhabib, Seyla. 2009. Claiming rights across borders: International human rights and democratic sovereignty. *American Political Science Review*, 103(4), 691–704.

Bennett, Jane. 2010. *Vibrant Matter: A Political Ecology of Things*. Durham, NC: Duke University Press.

Berg, Maggie and Barbara K. Seeber (eds.). 2016. *The Slow Professor: Challenging the Culture of Speed in the Academy.* Toronto: University of Toronto Press.

Berubé, Michael and Cary Nelson. 1995. *Higher Education Under Fire: Politics, Economics and the Crisis of the Humanities.* New York: Routledge.

Bhabha, Homi. 1994. *The Location of Culture.* New York: Routledge.

Bhabha, Homi. 1996. Unsatisfied: Notes on vernacular cosmopolitanism. In: Laura Garcia-Morena and Peter C. Pfeifer (eds.) *Text and Nation.* London: Camden House.

Bignall, Simone, Steve Hemming and Daryle Rigney. 2016. Three ecosophies for the Anthropocene: Environmental governance, continental posthumanism and indigenous expressivism. *Deleuze Studies*, 10(4), 455–78.

Bignall, Simone and Paul Patton. 2010. *Deleuze and the Postcolonial.* Edinburgh: Edinburgh University Press.

Bleck, Nancy, Katherine Dodds and Chief Bill Williams. 2013. *Picturing Transformations.* Vancouver: Figure 1 Publishing.

Bono, James J., Tim Dean and Ewa P. Ziarek. 2008. *A Time for the Humanities: Futurity and the Limits of Autonomy.* New York: Fordham University Press.

Bonta, Mark and John Protevi. 2004. *Deleuze and Geophilosophy: A Guide and Glossary.* Edinburgh: Edinburgh University Press.

Bostrom, Nick. 2014. *Superintelligence: Paths, Dangers, Strategies.* Oxford: Oxford University Press.

Bozalek, Vivienne, Rosi Braidotti, Tamara Shefer and Michalinos Zembylas (eds.). 2018. *Socially Just Pedagogies: Posthumanist, Feminist and Materialist Perspectives in Higher Education.* London: Bloomsbury Academic.

Brah, Avtar. 1996. *Cartographies of Diaspora: Contesting Identities.* London: Routledge.

Braidotti, Rosi. 1991. *Patterns of Dissonance: On Women in Contemporary French Philosophy.* Cambridge: Polity.

Braidotti, Rosi. 1994. *Nomadic Subjects: Embodiment and Sexual Difference in Contemporary Feminist Theory.* New York: Columbia University Press.

Braidotti, Rosi. 2002. *Metamorphoses: Towards a Materialist Theory of Becoming.* Cambridge: Polity.

Braidotti, Rosi. 2006. *Transpositions: On Nomadic Ethics.* Cambridge: Polity.

Braidotti, Rosi. 2011a. *Nomadic Subjects: Embodiment and Sexual Difference in Contemporary Feminist Theory.* New York: Columbia University Press.

Braidotti, Rosi. 2011b. *Nomadic Theory: The Portable Rosi Braidotti*. New York: Columbia University Press.

Braidotti, Rosi. 2013. *The Posthuman*. Cambridge: Polity.

Braidotti, Rosi. 2014. The untimely. In: Bolette Blaagaard and Iris van der Tuin (eds.) *The Subject of Rosi Braidotti: Politics and Concepts*. New York: Bloomsbury Academic, pp. 227–50.

Braidotti, Rosi. 2015. Posthuman feminist theory. In: Lisa Disch and Mary Hawkesworth (eds.) *The Oxford Handbook of Feminist Theory*. Oxford: Oxford University Press, pp. 673–88.

Braidotti, Rosi. 2016a. The contested posthumanities. In: Braidotti, Rosi and Gilroy, Paul (eds.) *Contesting Humanities*. London and New York: Bloomsbury Academic.

Braidotti, Rosi. 2016b. The critical posthumanities; Or, Is media-natures to naturecultures as Zoe is to Bios? *Cultural Politics*, 12(3), 380–90.

Braidotti, Rosi. 2017. Posthuman, all too human. *The 2017 Tanner Lectures on Human Values*. Utah: Whitney Humanities Center, Yale University and the Tanner Foundation.

Braidotti, Rosi. 2018. A theoretical framework for the critical posthumanities. *Theory, Culture & Society*, https://doi.org/10.1177/0263276418771486

Braidotti, Rosi and Simone Bignall (eds.). 2018. *Posthuman Ecologies*. London: Rowman & Littlefield International.

Braidotti, Rosi and Paul Gilroy (eds.). 2016. *Contesting Humanities*. London: Bloomsbury Academic.

Braidotti, Rosi and Maria Hlavajova (eds.). 2018. *Posthuman Glossary*. London: Bloomsbury Academic.

Brown, Nathan. 2016. Avoiding communism: A critique of Nick Srnicek and Alex Williams' inventing the future. *Parrhesia*, 25, 155–71.

Brown, Wendy. 2015. *Undoing the Demos: Neoliberalism's Stealth Revolution*. New York: Zone Books.

Bruns, Gerald L. 2010. *On Ceasing to Be Human*. Stanford, CA: Stanford University Press.

Bryant, Levi. 2011. *The Democracy of Objects*. Ann Arbor, MI: Open Humanities Press.

Bryld, Mette and Nina Lykke. 2000. *Cosmodolphins: Feminist Cultural Studies of Technology, Animals and the Sacred*. New York: Zed Books.

Burgess, J. Peter. 2014. *The Future of Security Research in the Social Sciences and the Humanities*. Strasbourg, France: European Science Foundation.

Burns, Lorna and Birgit Kaiser (eds.). 2012. *Postcolonial Literatures and Deleuze: Colonial Pasts, Differential Futures.* London: Palgrave Macmillan.

Butler, Judith. 2004. *Precarious Life: The Powers of Mourning and Violence.* New York: Verso Books.

Cameron, Fiona R. 2018. Posthuman museum practices. In: Rosi Braidotti and Maria Hlavajova (eds.) *Posthuman Glossary.* London: Bloomsbury Academic, pp. 349–52.

Carroll, Joseph. 2004. *Literary Darwinism: Evolution, Human Nature and Literature.* New York: Routledge.

Castells, Manuel. 2010. *The Information Age: Economy, Society and Culture. Volume 1: The Rise of the Network Society,* 2nd edn. Oxford: Wiley-Blackwell.

Césaire, Aimé. 1981. *Toussaint Louverture.* Paris: Présence Africaine.

Chakrabarty, Dipesh. 2009. The climate of history: Four theses. *Critical Enquiry,* 35, 197–222.

Chomsky, Noam. 2014. The death of American universities. *Jacobin Magazine.* Available at: <https://www.jacobinmag.com/2014/03/the-death-of-american-universities/>.

Citton, Yves and Frédéric Lordon. 2008. *Spinoza et les sciences sociales.* Paris: Editions Amsterdam.

Clark, Nigel. 2008. Aboriginal cosmopolitanism. *International Journal of Urban and Regional Research,* 32(3), 737–44.

Clark, Nigel and Yasmin Gunaratnam. 2017. Earthing the *Anthropos*? From 'socializing the Anthropocene' to geologizing the social. *European Journal of Social Theory,* 20(1), 146–63.

Clark, Nigel and Kathryn Yusoff. 2017. Geosocial formations and the Anthropocene. *Theory, Culture & Society,* 34(2–3), 3–23.

Clarke, Adele. 2018. Introducing making kin, not population. In: Adele E. Clarke and Donna Haraway (eds.) *Making Kin, Not Population.* Chicago, IL: Prickly Paradigm Press.

Clarke, Bruce. 2008. *Posthuman Metamorphosis: Narrative and Systems.* New York: Fordham University Press.

Clarke, Bruce. 2017. Rethinking Gaia: Stengers, Latour, Margulis. *Theory, Culture & Society,* 34(4), 3–26.

Clarke, Bruce and Manuela Rossini (eds.). 2016. *The Cambridge Companion to Literature and The Posthuman.* Cambridge: Cambridge University Press.

Clover, Joshua and Juliana Spahr. 2014. *#Misanthropocene: 24 Theses.* Oakland, CA: Commune Editions.

Coetzee, J.M. 2013. Take a stand on academic freedom. *University World News,* 29 November. Available at: <http://www.university-worldnews.com/article.php?story=20131126223127382>.

Cohen, Tom, Claire Colebrook and J. Hillis Miller. 2012. *Theory and the Disappearing Future: On De Man, on Benjamin.* New York: Routledge.

Cohen, Tom, Claire Colebrook and J. Hillis Miller. 2016. *Twilight of the Anthropocene Idols.* London: Open Humanities Press.

Cole, David R. and Joff P.N. Bradley (eds.). 2018. *Principles of Transversality in Globalization and Education.* New York: Springer.

Cole, Jonathan, Elinor Barber and Stephen Graubard (eds.). 1993. *The Research University in a Time of Discontent.* Baltimore, MD: John Hopkins University Press.

Colebrook, Claire. 2014a. *Death of the Posthuman.* Ann Arbor, MI: Open Humanities Press/University of Michigan Press.

Colebrook, Claire. 2014b. *Sex After Life: Essays on Extinction, Vol. 2.* Ann Arbor, MI: Open Humanities Press.

Coleman, Rebecca and Jessica Ringrose. 2013. *Deleuze and Research Methods.* Edinburgh: Edinburgh University Press.

Collini, Stefan. 2012. *What Are Universities For?* London: Penguin Books.

Coole, Diana and Samantha Frost (eds.). 2010. *New Materialisms: Ontology, Agency and Politics.* Durham, NC: Duke University Press.

Cooper, Melinda. 2008. *Life as Surplus: Biotechnology and Capitalism in the Neoliberal Era.* Seattle, WA: University of Washington Press.

Cooper, Melinda and Catherine Waldby. 2014. *Clinical Labor: Tissue Donors and Research Subjects in the Global Bioeconomy.* Durham, NC: Duke University Press.

Creed, Barbara. 1993. *The Monstrous-Feminine: Film, Feminism, Psychoanalysis.* New York: Routledge.

Creed, Barbara. 2009. *Darwin's Screens: Evolutionary Aesthetics, Time and Sexual Display in the Cinema.* Melbourne: Melbourne University Press.

Crist, Eileen. 2013. On the poverty of our nomenclature. *Environmental Humanities,* 3, 29–47.

Critchley, Simon. 2014. *The Faith of the Faithless.* London: Verso Books.

Crutzen, P. J. and E. F. Stoermer. 2000. The Anthropocene. *Global Change Newsletter,* 41, 17–18.

Davis, Heather and Etienne Turpin (eds.). 2015. *Art in the Anthropocene: Encounters Among Aesthetics, Politics, Environments and Epistemologies.* London: Open Humanities Press.

de Fontenay, Elizabeth. 1998. *Le silence des bêtes.* Paris: Fayard.

de Graef, Ortwin. 2016. 'Muscular Humanities' presentation at the European Consortium of Humanities Institutes and Centres (ECHIC), Annual Conference Macerata, 21–22 April.

De Sutter, Laurent. 2018. *Narcocapitalism*. Cambridge: Polity.

d'Eaubonne, Françoise. 1974. *Le féminisme ou la mort*. Paris: Pierre Horay.

DeLanda, Manuel. 2002. *Intensive Science and Virtual Philosophy*. New York: Continuum.

DeLanda, Manuel. 2016. *Assemblage Theory*. Edinburgh: Edinburgh University Press.

Deleuze, Gilles. 1983. *Nietzsche and Philosophy*. New York: Columbia University Press.

Deleuze, Gilles. 1984. *Kant's Critical Philosophy*. London: Athlone Press.

Deleuze, Gilles. 1988. *Spinoza: Practical Philosophy*. San Francisco, CA: City Lights Books.

Deleuze, Gilles. 1990. *Expressionism in Philosophy: Spinoza*. New York: Zone Books.

Deleuze, Gilles. 1993. *The Fold: Leibniz and the Baroque*. Minneapolis, MN: University of Minnesota Press.

Deleuze, Gilles. 1994. *Difference and Repetition*. London: Athlone Press.

Deleuze, Gilles. 1995a. *Negotiations*. New York: Columbia University Press.

Deleuze, Gilles. 1995b. The exhausted. *SubStance* 24(3), 3–28.

Deleuze, Gilles. 1998. *Essays Critical and Clinical*. London: Verso Books.

Deleuze, Gilles. 2003. *Pure Immanence: Essays on a Life*. New York: Zone Books.

Deleuze, Gilles. 2006. *Two Regimes of Madness: Texts and Interviews 1975–1995*. Cambridge, MA: MIT Press.

Deleuze, Gilles and Felix Guattari. 1977. *Anti-Oedipus*. New York: Viking Press.

Deleuze, Gilles and Felix Guattari. 1987. *A Thousand Plateaus: Capitalism and Schizophrenia*. Minneapolis, MN: University of Minnesota Press.

Deleuze, Gilles and Felix Guattari. 1994. *What is Philosophy?* New York: Columbia University Press.

Derrida, Jacques. 2007. No apocalypse, not now: Full speed ahead, seven missiles, seven missives. In: Peggy Kamuf and Elizabeth Rottenberg (eds.) *Psyche: Inventions of the Other*. Stanford, CA: Stanford University Press, pp. 387–409.

Derrida, Jacques. 2008. *The Animal That Therefore I Am*. New York: Fordham University Press.

Descola, Philippe. 2009. Human natures. *Social Anthropology*, 17(2), 145–57.

Descola, Philippe. 2013. *Beyond Nature and Culture*. Chicago, IL: University of Chicago Press.

Dolphijn, Rick and Iris van der Tuin (eds.). 2012. *New Materialism: Interviews and Cartographies*. Ann Arbor, MI: Open Humanities Press.

Donoghue, Frank. 2008. *The Last Professors: The Corporate University and the Fate of the Humanities*. New York: Fordham University Press.

Donovan, Josephine and Carol J. Adams (eds.). 1996. *Beyond Animal Rights: A Feminist Caring Ethic for the Treatment of Animals*. New York: Continuum.

Donovan, Josephine and Carol J. Adams (eds.). 2007. *The Feminist Care Tradition in Animal Ethics*. New York: Columbia University Press.

Douzinas, Costas. 2017. *Syriza in Power: Reflections of a Reluctant Politician*. Cambridge: Polity.

Epstein, Mikhail. 2012. *The Transformative Humanities: A Manifesto*. New York: Bloomsbury Academic.

Fanon, Frantz. 1967. *Black Skin, White Masks*. New York: Grove Press.

Felski, Rita. 2015. *The Limits of Critique*. Chicago, IL: University of Chicago Press.

Ferrando, Francesca. 2013. From the eternal recurrence to the posthuman multiverse. *The Agonist*, 4(1–2), 1–11.

Flannery, Tim. 1994. *The Future Eaters*. New York: Grove Press.

Foucault, Michel. 1970. *The Order of Things: An Archaeology of Human Sciences*. New York: Pantheon Books.

Foucault, Michel. 1977. Preface. In: Gilles Deleuze and Felix Guattari, *Anti-Oedipus*. New York: Viking Press.

Foucault, Michel. 1995. *Discipline and Punish*. New York: Pantheon Books.

Foucault, Michel. 2008. *The Birth of Biopolitics: Lectures at the Collège de France 1978–1979*. London: Palgrave Macmillan.

Foucault, Michel and Gilles Deleuze. 1977. Intellectuals and power: A conversation between Foucault and Deleuze. In: Donald Bouchard (ed.) *Language, Counter-Memory and Practice*. Ithaca, NY: Cornell University Press, pp. 205–17.

Franklin, Sarah, Celia Lury and Jackie Stacey. 2000. *Global Nature, Global Culture*. Thousand Oaks, CA: Sage Publications.

Fromm, Erich. 2001 [1941]. *Fear of Freedom*. New York: Routledge.

Fukuyama, Francis. 1989. The end of history? *The National Interest*, 16, 3–18.

Fukuyama, Francis. 2002. *Our Posthuman Future: Consequences of the Biotechnological Revolution*. London: Profile Books.

Fuller, Matthew. 2005. *Media Ecologies: Materialist Energies in Art and Technoculture*. Cambridge, MA: MIT Press.

Fuller, Matthew. 2008. *Software Studies: A Lexicon*. Cambridge, MA: MIT Press.

Fuller, Matthew. 2018. *How to Sleep: The Art, Biology and Culture of Unconsciousness*. London: Bloomsbury Academic.

Fuller, Matthew and Andrew Goffey. 2013. *Evil Media*. Cambridge, MA: MIT Press.

Gabrys, Jennifer. 2011. *Digital Rubbish: A Natural History of Electronics*. Ann Arbor, MI: University of Michigan Press.

Galison, Peter. 1997. *Image and Logic: A Material Culture of Microphysics*. Chicago, IL: University of Chicago Press.

Galison, Peter. 2004. Specific theory. *Critical Inquiry*, 30(2), 379–83.

Gatens, Moira and Genevieve Lloyd. 1999. *Collective Imaginings*. New York: Routledge.

Genosko, Gary. 2018. Four elements. In: Rosi Braidotti and Maria Hlavajova (eds.) *Posthuman Glossary*. London: Bloomsbury Academic, pp. 167–9.

Ghosh, Amitav. 2016. *The Great Derangement: Climate Change and the Unthinkable*. Chicago, IL: University of Chicago Press.

Giffney, Noreen and Myra J. Hird. 2008. *Queering the Non/Human*. London: Routledge.

Gill, Rosalind. 2010. Breaking the silence: The hidden injuries of the neoliberal universities. In: Rosalind Gill and Roisin Ryan-Flood (eds.) *Secrecy and Silence in the Research Process: Feminist Reflections*. New York: Routledge, pp. 228–44.

Gilroy, Paul. 2000. *Against Race*. Cambridge, MA: Harvard University Press.

Gilroy, Paul, 2016. *The Black Atlantic and the Re-enchantment of Humanism*. Salt Lake City, UT: University of Utah Press.

Glissant, Edouard. 1997. *Poetics of Relation*. Ann Arbor, MI: University of Michigan Press.

Glotfelty, Cheryll and Harold Fromm (eds.). 1996. *The Ecocriticism Reader*. Athens, GA: University of Georgia Press.

Goodley, Dan, Rebecca Lawthom, Kirsty Liddiard and Katherine Runswick-Cole. 2018. Posthuman disability and dishuman studies. In: Rosi Braidotti and Maria Hlavajova (eds.) *Posthuman Glossary*. London: Bloomsbury Academic, pp. 342–5.

Goodley, Dan, Rebecca Lawthom and Katherine Runswick-Cole. 2014. Posthuman disability studies. *Subjectivity*, 7(4), 341–61.

Gouges, Olympe de. 1791. *The Declaration of the Rights of Woman*. Available at <http://chnm.gmu.edu/revolution/d/293/>.

Gray, John. 2002. *Straw Dogs*. London: Granta Books.

Grewal, Inderpal and Caren Kaplan. 1994. *Scattered Hegemonies: Postmodernity and Transnational Feminist Practices*. Minneapolis, MN: University of Minnesota Press.

Griffin, Susan. 1978. *Woman and Nature: The Roaring Inside Her*. New York: Harper & Row.

Grosz, Elizabeth. 1995. *Space, Time and Perversion: Essays on the Politics of Bodies*. New York: Routledge.

Grosz, Elizabeth. 2011. *Becoming Undone: Darwinian Reflections on Life, Politics, and Art*. Durham, NC: Duke University Press.

Gruen, Lori and Kari Weil. 2012. Animal Others – Editors' introduction. *Hypatia*, 27(3), 477–87.

Grusin, Richard. 2017. *Anthropocene Feminism*. Minneapolis, MN: University of Minnesota Press.

Guattari, Felix. 1995. *Chaosmosis: An Ethico-aesthetic Paradigm*. Sydney: Power Publications.

Guattari, Felix. 2000. *The Three Ecologies*. London: Athlone Press.

Habermas, Jürgen. 2003. *The Future of Human Nature*. Cambridge: Polity.

Halberstam, J. Jack. 2012. *Gaga Feminism*. Boston, MA: Beacon Press.

Halberstam, Judith M. and Ira Livingston (eds.). 1995. *Posthuman Bodies*. Bloomington, IN: Indiana University Press.

Hall, Stuart. 1979. The great moving right show. *Marxism Today*, January, 14–20.

Hallward, Peter. 2006. *Out of this World: Deleuze and the Philosophy of Creation*. London: Verso Books.

Hanafin, Patrick. 2018. Posthuman rights, a micropolitics of. In: Rosi Braidotti and Maria Hlavajova (eds.) *Posthuman Glossary*. London: Bloomsbury Academic, pp. 352–5.

Haraway, Donna. 1985. A manifesto for cyborgs: Science, technology, and socialist feminism in the 1980s. *Socialist Review*, 5(2), 65–107.

Haraway, Donna. 1988. Situated knowledges: The science question in feminism as a site of discourse on the privilege of partial perspective. *Feminist Studies*, 14(3), 575–99.

Haraway, Donna. 1990. *Simians, Cyborgs and Women*. London: Free Association Press.

Haraway, Donna. 1997. *Modest_Witness@Second_Millennium. FemaleMan©_Meets_ Oncomouse™*. New York: Routledge.

Haraway, Donna. 2003. *The Companion Species Manifesto: Dogs, People and Significant Otherness*. Chicago, IL: Prickly Paradigm Press.

Haraway, Donna 2004 [1992]. The promises of monsters: A

regenerative politics for inappropriate/d Others. In: *The Haraway Reader*. New York: Routledge, pp. 63–124.

Haraway, Donna. 2016. *Staying with the Trouble: Making Kin in the Chthulucene*. Durham, NC: Duke University Press.

Harding, Sandra. 1986. *The Science Question in Feminism*. Ithaca, NY: Cornell University Press.

Harding, Sandra. 1991. *Whose Science? Whose Knowledge?* Ithaca, NY: Cornell University Press.

Hardt, Michael and Antonio Negri. 2000. *Empire*. Cambridge, MA: Harvard University Press.

Harman, Graham. 2010. *Towards Speculative Realism*. Washington, DC: Zero Books.

Harman, Graham. 2014. *Bruno Latour: Reassembling the Political*. London: Pluto Press.

Hayles, N. Katherine. 1999. *How We Became Posthuman: Virtual Bodies in Cybernetics, Literature and Informatics*. Chicago, IL: University of Chicago Press.

Hayles, N. Kathrine. 2005. *My Mother Was a Computer: Digital Subjects and Literary Texts*. Chicago, IL: University of Chicago Press.

Herbrechter, Stefan. 2013. *Posthumanism: A Critical Analysis*. New York: Bloomsbury Academic.

Hester, Helen. 2018. *Xenofeminism*. Cambridge: Polity.

Hill Collins, Patricia. 1991. *Black Feminist Thought*. New York: Routledge.

Hird, Myra J. and Celia Roberts. 2011. Feminism theorizes the nonhuman. *Feminist Theory*, 12(2), 109–17.

Holland, Eugene. 2011. *Nomad Citizenship: Free-Market Communism and the Slow-Motion General Strike*. Minneapolis, MN: University of Minnesota Press.

hooks, bell. 1981. *Ain't I a Woman: Black Women and Feminism*. Boston, MA: South End Press.

hooks, bell. 1990. Postmodern blackness. In: *Yearning: Race, Gender and Cultural Politics*. Toronto: Between the Lines.

Hörl, Erich. 2013. A thousand ecologies: The process of cyber-neticization and general ecology. In: Diedrich Diederichsen and Anselm Franke (eds.) *The Whole Earth: California and the Disappearance of the Outside*. Berlin: Sternberg Press, pp. 121–30.

Hörl, Erich. 2018. General ecology. In: Rosi Braidotti and Maria Hlavajova (eds.) *Posthuman Glossary*. London: Bloomsbury Academic, pp. 172–4.

Hörl, Erich and James Burton (eds.). 2017. *General Ecology: The New Ecological Paradigm*. London: Bloomsbury Academic.

Huggan, Graham and Helen Tiffin. 2009. *Postcolonial Ecocriticism: Literature, Animals, Environment*. New York: Routledge.

Huntington, Samuel. 1996. *The Clash of Civilizations and the Remaking of World Order*. New York: Simon and Schuster.

Irigaray, Luce. 1984. *This Sex Which is Not One*. Ithaca, NY: Cornell University Press.

Irigaray, Luce. 1993. *An Ethics of Sexual Difference*. Ithaca, NY: Cornell University Press.

Käll, Jannice. 2017. A posthuman data subject? The right to be forgotten and beyond. *German Law Journal*, 18(5), 1145–62.

Kelly, Joan. 1979. The double-edged vision of feminist theory. *Feminist Studies*, 5(1), 216–27.

King, Katie. 2011. *Networked Reenactments: Stories Transdisciplinary Knowledges Tell*. Durham, NC: Duke University Press.

Kirby, Vicki. 2011. *Quantum Anthropologies: Life at Large*. Durham, NC: Duke University Press.

Kirksey, Eben and Stefan Helmreich. 2010. The emergence of multispecies ethnography. *Cultural Anthropology*, 25(4), 545–76.

Klein, Naomi. 2014. *This Changes Everything: Capitalism vs. The Climate*. New York: Simon and Schuster.

Kolbert, Elizabeth. 2014. *The Sixth Extinction*. New York: Henry Holt Company.

Kristeva, Julia. 1980. *Desire in Language: A Semiotic Approach to Literature and Art*. New York: Columbia University Press.

Kroker, Arthur. 2014. *Exits to the Posthuman Future*. Cambridge: Polity.

Kurzweil, Ray. 2006. *The Singularity is Near*. New York: Penguin Putnam.

Laboria Cuboniks. 2015. *The Xenofeminist Manifesto*. Available at <http://tripleampersand.org/after-accelerationism-the-xeno feminist-manifesto/>.

Lambert, Gregg. 2001. *Report to the Academy*. Aurora, CO: The Davis Group Publisher.

Land, Nick. 1992. *The Thirst for Annihilation: Georges Bataille and Virulent Nihilism (an Essay in Atheistic Religion)*. London: Routledge.

Land, Nick. 1993. Making it with Deleuze: Remarks on Thanatos and Desiring-Production. *Journal of the British Society for Phenomenology*, 24(1), 66–76.

Last, Angela. 2017. We are the world? Anthropocene cultural production between geopoetics and geopolitics. *Theory, Culture & Society*, 34(2–3), 147–68.

Latour, Bruno. 1991. *We Have Never Been Modern*. Cambridge, MA: Harvard University Press.

Latour, Bruno. 2004. Why has critique run out of steam? *Critical Inquiry*, 30(2), 225–48.

Latour, Bruno. 2005. *Reassembling the Social: An Introduction to Actor-Network-Theory*. Oxford: Oxford University Press.

Latour, Bruno. 2017. *Facing Gaia: Eight Lectures on the New Climatic Regime*. Cambridge: Polity.

Lau, Carolyn. 2018. Posthuman literature and criticism. In: Rosi Braidotti and Maria Hlavajova (eds.) *Posthuman Glossary*. London: Bloomsbury Academic, pp. 347–9.

Lazzarato, Maurizio. 2012. *The Making of the Indebted Man: An Essay on the Neoliberal Condition*. Los Angeles, CA: Semiotext(e).

Lilla, Mark. 2017. *The Once and Future Liberal*. New York: HarperCollins.

Lillywhite, Austin. 2017. Relational matters: A critique of speculative realism and a defense of non-reductive materialism. *Chiasma*, 4(1), 13–39.

Livingston, Julie and Jasbir K. Puar. 2011. Interspecies. *Social Text*, 29(1), 3–14.

Lloyd, Genevieve. 1984. *The Man of Reason: Male and Female in Western Philosophy*. London: Methuen.

Lloyd, Genevieve. 1994. *Part of Nature: Self-knowledge in Spinoza's Ethic*. Ithaca, NY: Cornell University Press.

Lloyd, Genevieve. 1996. *Spinoza and the Ethics*. New York: Routledge.

Lorimer, Jamie. 2017. The Anthropo-scene: a guide for the perplexed. *Social Studies of Science*, 47(1), 117–42.

Louverture, Toussaint. 2011 [1794]. *Lettres à la France*. Bruyères-le-Châtel: Nouvelle Cité.

Lovelock, James. 2009. *The Vanishing Face of Gaia: A Final Warning*. New York: Basic Books.

Lury, Celia, Luciana Parisi and Tiziana Terranova. 2012. Introduction: The becoming topological of culture. *Theory, Culture & Society*, 29(4–5), 3–35.

Lykke, Nina. 2011. This discipline which is not one: Feminist studies as a post-discipline. In: Nina Lykke, Rosemarie Buikema and Gabriele Griffin (eds.) *Theories and Methodologies in Postgraduate Feminist Research: Researching Differently*. New York: Routledge, pp. 137–51.

Lykke, Nina. 2018. Postdisciplinarity. In: Rosi Braidotti and Maria Hlavajova (eds.) *Posthuman Glossary*. London: Bloomsbury Academic, pp. 332–5.

Lyotard, Jean-François. 1979. *The Postmodern Condition: A Report on Knowledge*. Minneapolis, MN: University of Minnesota Press.

Lyotard, Jean-François. 1989. *The Inhuman: Reflections on Time*. Oxford: Blackwell.

MacCormack, Patricia. 2014. *The Animal Catalyst: Towards Ahuman Theory*. New York: Bloomsbury Academic.

Macfarlane, Robert. 2016. Generation Anthropocene: How humans have altered the planet forever. *The Guardian*, 1 April. Available at: <https://www.theguardian.com/books/2016/apr/01/generation-anthropocene-altered-planet-for-ever>.

Macherey, Pierre. 2011. *Hegel or Spinoza*. Minneapolis, MN: University of Minnesota Press.

MacKenzie, Adrian. 2002. *Transductions: Bodies and Machines at Speed*. New York: Continuum.

MacKinnon, Catherine A. 2007. *Are Women Human?* Cambridge, MA: Harvard University Press.

Mahdawi, Arwa. 2018. We live in an age of anxiety – and we can't blame it all on Trump. *The Guardian*, 7 August.

Margulis, Lynn and Dorion Sagan. 1995. *What Is Life?* Berkeley, CA: University of California Press.

Marks, John. 1998. *Gilles Deleuze: Vitalism and Multiplicity*. London: Pluto Press.

Massumi, Brian. 1992. Everywhere you want to be: An introduction to fear. In: Joan Broadhurst (ed.) *Deleuze and the Transcendental Unconscious*. Warwick: Warwick Journal of Philosophy, pp. 175–215.

Massumi, Brian. 1998. Sensing the virtual, building the insensible. *Architectural Design*, 68(5/6), 16–24.

Massumi, Brian. 2002. *Parables for the Virtual: Movement, Affect, Sensation*. Durham, NC: Duke University Press.

Matheron, Alexandre. 1969. *Individu et communauté chez Spinoza*. Paris: Les Editions de Minuit.

Mazzei, Lisa A. and Kate McCoy. 2010. Thinking with Deleuze in qualitative research. *International Journal of Qualitative Studies in Education*, 23(5), 503–9.

Mbembe, Achille. 2003. Necropolitics. *Public Culture*, 15(1), 11–40.

Mbembe, Achille. 2017a. *Critique of Black Reason*. Durham, NC: Duke University Press.

Mbembe, Achille. 2017b. Negative Messianism marks our times. *The Guardian*, 3 February.

McNeil, Maureen. 2007. *Feminist Cultural Studies of Science and Technology*. London: Routledge.

Menand, Louis (ed.). 1996. *The Future of Academic Freedom*. Chicago, IL: University of Chicago Press.

Merchant, Carolyn. 1980. *The Death of Nature: Women, Ecology, and the Scientific Revolution*. New York: HarperCollins.

Midgley, Mary. 1996. *Utopias, Dolphins, and Computers: Problems of Philosophical Plumbing*. New York: Routledge.

Mies, Maria and Vandana Shiva. 1993. *Ecofeminism*. New York: Zed Books.

Mignolo, Walter. 2011. *The Darker Side of Western Modernity: Global Futures, Decolonial Options*. Durham, NC: Duke University Press.

Moore, Jason. 2013. Anthropocene, Capitalocene, and the myth of industrialization. *World-Ecological Imaginations: Power and Production in the Web of Life*, 16 June. Available at: <https://jasonwmoore.wordpress.com/2013/06/16/anthropocene-capitalocene-the-myth-of-industrialization/>.

Moreton-Robinson, Aileen. 2003. I still call Australia home: Indigenous belongings and place in a white postcolonizing society. In: Sara Ahmed, Claudia Castada, Anne-Marie Fortier and Mimi Sheller (eds.) *Uprootings/Regroundings: Questions of Home and Migration*. London: Bloomsbury Academic, pp. 23–40.

Moreton-Robinson, Aileen. 2009. Introduction: Critical indigenous theory. *Cultural Studies Review*, 15(2), 11–12.

Morton, Timothy. 2013. *Hyperobjects: Philosophy and Ecology after the End of the World*. Minneapolis, MN: University of Minnesota Press.

Morton, Timothy. 2016. *Dark Ecology: For a Logic of Future Coexistence*. New York: Columbia University Press.

Moulier-Boutang, Yann. 2012. *Cognitive Capitalism*. Cambridge: Polity.

Mullarkey, John. 2013. Animal spirits: Philosophomorphism and the background revolts of cinema. *Angelaki*, 18(1), 11–29.

Nakamura, Lisa. 2002. *Cybertypes: Race, Ethnicity and Identity on the Internet*. New York: Routledge.

Nakata, Martin. 2007. *Disciplining the Savages, Savaging the Disciplines*. Canberra: Aboriginal Studies Press.

Nancy, Jean-Luc. 2015. *After Fukushima: The Equivalence of Catastrophes*. New York: Fordham University Press.

Nayar, Pramod K. 2013. *Posthumanism*. Cambridge: Polity.

Negri, Antonio. 1991. *The Savage Anomaly: The Power of Spinoza's Metaphysics and Politics*. Minneapolis, MN: University of Minnesota Press.

New York Times Editorial Board. 2014. Notes from the Plasticene epoch: From ocean to beach, tons of plastic pollution. *The New York Times*, 15 June, SR10.

Nixon, Robert. 2011. *Slow Violence and the Environmentalism of the Poor*. Cambridge, MA: Harvard University Press.

Noys, Benjamin. 2010. *The Persistence of the Negative*. Edinburgh: Edinburgh University Press.

Noys, Benjamin. 2014. *Malign Velocities: Accelerationism and Capitalism*. Washington, DC: Zero Books.

Noys, Benjamin and Timothy S. Murphy. 2016. Introduction: Old and new weird. *Genre*, 49(2), 117–34.

Nussbaum, Martha C. 1999. *Cultivating Humanity: A Classical Defense of Reform in Liberal Education*. Cambridge, MA: Harvard University Press.

Nussbaum, Martha C. 2010. *Not for Profit: Why Democracy Needs the Humanities*. Princeton, NJ: Princeton University Press.

Papadopoulos, Dimitris. 2010. Insurgent posthumanism. *Ephemera*, 10(2), 134–51.

Parikka, Jussi. 2015a. *A Geology of Media*. Minneapolis, MN: University of Minnesota Press.

Parikka, Jussi. 2015b. *The Anthrobscene*, Minneapolis, MN: University of Minnesota Press.

Parisi, Luciana. 2004. *Abstract Sex: Philosophy, Bio-Technology, and the Mutation of Desire*. London: Continuum Press.

Parisi, Luciana. 2013. *Contagious Architecture: Computation, Aesthetics, and Space*. Cambridge, MA: MIT Press.

Parr, Adrian. 2013. *The Wrath of Capital*. New York: Columbia University Press.

Parr, Adrian. 2018. *Birth of a New Earth*. New York: Columbia University Press.

Patton, Paul. 2000. *Deleuze and the Political*. New York: Routledge.

Pell, Richard. 2015. PostNatural histories. In: Heather Davis and Etienne Turpin (eds.) *Art in the Anthropocene: Encounters Among Aesthetics, Politics, Environments and Epistemologies*. London: Open Humanities Press, pp. 299–316.

Pepperell, Robert. 2003. The Posthuman Manifesto. *Intellect Quarterly*, Winter. Available at: <https://www.intellectbooks.co.uk/File:download,id=412/Pepperell2.PDF>.

Peterson, Christopher. 2013. *Bestial Traces: Race, Sexuality, Animality*. New York: Fordham University Press.

Peterson, Jordan. 2018. *12 Rules for Life: An Antidote to Chaos*. Toronto: Penguin Random House.

Pinker, Steven. 2007. *The Stuff of Thought*. New York: Viking Press.

Ponzanesi, Sandra and Koen Leurs. 2014. Introduction to the special issue: On digital crossings in Europe. *Crossings, Journal of Migration and Culture*, 4(1), 3–22.

Pope Francis. 2015. Encyclical Letter *Laudato si': On Care for our Common Home*. Rome: The Vatican Press.

Povinelli, Elizabeth A. 2016. *Geontologies: A Requiem to Late Liberalism*. Durham, NC: Duke University Press.

Preciado, Paul. 2013. *Testo Junkie: Sex, Drugs and Biopolitics in the Pharmacopornographic Era*. New York: The Feminist Press at the City University of New York.

Protevi, John. 2001. *Political Physics: Deleuze, Derrida and the Body Politic*. London: Athlone Press.

Protevi, John. 2009. *Political Affect: Connecting the Social and the Somatic*. Minneapolis, MN: University of Minnesota Press.

Protevi, John. 2013. *Life, War, Earth*. Minneapolis, MN: University of Minnesota Press.

Protevi, John. 2018. Geo-hydro-solar-bio-techno-politics. In: Rosi Braidotti and Maria Hlavajova (eds.) *Posthuman Glossary*. London: Bloomsbury Academic, pp. 175–8.

Puar, Jasbir K. 2007. *Terrorist Assemblages: Homonationalism in Queer Times*. Durham, NC: Duke University Press.

Radman, Andrej and Heidi Sohn (eds.). 2017. *Critical and Clinical Cartographies: Architecture, Robotics, Medicine, Philosophy*. Edinburgh: Edinburgh University Press.

Raffnsoe, Sverre. 2013. *The Human Turn: The Makings of a Contemporary Relational Topography*. Frederiksberg: Copenhagen Business School Press.

Rajan, Kaushik Sunder. 2006. *Biocapital: The Constitution of Postgenomic Life*. Durham, NC: Duke University Press.

Readings, Bill. 1996. *The University in Ruins*. Cambridge, MA: Harvard University Press.

Redfield, Marc. 2016. *Theory at Yale: The Strange Case of Deconstruction in America*. New York: Fordham University Press.

Reich, Wilhelm. 1970. *The Mass Psychology of Fascism*. New York: Farrar, Straus and Giroux.

Rich, Adrienne. 1987. *Blood, Bread and Poetry*. London: Virago Press.

Ringrose, Jessica, Katie Warfield and Shiva Zarabadi. 2019. *Feminist Posthumanisms, New Materialisms and Education*. New York: Routledge.

Roden, David. 2014. *Posthuman Life: Philosophy at the Edge of the Human*. New York: Routledge.

Roden, David. 2018. Speculative posthumanism. In: Rosi Braidotti and Maria Hlavajova (eds.) *Posthuman Glossary*. London: Bloomsbury Academic, pp. 398–401.

Roets, Griet and Rosi Braidotti. 2012. Nomadology and subjectivity: Deleuze, Guattari and critical disability studies. In: Dan Goodley, Bill Hughes and Lennard Davis (eds.) *Disability and*

Social Theory: New Developments and Directions. London: Palgrave Macmillan, pp. 161–78.

Rorty, Richard. 1998. *Achieving Our Country: Leftist Thought in Twentieth-Century America*. Cambridge, MA: Harvard University Press.

Rose, Nikolas. 2007. *The Politics of Life Itself*. Princeton, NJ: Princeton University Press.

Rose, Nikolas. 2013. The human sciences in a biological age. *Theory, Culture & Society*, 30(1), 3–34.

Rose, Nikolas. 2016. Reading the human brain: How the mind became legible. *Body and Society*, 22(2), 140–77.

Rosendahl Thomsen, Mads. 2013. *The New Human in Literature: Posthuman Visions of Changes in Body, Mind, and Society after 1900*. London: Bloomsbury Academic.

Rust, Stephen A. and Carter Soles. 2014. Ecohorror special cluster: 'Living in fear, living in dread, pretty soon we'll all be dead'. *ISLE: Interdisciplinary Studies in Literature and Environment*, 21(3), 509–12.

Ryan, Marie-Laure, Lori Emerson and Benjamin J. Robertson (eds.). 2014. *The Johns Hopkins Guide to Digital Media*. Baltimore, MD: Johns Hopkins University Press.

Said, Edward. 1994. *Culture and Imperialism*. London: Vintage.

Said, Edward. 2004. *Humanism and Democratic Criticism*. New York: Columbia University Press.

Sassen, Saskia. 2014. *Expulsions: Brutality and Complexity in the Global Economy*. Cambridge, MA: Harvard University Press.

Savage, Michael. 2018. Richest 1% on target to own two-thirds of all wealth by 2030. *The Guardian*, 7 April.

Sayers, Jentery. 2018. *The Routledge Companion to Media Studies and Digital Humanities*. London: Routledge.

Schreibman, Susan, Ray Siemens and John Unsworth. 2004. *A Companion to Digital Humanities*. Oxford: Blackwell.

Schwab, Klaus. 2015. The fourth industrial revolution. *Foreign Affairs*, 12 December.

Scranton, Roy. 2015. *Learning to Die in the Anthropocene*. San Francisco, CA: City Lights Books.

Semetsky, Inna. 2008. *Nomadic Education: Variations on a Theme by Deleuze and Guattari*. Rotterdam: Sense Publishers.

Semetsky, Inna and Diana Masny (eds.). 2013. *Deleuze and Education*. Edinburgh: Edinburgh University Press.

Serres, Michel. 2008. *The Natural Contract*. Ann Arbor, MA: University of Michigan Press.

Shildrick, Margrit. 2009. *Dangerous Discourses of Disability, Subjectivity and Sexuality*. London: Palgrave Macmillan.

Shiva, Vandana. 1993. *Monocultures of the Mind*. London: Palgrave Macmillan.

Shiva, Vandana. 1997. *Biopiracy: The Plunder of Nature and Knowledge*. Boston, MA: South End Press.

Shumway, David R. 1997. The star system in literary studies. *PMLA*, 112(1), 85–100.

Skinner, Quentin. 2012. *Liberty Before Liberalism*. Cambridge: Cambridge University Press.

Sloterdijk, Peter. 2009. *Rules for the Human Zoo*: A response to the *Letter on Humanism*. *Environment and Planning D: Society and Space*, 27(1), 12–28.

Small, Helen. 2013. *The Value of the Humanities*. Oxford: Oxford University Press.

Smelik, Anneke and Nina Lykke (eds.). 2008. *Bits of Life: Feminism at the Intersections of Media, Bioscience, and Technology*. Seattle, WA: University of Washington Press.

Snow, C. P. 1998 [1959]. *The Two Cultures*. Cambridge: Cambridge University Press.

Sobchack, Vivian. 2004. *Carnal Thoughts: Embodiment and Moving Image Culture*. Berkeley, CA: University of California Press.

Spinoza, Benedict de. 1996 [1677]. *Ethics*. London: Penguin Classics.

Spivak, Gayatri C. 1988. Can the subaltern speak? In: Cary Nelson and Lawrence Grossberg (eds.) *Marxism and the Interpretation of Culture*. Chicago, IL: University of Illinois Press.

Spivak, Gayatri C. 1990. *The Post-Colonial Critic: Interviews, Strategies, Dialogues*. New York: Routledge.

Spivak, Gayatri C. 1999. *A Critique of Postcolonial Reason: Toward a History of the Vanishing Present*. Cambridge, MA: Harvard University Press.

Spivak, Gayatri C. 2003. *Death of a Discipline*. New York: Columbia University Press.

Srnicek, Nick. 2016. *Platform Capitalism*. Cambridge: Polity.

Srnicek, Nick and Alex Williams. 2015. *Inventing the Future: Postcapitalism and a World without Work*. London: Verso Books.

St. Pierre, Elizabeth A. 2016. The empirical and the new empiricisms. *Cultural Studies ↔ Critical Methodologies*, 16(2), 111–24.

Stengers, Isabelle. 1997. *Power and Invention: Situating Science*. Minneapolis, MN: University of Minnesota Press.

Stengers, Isabelle. 2011. *Thinking with Whitehead*. Cambridge, MA: Harvard University Press.

Sterling, Bruce. 2012. *The Manifesto of Speculative*

Posthumanism. Available at <http://www.wired.com/2014/02/manifesto-speculative-posthumanism/>.

Stimpson, Catherine. R. 2016. The nomadic humanities. *Los Angeles Review of Books*, 12 July.

Stoler, Ann Laura. 1995. *Race and the Education of Desire: Foucault's* History of Sexuality *and the Colonial Order of Things*. Durham, NC: Duke University Press.

Strom, Kathryn J. 2015. Teaching as assemblage: Negotiating learning and practice in the first year of teaching. *Journal of Teacher Education*, 66(4), 321–33.

Strom, Kathryn, Eric Haas, Arnold Danzig, Eligio Martinez and Kathleen McConnell. 2018. Preparing educational leaders to think differently in polarized, post-truth times. *Educational Forum*, 82(3), 259–77.

Stryker, Susan and Aren Aizura (eds.). 2013. *The Transgender Studies Reader 2*. New York: Routledge.

Stryker, Susan and Stephen Whittle (eds.). 2006. *The Transgender Studies Reader 1*. New York: Routledge.

Szerszynski, B. 2017. Gods of the Anthropocene: Geo-spiritual formations in the Earth's new epoch. *Theory, Culture & Society*, 34(2–3), 253–75.

Terranova, Tiziana. 2004. *Network Culture*. London: Pluto Press.

Terranova, Tiziana. 2018. Hypersocial. In: Rosi Braidotti and Maria Hlavajova (eds.) *Posthuman Glossary*. London: Bloomsbury Academic, pp. 195–7.

Thompson, John. 2005. Survival strategies for academic publishing. *The Chronicle Review*, 17 June, B6–B9.

Thompson, John. 2010. *Merchants of Culture: The Publishing Business in the Twenty-First Century*. Cambridge: Polity.

Todd, Zoe. 2015. Indigenizing the Anthropocene. In: Heather Davis and Etienne Turpin (eds.) *Art in the Anthropocene: Encounters Among Aesthetics, Politics, Environments and Epistemologies*. London: Open Humanities Press, pp. 241–54.

Todd, Zoe. 2016. An indigenous feminist's take on the ontological turn: 'Ontology' is just another word for colonialism. *Journal of Historical Sociology*, 29(1), 4–22.

Toscano, Alberto. 2005. Axiomatic. In: Adrian Parr (ed.) *The Deleuze Dictionary*. Edinburgh: Edinburgh University Press, pp. 17–18.

Tsing, Anna Lowenhaupt. 2015. *The Mushroom at the End of the World: On the Possibility of Life in Capitalist Ruins*. Princeton, NJ: Princeton University Press.

Tsing, Anna Lowenhaupt, Heather Anne Swanson, Elaine Gain and Nils Bubandt (eds.). 2017. *Arts of Living on a Damaged Planet*. Minneapolis, MN: University of Minnesota Press.

Ulstein, Gry. 2017. Brave new weird: Anthropocene monsters in Jeff VanderMeer's *The Southern Reach*. *Concentric: Literary and Cultural Studies*, 41(3), 71–96.

Ulstein, Gry. 2019. Age of Lovecraft: Anthropocene monsters in new weird narrative. *Nordlit*, 42.

van Dooren, Thom. 2014. *Flight Ways: Life and Loss at the Edge of Extinction*. New York: Columbia University Press.

Vattimo, Gianni and Pier Aldo Rovatti (eds.). 2012. *Weak Thought*. Albany, NY: State University of New York Press.

Viswanathan, Gauri (ed.). 2001. *Power, Politics and Culture: Interviews with Edward Said*. London: Bloomsbury.

Viveiros de Castro, Eduardo. 1998. Cosmological deixis and Amerindian perspectivism. *Journal of the Royal Anthropological Institute*, 4(3), 469–88.

Viveiros de Castro, Eduardo. 2009. *Cannibal Metaphysics: For a Post-structural Anthropology*. Minneapolis, MN: Univocal Publishing.

Viveiros de Castro, Eduardo. 2015. *The Relative Native: Essays on Indigenous Conceptual Worlds*. Chicago, IL: HAU Press.

Walker, Jeremy and Melinda Cooper. 2018. Resilience. In: Rosi Braidotti and Maria Hlavajova (eds.) *Posthuman Glossary*. London: Bloomsbury Academic, pp. 385–8.

Wamberg, Jacob. 2012. Dehumanizing Danto and Fukuyama: Towards a post-Hegelian role for art in evolution. In: Kasper Lippert-Rasmussen, Mads Rosendahl Thomsen and Jacob Wamberg (eds.) *The Posthuman Condition*. Aarhus: Aarhus University Press.

Wamberg, Jacob and Mads Rosendahl Thomsen. 2016. The Posthuman in the Anthropocene: A look through the aesthetic field. *European Review*, 25(1), 150–65.

Warner, Marina. 2014. Why I quit. *London Review of Books*, 36(17), 42–3.

Warner, Marina. 2015. Learning my lesson. *London Review of Books*, 37(6), 8–14.

Wekker, Gloria. 2016. *White Innocence*. Durham, NC: Duke University Press.

Wennemann, Daryl J. 2013. *Posthuman Personhood*. Lanham, MD: University Press of America.

West, Cornell. 2018. America is spiritually bankrupt. We must fight back together. *The Guardian*, 14 June.

Whyte, Kyle P. 2013. On the role of traditional ecological knowledge as a collaborative concept: A philosophical study. *Ecological Processes* 2(7).

Whyte, Kyle P. 2016. Is it colonial déjà vu? Indigenous peoples and climate injustice. In: Joni Adamson, Michael Davis and Hsinya Huang (eds.) *Humanities for the Environment: Integrating Knowledges, Forging New Constellations of Practice*. Abingdon-on-Thames: Earthscan Publications, pp. 88–104.

Whyte, Kyle P. 2017. Indigenous climate change studies: Indigenizing futures, decolonizing the Anthropocene. *English Language Notes*, 55(1–2), 153–62.

Williams, Alex and Nick Srnicek. 2014. #Accelerate: Manifesto for accelerationist politics. In: Robin MacKay and Armen Avanessian (eds.) *#Accelerate#: The Accelerationist Reader*. Falmouth: Urbanomic Media.

Williams, Jeffrey. 2014. *How To Be an Intellectual: Essays on Criticism, Culture & the University*. New York: Fordham University Press.

Wilson, Margaret. 1990. Comments on J.-M. Beyssade: 'De l'émotion intérieure chez Descartes à l'affect actif spinoziste'. In: Edwin Curley and Pierre-François Moreau (eds.) *Spinoza: Issues and Directions*. Leiden: E. J. Brill, pp. 191–5.

Wolfe, Cary (ed.). 2003. *Zoontologies: The Question of the Animal*. Minneapolis, MN: University of Minnesota Press.

Wolfe, Cary. 2010. *What is Posthumanism?* Minneapolis, MN: University of Minnesota Press.

Wolfendale, Peter. 2014. *Object-Oriented Philosophy*. Falmouth: Urbanomic Media.

Woolf, Virginia. 1939. *Three Guineas*. London: Hogarth Press.

Wuerth, Ingrid. 2017. International law in the post-human rights era. *Texas Law Review*, 96(279), 279–349.

Wynter, Sylvia. 2015. *On Being Human as Praxis*. Durham, NC: Duke University Press.

Young, Robert J. C. 1990. *White Mythologies: Writing History and the West*. New York: Routledge.

Young, Robert J. C. 1995. *Colonial Desire: Hybridity in Theory, Culture and Race*. New York: Routledge.

Yusoff, Kathryn. 2015. Geologic subjects: Nonhuman origins, geomorphic aesthetics and the art of becoming inhuman. *Cultural Geographies*, 22(3), 383–407.

Žižek, Slavoj. 2016. Trump is really a centrist liberal. *The Guardian*, 28 April.

Zuboff, Shoshana. 2019. *The Age of Surveillance Capitalism*. London: Profile Books.

Zylinska, Joanna. 2014. *Minimal Ethics for the Anthropocene*. London: Open Humanities Press.

Index

Guattari, Felix 8, 12, 29, 30, 33, 36
  and affirmative ethics 172
  and posthuman knowledge production 76, 88, 96, 97
  and the posthuman subject 42, 50, 63, 64
  and posthuman thought 118, 126, 143, 144
  see also ecosophy; transversality

Haraway, Donna 31, 48, 78, 82, 85, 95, 109, 150
Harman, Graham 56, 60
Hastac Scholars Forum 163
Hayles, Katherine 101
health and fitness discourse 15–16
heterogeneity 19, 52–3, 61, 90, 116, 155
  and knowledge production 153
  and political resistance 151
  and time 65, 69
  see also assemblage(s); complexity; multiplicity
heterogenesis 51
Hörl, Erich 77, 98
Huggan, Graham 80, 160
human rights 6, 128–9, 135
humane/inhumane 8, 42, 61, 76, 142
human/non-human distinction 6–7
  and digital technology 13–14
  dis-identification with 140
  non-Western 7
  see also animals
Humanism 38, 39
  and affirmative ethics 159–60

anti-Humanism 11, 60–1, 159–60
  and the Critical PostHumanities 107–8
  critiques of 8–11, 12
  and disability studies 139
  humanist universalism 159
  neo-humanism 108
  and posthuman pedagogy 141
  and posthuman subjectivity 43, 49, 58–9, 67, 69
  Socialist Humanism 86
  trans-humanism 59–60
  see also Eurocentric Humanism
Humanities 6, 100
  and the Critical PostHumanities 111
  and posthuman knowledge production 79, 91–2
  and posthuman subjectivity 58
  and the posthuman university 146, 148
  and theory fatigue 19, 20, 23, 24, 25, 27, 28
humans in posthuman times 11–12

imaginary *see* social imaginary
imagination *see* creative imagination
immanence
  and affirmative ethics 156, 157, 165–6, 169
  and the Critical PostHumanities 103, 108, 113, 114, 125
  materialist immanence 38
  and posthuman knowledge production 87, 90
  and posthuman subjectivity